# Jesus in Global Contexts

# Jesus in Global Contexts

Priscilla Pope-Levison
John R. Levison

Westminster/John Knox Press
Louisville, Kentucky

Scripture quotations from the New Revised Standard Version of the Bible are copyright © 1989 by the Division of Christian Education of the National Council of the Churches of Christ in the U.S.A., and are used by permission.

Book design by Gene Harris

First edition

Published by Westminster/John Knox Press
Louisville, Kentucky

This book is printed on acid-free paper that meets the American National Standards Institute Z39.48 standard. ∞

PRINTED IN THE UNITED STATES OF AMERICA

9  8  7  6  5  4  3  2  1

Library of Congress Cataloging-in-Publication Data
Pope-Levison, Priscilla, 1958–
    Jesus in global contexts / Priscilla Pope-Levison,
John R. Levison. — 1st ed.
        p.   cm.
    Includes bibliographical references and indexes.
    ISBN 0-664-25165-X

    1. Jesus Christ—History of doctrines—20th century.
2. Christianity and culture.  I. Levison, John R.  II. Title.
BT202.P59 1992
232—dc20                                        91-47577

To our beloved teachers

Gerald F. Hawthorne

and

Steven G. Mackie

# Contents

# Acknowledgments

Several libraries have been essential to this research: the Melville J. Herskovits Library of African Studies, Northwestern University; the Centre for the Study of Christianity in the Non-Western World, University of Edinburgh, New College; Methodist Theological School in Ohio; and the University Library of Cambridge University. Librarians at North Park College and Theological Seminary, Sonia Bodi and Ann Briody, loaned us hundreds of books for hundreds of days.

North Park College and Theological Seminary provided us with generous faculty development grants for travel to Kenya. Conversations with Dr. Jesse Mugambi and correspondence with Dr. José Chipenda prepared us for our trip. In Africa, our gracious hosts were Rev. Phyllis Bird of the All Africa Conference of Churches and Dr. Rollin Grams of Nairobi Evangelical Graduate School of Theology. Phyllis and her administrative assistant, Samu, arranged meetings with Father Bethuel of Christ the King Cathedral in Nakuru, Father Charles Nyamiti of the Catholic Higher Institute of East Africa, Dr. Teresia Hinga of Kenyatta University, and Samita Zacharia, Alice Shitsimi, and Hezekiah Timotheo Shitsimi, who made it possible for us to attend a worship service of the African Church of the Holy Spirit.

Writing this book demanded sequestering ourselves for several summers, uninterrupted by college and seminary

responsibilities. In this respect, we are indebted to Dr.
Ernst Bammel, of Cambridge University, who arranged for
us to stay at St. Edmund's College during the summer of
1989, and to Priscilla's parents for the perennial offer of
their cottage.

We are especially grateful to our editor, Cynthia Thomp-
son, for blending perceptive criticism with timely encour-
agement. Much of the pleasure of writing this book has
been in the opportunity to work with her. In addition, two
North Park friends, Marla Parker and Amy Wohl, worked
to prepare this manuscript for publication.

We also want to thank each other for hours when we sat
knee to knee and discussed mind to mind even when we did
not see eye to eye. We delight as well in the recollection of
fun memories that arose as we wrote this book: noon naps in
Edinburgh's Princes Street Gardens; tea and scones at Cambridge University Library; "editorial conferences"—picnic
lunches at the Michigan Dunes; and a dugout canoe ride to
snorkel off the coast of Kenya. Even more, there are the
daily memories of being married to our closest colleague
and friend.

Chapter 1

# Conversations
# in Christology

Conversations can be unsettling. The first white South African to live in a black township recalls an unsettling conversation he had with the great Swiss theologian Karl Barth in the mid-1960s. At that time, Nico Smith was a proponent of apartheid and a member of the Broederbund, an exclusive, secret Afrikaner nationalist organization. Barth asked Smith, "Tell me, are you free to preach the gospel in South Africa?" "Of course!" Smith replied. "We have freedom of religion in South Africa." "No," Barth retorted, "that is not the type of freedom I am asking about. Are you free in yourself? Say, for instance, you became convinced of a certain meaning of the gospel which might not be the way your family and friends understand the gospel. Would you feel free to say, 'This is how I understand the gospel and how I must preach it'?" Continuing to press the point, Barth added: "You may arrive at a point where your convictions about the gospel contradict what your government believes. Will you then also feel free to preach the gospel?"

Barth's questions plagued Nico Smith as he began to wonder whether he was free to preach against apartheid. Eventually, in 1982, the conversation with Barth contributed to his becoming the pastor of the Black Dutch Reformed Church located in the black township of Mamelodi. There, he and his spouse, Dr. Ellen Smith, settled.[1]

This book may be unsettling for those who have not yet heard the conversations about Christ in other contexts. For in this book is a panoply of Christologies from Asia, Africa, Latin America, and North America. It may be unsettling to read about Jesus as an African ancestor or the cosmic Christ or the Black Messiah. It may be unsettling, but several developments in the global dialogue and theories of interpretation necessitate just such a conversation.

## The Locus of Conversation Has Shifted

One of the most important . . . events in the whole of Christian history, has occurred within the lifetime of people not yet old. It has not reached the textbooks, and most Christians, including many of the best informed, do not know it has happened. It is nothing less than a complete change in the centre of gravity of Christianity, so that the heartlands of the Church are no longer in Europe, decreasingly in North America, but in Latin America, in certain parts of Asia, and . . . in Africa.[2]

In the midst of doctoral research on evangelism in Latin American liberation theology, one of the authors had a lengthy conversation with a seminary administrator and a denominational evangelist. Both agreed that liberation theology is a passing fad and wondered what she would teach in ten years when it would become obsolete. They encouraged her to branch out into "theology"—perhaps John Wesley's, her denominational heritage. What they did not acknowledge is the shift in Christianity's center of gravity. This shift from the First World to the Third World is not only demographic but also theological.

The inability of First World Christians to recognize this theological shift is not altogether surprising. First of all, much of Third World theology, especially in its early stages, closely resembled its mentor. Most Third World theologians have undertaken their theological training at Western universities, such as Louvain, Tübingen, or Cambridge. There they study classical Western traditions and ideologies under the tutelage of Western theologians. The imprint of this thorough Westernization is difficult to transcend.[3] Nevertheless Third World theologians prefer to regard Western theology as a conversation partner rather than the standard. A Filipino theologian explains: "I hope we are beyond the stage where 'indigenizing theology' means translating the western theological works written in Latin, French, German, or English into our native dialects. . . . Neither should producing an indigenous theology mean 'applying' the theology of Athanasius, Ambrose, Pannenberg, Rahner, or Vatican II 'to the local situation.'"[4]

The second reason for the hiddenness of the theological shift from the First World is that many Third World theological works are not easily accessible to Western Christians, since they are published in places such as Kinshasa, Zaire, or Bangalore, India, rather than in New York City or London. One prominent African theologian, in a personal conversation, stated that he intentionally publishes his books in Africa to make them affordable for other Africans, although he well knows that his books will be less accessible to a First World audience.

Third, the grass-roots origin of Third World theology rarely reaches a publisher. It transpires in a community enterprise, not an academic setting, where it is oral and artistic rather than literary.[5] Community gatherings might include village Bible studies, laity training centers, or pastors' retreats. In these settings, the community's role in the theological task is "often one of raising the questions, of providing the experience of having lived with those questions . . . and of recognizing which solutions are indeed genuine, authentic, and commensurate with their experience."[6]

Nevertheless, these three factors—theological education, publication, and production—cannot conceal from First World Christians the vast amount of theological activity that is pouring from the oppressed peoples of Latin America, Asia, Africa, and North America. The Ecumenical Association of Third World Theologians (EATWOT) itself has gathered up to eighty theologians at one time to discuss Third World theology. The Association first met in Dar es Salaam, Tanzania, in 1976, and subsequent meetings have taken place in Accra, Ghana; Wennappuwa, Sri Lanka; New Delhi, India; Geneva, Switzerland; and Oaxtepec, Mexico. Looking back on the first EATWOT meeting, a participant describes its significance as "the sign of a new stage in the history of theology. It was the start of a geographical, cultural and theological displacement. Henceforth theology was removed from the 'centre' to the 'periphery.'"[7]

The magnitude of this theological shift from the First World to the Third World behooves the former to converse with the latter. Are Western theologians willing to sit at the feet of their pupils and be mentored? From the vantage point of Third World theologians, the time has arrived. "We have eaten theology with you; we have drunk theology with you; we have dreamed theology with you. . . . We know you theologically. The question is, do you know us theologically? Would you like to know us theologically?"[8]

## The Model of Conversation Has Changed

This shift to the Third World has found a surprising ally in contemporary models of literary interpretation. Prior to this development, the Enlightenment model of interpretation that dominated biblical scholarship for nearly two centuries was a monologue: the Bible speaks to its interpreters who listen. The task of the scholar has been to uncover the original meaning of the Bible by means of linguistic and historical analysis. This task demanded that the interpreter jettison all bias so as not to distort the Bible's original meaning with modern questions.

This model of monologue has been displaced by the model of dialogue between text and interpreter because it is evident that what the Bible *says* is determined to a great extent by what the interpreter *asks*.[9] The inevitable role of bias was exposed by Albert Schweitzer in his monumental survey of contemporary lives of Jesus at the dawn of the twentieth century. With flair and precision, Schweitzer demonstrated that "each successive epoch of theology . . . found its own thoughts in Jesus."[10] Even the resolute Germanic spirit, which Schweitzer otherwise praised, evokes a bias that "leads it to project back into history what belongs to our own time. . . . The consequence is that it creates the historical Jesus in its own image."[11]

The bias that Schweitzer encountered in life of Jesus research has become standard fare for the process of interpretation. The consensus of philosophers as noteworthy as Dilthey, Heidegger, and Gadamer, as well as theologians as prominent as Bultmann, Lonergan, and Tracy, confirms that the context of interpreters inevitably shapes their approaches to literary texts. "The fact is that no interpreter enters into the attempt to understand any text or historical event without prejudgments formed by the history of the effects of her or his culture. There does not exist any exegete or historian as purely autonomous as the Enlightenment model promised."[12]

This observation provides theoretical support for contextual Christology, for its implication is that "*the modern interpreter, no less than the text, stands in a given historical context and tradition.*"[13] Not only the text from the past but also the interpreter's context in the present requires study.

Contextual theologians study this contemporary context. Context is the starting point of theological reflection. Context is the here and now of the present situation which ensures that theology will heed the "cry for the recognition of the significance of this time and this place."[14] The extensive context for theology includes the political, economic, social, religious, and cultural realms. Contextual theology begins with a social analysis of the context. "No theological method is adequate apart from a critical analysis of all the major structures of oppression, . . . an analysis which links the economic, political, social, cultural, and religious dimensions of our realities, which helps us to understand better our particular contexts."[15] Beginning with the context rather than with the text ensures theology's relevance to any situation in which theological reflection is undertaken.

An adequate theological interpretation requires a creative dialogue between text and context, between present and past. This is a model of interpretation as *conversation.*[16] This model recognizes that the interpreter engages the Bible as a dialogue partner with specific questions that arise from his or her context. The goal of interpretation is to allow the conversation between the Bible and its interpreters to develop a life of its own. Deepest insight and relevance lie neither in the original meaning of the Bible alone nor in the contemporary context but in the to-and-fro of question and answer between them. The relationship

between them can be understood as the fusion of two horizons. The text represents the first horizon, and the context,
the second horizon. The ultimate goal of interpretation is
to fuse these horizons in a way that is contiguous with the
past and relevant to the present. The process of interpretation is like a concert, in which a musical score and an orchestra's creative interpretation fuse to generate an artistic
presentation in its own right. Such a concert requires an
excellent score and a talented orchestra; if the score is dull
or the orchestra lackluster, the concert will fail. But the
genius of a successful concert goes beyond both score and
orchestra and occurs in their creative meeting.[17]

This model of interpretation can be illustrated by the African portrait of Jesus as Elder Brother. In the Bible, the
first horizon, Jesus is first-born. In many African cultures,
the second horizon, the elder brother is the first within a
family to become a full member of the tribe by completing
the rites of passage (e.g., birth, initiation into adulthood,
marriage). These are obviously two distinct horizons: elder
brother is hardly a dominant biblical designation for Jesus,
nor is Jesus an African by birth. However, in the fusion of
biblical and African horizons, Jesus becomes Elder
Brother. As Elder Brother, Jesus is transformed to become
truly African, enmeshed in the kinship fibers of tribal African life. The African rites of passage are transformed because Jesus fulfills them with the ultimate rite, the
resurrection. The result, therefore, is a creative fusion that
goes beyond both horizons.

## The Conversation Requires Expansion

Since every interpretation is a creative fusion of text and
context, no interpretation is universal, because each context is unique. The importance of context for theology can
be encapsulated by two theses: "(1) All theologies are con-
textually conditioned. . . . (2) It may take others to show
us how conditioned, parochial, or ideologically captive our
own theology is."[18]

The first thesis eradicates any theology's claim to do
theology on behalf of another context; it denounces any
attempt to universalize theology. All theologies are influ-

enced by and committed to a specific context, just as all theologians are shaped by their social location. "Theology is not a set of timeless truths, no matter how much the goal of achieving such truths may have been sought by theologians in the past. It is rather a certain kind of reflection on what is going on in very specific situations—Palestine, Rome, Constantinople, Geneva, Canterbury, Copenhagen, Hell's Kitchen."[19] Helmut Thielicke concurs when he writes that Christian truth "has nothing to do whatever with timeless truth. . . . Every word, including God's Word, implies a recipient. . . . This Word is historical not merely in the sense of being grounded in history, but also as it is addressed to historical situations."[20]

With respect to the second thesis, Third World theologians have attempted to demonstrate to the First World that Western theology is captive to its own context, even though it was exported to countless contexts around the globe. Western theology is founded on Western traditions, such as Aristotelian philosophy and Roman law, and it usually assumes a Western systematic, scholarly, and discursive form. For reasons such as these, many Third World theologians charge that "the 'universal theology' of the Church was in fact a geographically localised and culturally conditioned interpretation. Theology was not universal but European."[21] Even the renowned European theologian Edward Schillebeeckx admits, "Previously, one almost took for granted that the theology of the Western churches was supraregional and was, precisely in its Western form, universal and therefore directly accessible for persons from other cultures. But especially with the emergence of liberation theology . . . Western theologians came to the realization that their own theology has just as much sociocultural bias as any other."[22]

The theological task, then, demands ongoing conversations between theologies. These conversations frequently occur within organizations such as the World Council of Churches (WCC) and the Ecumenical Association of Third World Theologians (EATWOT). The purpose of these organizations is to facilitate a multipartner, multicontextual conversation, not to produce a "universal" theology that is applicable in all contexts, but simply to enrich and to ex-

pand each other's theologies. One participant in the first
EATWOT meeting reflects on those conversations: "Challenged by the differences we found among ourselves, we
have come out of this Assembly more open and better dis-
posed to stimulate dialogue and exchange, to allow ourselves to be reached and influenced by difference and
otherness. In this way we—speaking from the powerlessness and fragility of the situation of the Third World—feel
more capable of daring to devise and create something
new."[23]

## Preparing to Overhear the Conversations

### *The Participants*

Interpreting Christologies from four regions is a daunt-
ing responsibility that requires from us relatively strict ad-
herence to specific criteria of selection. We recognize that
this decision necessitates the exclusion of some portraits of
Jesus, despite their influence among oppressed peoples
throughout the world. With rare exception, we have selected Christian contextual theologians to represent the
conversations in Christology that are taking place in Asia,
Africa, Latin America, and among North American feminists and blacks.

—They are *Christian* contextual theologians who, with
rare exception, take seriously the Bible and Christian tradition. This criterion entails excluding Muslim, Jewish, and
Buddhist conceptions of Christ that have arisen in the context of interreligious dialogue.

—They are Christian *contextual* theologians whose
starting point is their own context. These theologians consciously use their own context in conversation with the Bible and Christian tradition. On the basis of this criterion,
the Christologies of Pentecostalism, and movements like
it, will not be included, despite rapid growth in the Third
World. This criterion also means that we shall exclude
scholars whose theologies closely resemble the classical,
historical-critical scholarship of the West.

—They are Christian contextual *theologians*, with only a
few exceptions.[24] This criterion requires the exclusion of

popular forms of religion, whether dramatic or literary or artistic, except as they are interpreted by contextual theologians. It should be noted that these theologians usually attempt to integrate the popular religiosity of their context into their theological method.

Dividing the conversations of these theologians into four regionwide groupings has the obvious drawback of joining countries that confront vastly different issues. For instance, the Asian grouping associates the Philippines, which has a low per capita income and a 90 percent Christian majority, with Japan, which has one of the highest per capita incomes in the world and a 1 to 2 percent Christian minority. Nevertheless the theologians and churches in these regions have provided the pattern for the organization of this book into the regions of Latin America, Asia, Africa, and North America. The Ecumenical Association of Third World Theologians organizes itself regionally. Meetings have rotated between Africa, Asia, and Latin America, with one in Europe, and, at least initially, papers were grouped together according to these regions. In addition, two of these regions, Africa and Asia, promulgate this division with their long-standing, regionwide organization for theological and ecumenical inquiry. The All Africa Conference of Churches (AACC), founded in 1963, links the vast and culturally diverse African continent. Similarly, the Christian Conference of Asia (CCA) encompasses a region that extends as far west as Pakistan, as far north as Korea and Japan, and as far south as New Zealand and Australia. Even North American black and feminist theologians recognize a regional identity, as they converse primarily with other North American theologians. Despite its liabilities, therefore, the organization of this book will take its cue from theological and ecclesiastical organizations around the globe.

## The Contents

In order to facilitate contrast and comparison between conversations in Christology, each chapter has an identical outline: issues faced; sources and method; and portraits of Jesus. These three sections and the order in which they occur are not arbitrary, for they reflect the method that

many contextual theologians have in common: context influences sources and theological method, which in turn influence portraits of Jesus.[25]

—Each chapter begins with the most crucial issues that
must be addressed if theology is to be relevant within each
context.

—A second section delineates the sources and method of
theological reflection within each context. The one constant source is the Bible.

—The portraits of Jesus that develop within each context comprise the third and predominant section of each
chapter.

## The Authors' Conversation

We should confess at this early point our bias about this
material: we find these contextual Christologies alluring
and enlivening, and we introduce them to promote rather
than to reject them. We are also aware that writing this
book can be construed as yet another instance of oppressors' speaking *on behalf of* those whom they oppress: we
are white, middle-class Christians in the United Methodist
Church who have come to this conversation in the comfort-
able context of college and seminary teaching. Ironically,
our graduate educations may have been funded, even partially, by the economic legacies of British colonialism and
the tobacco industry in the southern United States.

Because we are aware of the possible charge of being
patronizing, we have set out to follow the three guidelines
that Robert McAfee Brown proffers in response to the
question, "Can 'oppressors' do theology today?" We have
attempted (1) to listen, (2) to interpret what we hear, and
(3) to see the world through eyes other than our own.[26]

Together we have listened in the quiet hush of university
libraries to the rage of Mary Daly; to the pragmatic passion
of Martin Luther King, Jr.; and to the incisive political acu-
men of Indian lawyer and theologian M. M. Thomas. We
have traveled to listen to residents of Managua, Nicaragua,
discuss Mark 13 in the light of the Sandinista Revolution; to
hear Bishop Ting of China speak on Chinese views of Jesus;
to feel the song and dance of an African Independent

Church; to sense, over a cup of Kenyan tea, the quiet humility of Charles Nyamiti, a leading East African Roman Catholic theologian; and to hear Allan Boesak preach shortly after he and Desmond Tutu had met with the president of the United States.

Now our responsibility is to describe what we have heard. This task will be precarious. One African theologian to whom we explained this book opposed the project at first; in a subsequent conversation he relented and urged, "Do not misrepresent us!" Our primary task in this book, therefore, is to describe accurately the viewpoints of these theologians. The reader should assume that we consider the material to be an accurate presentation of the theologians' points of view rather than our own. We recognize, of course, that even description, by selection and emphasis, contains interpretation. Nevertheless, we hope that our description will provide an accurate, brief introduction for people who may be unfamiliar with these Christologies. We have included extensive notes with the hope that readers will pursue further research based on primary sources.

We will not agree or disagree or proffer any critiques in the descriptive chapters on the various regions (chapters 2 through 5). Only the conclusion (chapter 6) will contain critique. Even here we intend to include only those critiques which arise out of the similarities and differences between these Christologies. We, as authors, will join the conversation as participants rather than arbiters or, at most, as facilitators of the conversation.

Through listening and interpreting, we have begun to *see the world through others' eyes*. These Christologies have broadened our vision, so that we are asking now the questions that we have heard these theologians ask. We have begun to press the political and economic questions into greater service: Why did a typhoon cause the death of over 100,000 people in Bangladesh, while the World Series in San Francisco could continue, practically unhindered, in the wake of a massive earthquake? Why was a North American city relatively prepared and villages in Bangladesh ill equipped for predictable disaster? We have begun to ask what a course on Western civilization would look like from the vantage point of slaves or Latin American Indians. Perhaps most important, we have begun to ask about the adequacy of our own Christologies. Have we separated Jesus from the economic, political, and racial spheres in order to keep him personally relevant? In short, these conversations in Christology have unsettled us.

## NOTES

1. Based on a personal conversation with Nico Smith, whom one of the authors presented in 1990 for an honorary doctorate from North Park College, Chicago.

2. Andrew F. Walls, "Towards Understanding Africa's Place in Christian History," in *Religion in a Pluralistic Society*, ed. John S. Pobee (Leiden: E. J. Brill, 1976), 180; quoted by William A. Dyrness, *Learning About Theology from the Third World* (Grand Rapids: Zondervan Publishing House, 1990), 13. After fifteen years, this quotation still applies.

3. This Western imprint is evident in three surveys of lives of Jesus that encompass Germany, North America, and Western culture. In 1906, Albert Schweitzer surveyed "German research upon the Life of Jesus" (*The Quest of the Historical Jesus: A Critical Study of Its Progress from Reimarus to Wrede* [New York: Macmillan Co., 1959], 399). Schweitzer did not cross the English Channel—let alone the Atlantic Ocean or the Mediterranean Sea—to analyze lives of Jesus. He ventured to France only to indict the French for perfuming the life of Jesus with sentimentality. Henry J. Cadbury criticized North American lives of Jesus for blatant anachronisms, e.g., portraying Jesus as a successful salesperson (*The Perils of Modernizing Jesus* [New York: Macmillan Co., 1937]). Half a century later Jaroslav Pelikan masterfully surveyed interpretations of Jesus in the history of culture (*Jesus Through the Centuries: His Place in the History of Culture* [New Haven, Conn.: Yale University Press, 1985]). Pelikan carefully defined culture to include literature, philosophy, and the fine arts as well as "the political, social, and economic history of the interpretation of Jesus" (ibid., 7). Yet he nowhere employed adjectives such as "Western" or "European" to identify *which* contexts he surveyed. The assumption must be that "culture" means "*Western* culture" because the only non-Western interpreter of Jesus who receives full attention is Mahatma Gandhi, who influ-

enced notable Western figures such as Martin Luther King, Jr. A reference to Gustavo Gutiérrez, the founder of Latin American liberation theology, occurs in an endnote (p. 257 n. 32). A year later, in the Netherlands, Anton Wessels surveyed several non-European portraits of Jesus. His book (*Images of Jesus: How Jesus Is Perceived and Portrayed in Non-European Cultures* [Grand Rapids: Wm. B. Eerdmans Publishing Co., 1990], based on a 1986 Dutch original) reflects the shift to the Third World, although a large portion of several chapters is devoted to European missionary and colonialist Christologies to which these non-European Christologies were a response.

4. Carlos Abesamis, "Doing Theological Reflection in a Philippine Context," in *The Emergent Gospel: Theology from the Underside of History*, Papers from the Ecumenical Dialogue of Third World Theologians, Dar es Salaam, August 5–12, 1976, ed. Sergio Torres and Virginia Fabella (Maryknoll, N.Y.: Orbis Books, 1978), 118.

5. Ernesto Cardenal, ed., *The Gospel in Solentiname* (Maryknoll, N.Y.: Orbis Books, 1976–1982), is a notable exception to this trend.

6. Robert Schreiter, *Constructing Local Theologies* (Maryknoll, N.Y.: Orbis Books, 1985), 17.

7. Sergio Torres Gonzalez, "Dar-es-Salaam 1976," in *Convergences and Differences*, ed. Leonardo Boff and Virgil Elizondo, Concilium (Edinburgh: T. & T. Clark, 1988), 111.

8. John S. Mbiti, "Theological Impotence and the Universality of the Church," in *Third World Theologies*, ed. Gerald H. Anderson and Thomas F. Stransky, Mission Trends No. 3 (New York: Paulist Press, 1976), 16–17.

9. Among biblical scholars, Rudolf Bultmann defended on philosophical grounds the positive value of preunderstanding that puts certain questions to the text. See "The Problem of Hermeneutics," in Rudolf Bultmann, *Essays Philosophical and Theological* (London: SCM Press, 1955), 234–261, esp. 252–256. On the importance of questions, Bultmann writes: "A comprehension—an interpretation—is . . . *constantly orientated to a particular formulation of a question, a particular 'objective'*" (ibid., 239). See also "Is Exegesis Without Presuppositions Possible?" in *Existence and Faith: Shorter Writings of Rudolf Bultmann*, ed. Schubert M. Ogden (London: Hodder & Stoughton, 1961), 289–296.

10. Schweitzer, *The Quest of the Historical Jesus*, 4.

11. Ibid., 312.

12. Robert M. Grant and David Tracy, *A Short History of the Interpretation of the Bible*, 2nd ed. (Philadelphia: Fortress Press, 1984), 156. All references to this book are from part two, written by David Tracy. On these philosophers and theologians, except for Tracy, see Anthony C. Thiselton, *The Two Horizons: New Testament Hermeneutics and Philosophical Description with Special Reference to Heidegger, Bultmann, Gadamer, and Wittgenstein* (Grand Rapids: Wm. B. Eerdmans Publishing Co., 1980).

13. Thiselton, *The Two Horizons*, 11.

14. Rodrigo Tano, *Theology in the Philippine Setting* (Quezon City: New Day Publishers, 1981), 45.

15. "Doing Theology in a Divided World: Final Statement of the Sixth EATWOT Conference," in *Doing Theology in a Divided World*, Papers from the Sixth International Conference of the Ecumenical Association of Third World Theologians, January 5–13, 1983, Geneva, Switzerland, ed. Virginia Fabella and Sergio Torres (Maryknoll: Orbis Books, 1985), 189.

16. Grant and Tracy, *A Short History*, 154–160, 181. Tracy here interprets H.-G. Gadamer, *Truth and Method*, 2nd ed. (New York: Crossroad, 1990).

17. Gadamer, *Truth and Method*, 101–121. Gadamer's basic image is that of a game: the players become unselfconsciously involved in the world of the game. He further construes this conception of play as a drama, in which the actors are as concerned with presentation as with the script, or a religious festival, in which the presentation of the festival is as significant as the original meaning of the festival. See also Thiselton's lucid discussion of key issues of interpretation in *The Two Horizons*, 10–23; and Gadamer, *Truth and Method*, 293–326.

18. Robert McAfee Brown, "Diversity and Inclusiveness," *Church and Society* 67 (1977), 52–53.

19. Robert McAfee Brown, "A Preface and a Conclusion," in *Theology in the Americas*, ed. Sergio Torres and John Eagleson (Maryknoll, N.Y.: Orbis Books, 1976), xviii.

20. As quoted by Thiselton, *The Two Horizons*, 98.

21. Torres, "Dar-es-Salaam 1976," 111. According to Charles Kraft, Western theology is an "'ethnic theology' specialized for Westerners" (*Christianity in Culture: A Study in Dynamic Biblical Theologizing in Cross-Cultural Perspective* [Maryknoll, N.Y.: Orbis Books, 1979]), 292.

22. Edward Schillebeeckx, "Foreword," in Schreiter, *Constructing Local Theologies*, ix.

23. Torres, "Dar-es-Salaam," 1976, 122.

24. Albert Cleage and Martin Luther King, Jr., are black preachers; preaching is a typical medium of black theology. Shusaku Endo is a Japanese Roman Catholic novelist; he is deeply committed to his context. In the preface to *A Life of Jesus* (New York: Paulist Press, 1973), Endo writes, "My way of depicting Jesus is rooted in my being a Japanese novelist" (p. 1).

25. Schreiter, *Constructing Local Theologies*, 4.

26. Brown, "A Preface and a Conclusion," xxiv–xxvi.

Chapter 2

# Jesus
# in Latin America

## Issue Faced

Although Latin America shares many problems with other Third World regions, Latin American liberation theologians cite *dependency* as the primary factor in Latin American oppression. A two-tiered dependency characterizes Latin America. The first tier consists of Latin America's dependency on foreign countries and foreign investments. This external dependency has been forged since colonization when its human and economic resources were ravaged by other countries. Many countries have been party to Latin America's dependency, including Spain, Portugal, Great Britain, the Soviet Union, and the United States of America. External dependency on other countries, the first tier, has created an internal dependency within the region, which constitutes the second tier. In this second tier, the poor majority are dependent on the ruling class, a slim minority who control the social, economic, and political spheres of life. These two tiers are intertwined, for the ruling class is closely linked with foreign powers and is dependent on these outsiders to maintain their control within Latin America. There is, then, a two-tiered, interdependent dependency.

In addition to being two-tiered, dependency in Latin America is also multidimensional. In its most common usage, dependency refers to economic dependency. However, economics are inseparable from other factors. "These economic developments have brought about transitions in the social order and class structure, and these changes in turn have crucially affected political change. We thus begin with a set of simplified causal relationships: economic changes produce social changes which furnish the context for political change."[1] Dependency in Latin America, therefore, includes the economic, social, and political spheres as well as, according to Latin American liberation theologians, the religious sphere.

*Economically*, Latin America provides for the needs of other nations rather than its own. It produces what foreign markets dictate, generally "foodstuffs and raw materials," rather than what it needs internally. Then, because it exports unfinished materials, Latin America is forced to import finished products. Often, however, the exchange is uneven and unpredictable, since the prices of Latin American export products are usually less, yet more unstable, than the higher prices of foreign imports.[2] In addition, indigenous artisans, who manufacture finished products, are displaced because of the quantity and quality of foreign imports. Thus, by catering to foreign markets, Latin America forfeits its economic self-determination.

This external economic dependency contributes to an internal *social stratification* because the ruling class is simultaneously dependent on outside investments and depended upon by the lower class. Latin American society is divided into three classes unequal in size. The lower class—workers, unemployed, urban and rural poor—comprises 80 to 85 percent of the population. They possess little power to change their social position, much less the social system of dependency. The middle class—roughly 10 to 15 percent, though the percentage varies between countries—consists of professional people and small business owners. Despite their prominent social position, they lack the power to alter the social stratification because of their dependence upon the ruling class.[3] The top 2 percent of the population is the ruling class, "urban industrialists, bankers, high executives, technocrats, and top officers in the armed forces."[4] They exercise control over agriculture, business, and corporations. Only the ruling class is in a position to bring about a social transformation from internal dependency, but it is precisely these people who preserve their social position through external dependency on foreign investors.

The ruling class is not, however, solely responsible for the economic and social dependency of Latin America. The more powerful foreign nations that desire the economic resources and strategic geographical position of Latin America greatly influence the *political* climate. The Kennedy Administration recognized the interrelationship of the economic, social, and political spheres in its development program for Latin America entitled Alliance for Progress. The program's impetus came in the aftermath of the Cuban Revolution and the fear that communism might spread in Latin America, the United States' backyard. Because its objective was to prevent revolution from below by reform from above,[5] the Alliance for Progress targeted cooperative governments as the recipients of economic and social development aid. Although the Alliance for Progress did not achieve its development goals, it correctly recognized the interplay between the dimensions of dependency.[6]

Liberation theologians add *religious* dependency to Latin America's other forms of dependency. Like the others, religious dependency is two-tiered. Externally, many Latin American churches receive significant subsidies from churches in other countries and consequently are influenced by them. We observed an example of religious dependency while in Latin America. One evening we worshiped in an expansive church building constructed with North American dollars. The extensive cost of upkeep and repairs compelled the small Pentecostal congregation to maintain its dependency on North American money. In addition, since the founding of the church, every minister has been a North American whose salary and language training was paid for by North American churches.

There is also internal religious dependency within Latin America. The church, particularly the Roman Catholic Church, depends on the ruling class for its salaries, building maintenance, and social programs for the poor. Such dependency restrains the church, an otherwise powerful social force in Latin America, from full participation in societal transformation.

This survey should make unmistakably clear the near-permanent dependency of Latin America, both externally and internally. These interrelated dependencies of the economic, social, political, and religious realms constitute the major issue that Latin American liberation theologians confront in their writings and with their lives.

## Sources and Method

Roman Catholic documents from several conferences provide an important source for Latin American liberation theology. Perhaps the two most influential for the emergence of liberation theology are the Vatican II document *Gaudium et Spes* (The Church in the Modern-Day World), and the Medellín document. In the mid-1960s when Vatican II "opened the window" (*aggiornamento*) for the Roman Catholic Church, *Gaudium et Spes* opened the window the widest. The three-step methodology of this document has been as influential as many of its conclusions. These steps are variously described as see/judge/act,[7] "fact/reflection/recommendations,"[8] or "socio-analytical/ hermeneutic/pastoral practice."[9] In the first step, the context is analyzed using social and behavioral sciences and economic theories. In the second step, the findings of step one are considered in the light of the Bible and tradition. In the third step, recommendations for action within the context, which was analyzed in step one and reflected on in step two, are made and implemented.

This same methodology was used at the 1968 meeting of the Latin American bishops in Medellín, Colombia. The Medellín conference commenced with an examination of the Latin American reality (step one). After reflecting biblically and theologically on the reality of their context (step two), the bishops recommended that the church be in solidarity with the poor (step three).[10] This prophetic declaration of its commitment to the poor by the Roman Catholic Church prompted Latin American liberation theologians to make one crucial modification in the three-step methodol-

✳ ogy. They require a *pre*-commitment to the poor which precedes step one and thereby influences every step. Thus these two documents, *Gaudium et Spes* and Medellín, provide a methodology and a commitment to the poor that liberation theologians incorporate at the start and throughout their theology.

### Step One

Fact

In the first step of the methodology, these theologians utilize Marxist ideas as an instrument for social analysis. Karl Marx recognized the existence of a class struggle.[11] At the top are the owners who control the means of production, and on the bottom are the workers who produce goods. These classes struggle against each other for power. When liberation theologians observe the Latin American context, they perceive an ongoing class struggle between the minority elite and the majority workers. Their Marxist analysis of the class struggle helps them to analyze their context.

### Step Two

Reflection

Marxism is also helpful as a source in step two, the reflection on the findings of step one. In his writings, Marx employed the term "praxis." Praxis is concrete engagement for the purpose of transformation.[12] Similarly, liberation theologians define praxis as "'transforming action,' not simply any kind of action, but rather a historical transformation. *Historical* praxis means a transforming change, a transforming action of history."[13] Gustavo Gutiérrez includes praxis in his definition of theology as "critical reflection on Christian praxis in the light of God's word."[14] For Latin American liberation theologians, theology is critical reflection on praxis.

✳ These theologians refine further precisely what constitutes praxis. Praxis is action on behalf of the poor. Liberation theology assumes a pre-commitment to the poor and praxis on their behalf. Having this pre-commitment reverses theology as it is traditionally done. Rather than be-
✳ ginning with theological foundations and terminology, the

Bible, or church tradition, liberation theology begins with praxis among the poor. Subsequently, theology reflects on this praxis, and a circular pattern is created: theology reflects on praxis and leads to a renewed praxis which leads to further theological reflection.[15]

Liberation theologians' praxis[16] draws them to the historical Jesus as the starting point for Christology. They are suspicious of other starting points that undervalue history as the locus of God's activity. This is why Jon Sobrino devotes the first nine pages of his *Christology at the Crossroads* to a critique of seven starting points that fail to provide sufficient foundation for addressing oppression.[17] They also reject images of Jesus that devalue this world, such as Jesus in his mother's arms at birth and death.[18] Their portrait of Jesus begins with his historical activity as a human being, before the early Christians began to worship him as Messiah or risen Lord.

Interest in the historical Jesus leads invariably to the Synoptic Gospels. Latin American liberation theologians tend to prefer Mark's and Luke's gospels to Matthew's, which they feel frequently blunts the political and economic edges of Jesus' proclamation of God's reign. For example, where Luke records, "Blessed are you who are *poor*," Matthew writes, "Blessed are the poor *in spirit*" (Luke 6:20; Matt. 5:3). Luke, in particular, provides the socioeconomic portrait of Jesus that most closely coincides with the issues of oppression that dominate Latin America.

The interest of Latin American liberation theologians in the historical Jesus separates them from scholars who are involved in the so-called quest of the historical Jesus. Liberation theologians are not on a quest to establish objective data to recover precisely what Jesus said and did.[19] Rather, they want to understand the relevance of the historical Jesus for their own Latin American context. In this respect, their approach to the Bible provides an example of the model of interpretation as conversation. *Understanding* Jesus, as opposed to *recovering* Jesus, requires holding together in creative fusion two distinct horizons: the historical Jesus of the Gospels and the historical context of contemporary Latin America.[20]

These theologians believe they have an advantage over

European and North American biblical scholars in the conversation between text and context. They observe that the situation of first-century Palestine is far more similar to the Latin American context than it is to North America and Europe. Therefore they contend that their situation enables them better to understand the significance of the historical Jesus.[21]

*Recommendations*

### Step Three

The third step of the methodology, which consists of recommendations for action on the basis of steps one and two, has resulted in a unanimous recommendation of conscientization. Conscientization originates from yet another important source for liberation theology: Paulo Freire's ideas on literacy training. Freire defines conscientization as "*development* of the awakening of critical awareness."[22] This detailed process entails becoming aware of one's context of oppression, shedding fatalism, and learning to control one's own destiny.

Conscientization is a difficult process because a "culture of silence" blankets the majority poor in Latin America.[23] This culture of silence is a direct result of the Latin American context of dependency, in which the poor have no opportunity for self-determination; in other words, the poor are what Freire calls "objects" rather than "subjects": "The integrated person is person as *subject*. In contrast, the adaptive person is person as *object*. . . . If a man is incapable of changing reality, he adjusts himself instead. Adaptation is behavior characteristic of the animal sphere; exhibited by man, it is symptomatic of his dehumanization."[24]

Liberation theologians exhort the church to conscientize the poor by proclaiming to them the good news that God is a liberating God who has a preference for them and in whose reign they have priority. The church demonstrates God's love for the poor when it puts itself in solidarity with them, as the documents from Medellín (1968) and Puebla (1980) decreed. Conscientization, when practiced by the church, implies a willingness to learn from the poor, to treat them as subjects, not objects, and to pave the way for their liberation.

Latin American base communities exemplify the conscientization process and the participation of the poor
which Freire discusses. Base communities began to emerge
in the 1960s, especially among the poor and the marginalized, because of the shortage of priests in Latin America.
At the Medellín conference, these communities were ap-
plauded as being an essential part of evangelization. Today,
base communities exist throughout Latin America, with
the strongest concentration in Brazil. Generally, base communities consist of twelve to fifteen persons who meet reg-
ularly to read the Bible and to reflect on it in the light of
their context. Their reflection frequently leads to praxis
aimed at ameliorating oppression. Praxis might entail community participation to construct a road or a well, or political involvement to effect substantive change.

Ideally, the theological reflection of base communities
is incorporated into "professional" liberation theology.
The three levels of liberation theology—professional
(trained theologians), pastoral (priests and ministers), and
popular (the people, especially in base communities)—
have been diagrammed as a tree: "Those who see only
professional theologians at work in it see only the
branches of the tree. They fail to see the trunk, which is
the thinking of priests and other pastoral ministers. . . .
The roots are the practical living and thinking—though
submerged and anonymous—going on in tens of thousands of base communities living out their faith and thinking it in a liberating key."[25]

## Main Emphases

### *Liberation*

In the mid-1960s, when liberation theology was initially
formulated, "development" was the catchword of the
times for the amelioration of the Latin American situation.
The Alliance for Progress purposed to develop Latin
America economically, socially, and politically. However,
dissonant voices questioned the sufficiency of development
and wondered whether it locked Latin America into dependent relationships with foreign corporations and gov-

ernments. Instead of development, these critics employed the word "liberation" to signify a radical break from dependent relationships and ineffective development programs. The word itself referred to contemporary events in Latin America. The Cuban Revolution had occurred only a few years earlier, in 1959, kindling hope for a new social order. Also, two revolutionary figures, Camilo Torres and Ernesto "Che" Guevara, were killed in 1966 and 1967, respectively, in their attempts for liberation through guerrilla movements. "'Liberation' thus implied a *revolutionary option* and a clear *political and ideological break* from nationalist-developmentalist reformism and from the new military regimes. It is within this *specific* historical context that we must understand the shift from a theology of *development* to a theology of *liberation.*"[26]

Liberation was adopted by many, including liberation theologians, as the alternative to development because it encapsulated the vision for a new social order for Latin America. Their reflection on liberation in the light of the historical Jesus led only to a further rejection of development, for Jesus had drawn a severe dichotomy between the old and new orders. He likened his ministry to new wine which cannot be poured into old wineskins without bursting them (Mark 2:21–22).

 Recognizing the many dimensions of dependency, Gutiérrez delineates three interdependent levels of liberation—liberation in the economic/political sphere, liberation from dehumanization, and liberation from sin.[27]

The first level addresses oppression of the poor by the rich, workers by owners, and majority by minority which is institutionalized in unjust economic, political, and social structures. Liberation on this level requires a structural transformation to create economic, political, and social freedom for the majority.

The second level addresses the oppression of dehumanization which "marks not only those whose humanity has been stolen, but also (though in a different way) those who have stolen it." As Freire notes, the culture of silence dehumanizes the poor and oppressed in Latin America who lack a critical consciousness of who they are and what their destiny as a subject, not an object, might be. Liberation allows them the freedom to voice the silence and to follow their "vocation of becoming more fully human."[28]

The third level addresses oppression from sin. Sin is the ultimate cause of all injustice and oppression for individuals and society; it infiltrates every dimension. Liberation from sin enables true communion with God and with neighbor to become a reality.

Jesus is seen as the liberator from each of these oppressions. He fought economic structures with his teaching, such as the parable of the workers who labored for different lengths of time but earned the same wage (Matt. 20:1–16). This parable is a frontal attack on the view that those with more money deserve it and, concomitantly, that the poor deserve their low economic status.[29] He fought social structures by eating meals with so-called sinners and prostitutes. He fought dehumanization by placing human need above even the most sacred traditions such as Sabbath purity (Mark 2:23–3:6). Therefore the oppressed were conscientized in his presence. Blind Bartimaeus, whom the crowds silenced, was given voice and healed by Jesus (Mark 10:46–52). An unnamed woman with a flow of blood and no financial resources touched Jesus and subsequently "told him the whole truth" (Mark 5:25–34). Jesus fought sin by denouncing everything—whether religious, political, economic, or social—that alienated people from God and from their neighbor. In other words, the "fundamental project" of Jesus was "to proclaim and be the instrument of the concrete realization of the absolute meaning of the world: i.e., liberation *from* every stigma (including suffering, division, sin and death) and liberation *for* real life, for open-ended communication of love, grace, and plenitude in God."[30]

"Integral liberation" is a phrase used to express this multidimensional liberation. Latin American bishops defined integral liberation in the Puebla document (PD) as liberation that "takes in all the different dimensions of life: the social, the political, the economic, the cultural, and all their interrelationships. Through all these dimensions must flow the transforming treasure of the Gospel" (PD:483). Integral liberation is *integral* because it touches all forms of oppression. Integral liberation is *liberation* because its purpose is to eliminate injustice.

## Reign of God

The most obvious characteristic about the reign of God is that it is God's reign. It is God who initiates and fulfills the reign of God. To underscore God's ultimate role in the reign, these theologians often use phrases such as "God's historical project"[31] or "God's absolute future and God's design for humanity."[32] The God of the reign is an active God who labors within human history to establish the reign. Certainly the historical concretization of God's activity is not without foundation. Liberation theologians frequently point to God's activity in creation, in the exodus, and especially in the person of Jesus.

The most palpable evidence of God's reign, according to Jesus, took place in his miracles: "But if it is by the finger of God that I cast out the demons, then the kingdom of God has come to you" (Luke 11:20; see Matt. 12:28). Through Jesus' miracles God came concretely to the aid of those whom no one else could help. Therefore the sick and demon-possessed whom Jesus healed become powerful symbols of God's gracious activity. Each healing is "concretely experienced as liberation from some type of oppression."[33] The miracles of Jesus, then, are not primarily a demonstration of Jesus' divinity.[34]  Rather, they are actions by which God liberates the oppressed for participation in the reign of God. They are the historical actualization of God's grace toward those who cannot improve their plight.

The central characteristic of God's reign is liberation. It is nothing less than a utopia of integral liberation, "the full liberation of creation—cosmic and human—from its iniquities, and the integral realization of God's design which is the insertion of everything in God's divine life."[35] It will consist of "a world in which the creative plan of God is finally fulfilled; where hunger, poverty, injustice, oppression, pain, even disease and death have been definitively overcome; it is a world from which evil has been rooted out forever."[36]

In the context of dependency and poverty, this utopian vision may appear unrealistic, but here liberation theologians are merely claiming their biblical inheritance. Early Israelite law codes portrayed God as a God who responds directly to the cries of the oppressed: "You shall not abuse any widow or orphan. If you do abuse them, when they cry out to me, I will surely heed their cry; my wrath will burn, and I will kill you with the sword. . . . And if your neighbor cries out to me, I will listen, for I am compassionate" (Ex. 22:22–24, 27b). The Hebrew prophets took these words seriously and stressed God's penchant for justice (e.g., Amos 2:6–8; Hos. 6:6; Micah 6:8). The prophets envisaged a utopia where God would establish justice and where nations would beat their swords into plowshares (Isa. 2:4).

Precisely this vision fired the imagination of Jesus to the point where he proclaimed the near presence of this reign: "The kingdom of God has come near; repent, and believe in the good news" (Mark 1:14–15).[37] He announced this vision in his initial sermon in the synagogue at Nazareth, where he read the assigned words from Isaiah 61:1–3 and then startlingly announced their fulfillment: "Today this scripture has been fulfilled in your hearing" (Luke 4:18–21). In essence, he proclaimed the historical realization of the year of Jubilee, to which Isaiah 61 had referred (Leviticus 25), when all debts were to be remitted and justice was to be restored to the oppressed. What the people had regarded as an ideal, Jesus understood as a historical project. He spent his ministry fulfilling this vision in a concrete historical context (see Matt. 11:2–6).

Jesus did not complete this historical project; the reign of God did not arrive. But he did anticipate "total liberation in a process embodying partial liberations that remain open to complete fulfillment."[38] This is apparent in the Beatitudes, in which the first blessing is a present reality but the following blessings remain in the future:

Blessed are you who are poor, for yours *is* the kingdom
   of God.
Blessed are you who are hungry now, for you *will* be filled.
Blessed are you who weep now, for you *will* laugh.

> Blessed are you when people hate you . . .
> for surely your reward is great *in heaven*.
>                 (Luke 6:20b–23a).[39]

There exists, then, a tension between what Jesus accomplished and what remains to be accomplished, between his effort and God's final intervention.

This tension between present, partial liberation and future, integral liberation is strengthened by the resurrection. On the one hand, the resurrection confirms the liberating efforts of Jesus by raising him to life. On the other hand, the resurrection foreshadows future liberation *in history* by its liberation of Jesus. The resurrection, therefore, validates the path of Jesus and anticipates the goal of that path. It does not, however, complete the process of liberation but opens the path to justice, for now "Jesus continues to exist among human beings, giving impetus to their struggle for liberation."[40]

The followers of Jesus therefore must do what Jesus did: effect partial liberations in order to anticipate the future, integral liberation that God will graciously accomplish. They must live "in a way that will really correspond with the coming kingdom . . . through a concrete praxis that follows in the footsteps of Jesus himself."[41] From this perspective, liberation theologians affirm unanimously that the fulfillment of God's reign demands, even depends upon, human labor.[42] Míguez Bonino asks the question, "Do historical happenings . . . have any value in terms of the Kingdom which God prepares and will gloriously establish in the Parousia of the Lord?"[43] His answer is, Yes! Yes, human labor within history has an impact on the reign of God. In fact, such labor has eternal status: "Every act, action, or plan, which, here and now on this earth, realizes God's plan, even if only partially, will have an eternal future."[44] Therefore the ultimate question is, How can one join in the activity of the kingdom?[45]


## Conversion

Entrance into the reign of God begins with conversion. While liberation theologians accept the typical understanding of conversion as an individual act, they prefer to emphasize its collective dimension. When an individual turns away from sin, that individual must also turn away from sins of a collective nature, such as "alliances with the oppressive structures of this world."[46] Similarly, in conversion an individual must turn toward God and neighbor. This turning creates changed relationships on the divine and human levels which have a collective impact. For instance, when converts turn toward the poor and make the poor their neighbors, then classes and groups in society begin to shift.

In this respect, Latin American liberation theologians appeal to Jesus' social analysis, which led him to address groups within his society. While some of what he says, such as, "The kingdom of God has come near; repent" (Mark 1:15), applied to all people, in fact his message varied according to his audience. God's reign arrives for everyone, but its arrival actually calls for different kinds of conversion for different social classes. This basic distinction is evident in the demands that Jesus placed upon the poor and the powerful.

Even though the reign of God arrives to create justice for the poor quite apart from their effort, Jesus still required of them a conversion of sorts. Their conversion consisted of beginning to believe that God could ameliorate their apparently hopeless situation. They must be converted from despair to hope in the recognition that the reign of God *is theirs* (Luke 6:20). In other words, the poor must be converted "so that they may *believe* in the good news, precisely because it is *so good*, so seemingly incredible and so different from their accustomed situation."[47]

The marvel of Jesus' ministry is that the poor did begin to hope in the liberation of God. The sick cried out to Jesus for healing, the sinful begged Jesus for forgiveness, the demon-possessed searched for release from Jesus, and the poor flocked around Jesus who himself gained a reputation as "a friend of tax collectors and sinners" (Matt. 11:19). In other words, the conscientized poor began to take the initiative to free themselves from oppression.

While the poor received the dawn of God's reign as good

news, the powerful received it as bad news. They recognized that this reign necessitated a restructuring of the society that accorded to them economic, social, and religious privileges. Therefore the basic question Jesus asked of the powerful as a group was whether they were prepared to yield their security to the God who reigns.[48]

On the socioeconomic level, this demand is illustrated by the rich young ruler whom Jesus commanded to sell his possessions, to give to the poor, and to follow Jesus. Matthew adds, "and you will have *treasure in heaven*" (Matt. 19:21), recalling similar words spoken to *all* people in the Sermon on the Mount: "Do not store up for yourselves treasures on earth . . . but store up for yourselves *treasures in heaven*" (Matt. 6:19–20). Thus Matthew is careful to apply universally, through the reiteration of the same phrase, what might otherwise be taken as a demand to only one rich man. Conversion for the powerful, then, requires yielding their socioeconomic security to God.

On the religious level, Jesus condemned the Jewish leaders as a group for their misuse of authority. "He hurls anathemas at the Pharisees for disregarding justice (Matt. 23:23), at the lawyers for imposing intolerable burdens (Matt. 23:4), at the learned for stealing the keys to knowledge (Luke 11:52), and at the rulers of this world for governing despotically (Matt. 20:26)."[49] These invectives reveal the basic unity between religious and socioeconomic charges. The Pharisees, for instance, by means of their interpretation of Torah, provided religious rationale for regarding poverty as the effect of sinfulness. In this way they helped to produce a class of oppressed people who were regarded as both socioeconomically oppressed and religiously impoverished. Consequently, Jesus challenged the Pharisees to a conversion that entailed a move "from the oppressive security of the letter of the law to the liberating insecurity of having to opt for the poor, even in the face of God's very word."[50]

Some leaders in the Roman Catholic Church in Latin America have begun to acknowledge the church's need for conversion. In the Puebla document, the bishops include a litany of the church's sins: "Not all of us in the Latin American Church have committed ourselves sufficiently to the poor. We are not always concerned about them, or in solidarity with them. Service to them really calls for constant conversion and purification among all Christians. That must be done if we are to achieve fuller identification each day with the poor Christ and our own poor" (PD:1140). However, liberation theologians claim that the church has not relinquished its dependence upon the ruling class, provides only timid and ineffective support of the poor, and is unwilling to denounce injustice. Therefore, just as Jesus demanded conversion of the Pharisees, lawyers, and other leaders, liberation theologians demand the conversion of the church. It must turn away from its sins and turn toward the poor, "to a preferential option for the poor, an option aimed at their integral liberation" (PD:1134).

## Preference for the Poor

This confession indicates that liberation theologians are not the only voices calling the church to a preference for the poor. As we have seen again and again, the centrality of the poor is found in the documents of the church, such as those from Medellín (1968) and Puebla (1980). The Puebla document includes a section entitled "A Preferential Option for the Poor," whose opening paragraph unhesitatingly supports Medellín's commitment to the poor: "With renewed hope in the vivifying power of the Spirit, we are going to take up once again the position of . . . Medellín, which adopted a clear and prophetic option expressing preference for, and solidarity with, the poor" (PD:1134). Who are the poor for whom the church stated its preference? The poor consist of two groups: the socioeconomically poor and the evangelically poor.[51]

The socioeconomically poor cannot obtain the basic necessities to sustain life.[52] These are the ones whom Jesus appointed to be the beneficiaries of God's reign: "Blessed are you who are poor, for yours is the kingdom of God" (Luke 6:20b). This blessing clearly refers to the socioeconomic poor, for Jesus proceeded to distinguish them from the wealthy, well fed, and well respected (Luke 6:24–26).[53] The Beatitudes are not the first statements to give preference to the poor. In his introductory sermon at Naz-

areth, Jesus had already included the poor alongside pris-
oners, the blind, and the oppressed as the fortunate
recipients of the good news of liberation (Luke 4:18–19).

Such explicit pronouncements are only one kind of gospel material that expresses Jesus' preference for the poor.
Throughout his ministry, Jesus employed bucolic images in
his parables, welcomed beggars, healed the diseased, and
ate with the sort of people that earned him the reputation
of being "a friend of tax collectors and sinners" (Matt.
9:10–13; 11:19; Mark 2:15–17). In his lengthy journey to
Jerusalem, according to Luke 9:51–19:10, the protagonists
of Jesus' teaching and the objects of Jesus' miracles were
the socially marginalized and the economically deprived:
Samaritans (Luke 10:25–37; 17:11–19); a beggar who sits
daily at a rich man's gate (Luke 16:19–31; cf. 12:13–21);
and a woman whose savings consist of a meager ten days'
wage of a common laborer (Luke 15:8–10). There can be
little doubt, then, that Jesus' sympathies lay with the poor.

But Jesus did far more than sympathize with the oppressed. He became their staunch advocate against their
oppressors. In particular, he fought two ideological battles.
 First, he argued that poverty was not the result of sin but of
injustice. Second, Jesus challenged the assumption that
poverty is inevitable.

Jesus had to fight the first ideological battle with his own
disciples who associated poverty and disease with sinfulness.
On two occasions the disciples expressed this opinion. While
passing a blind man, they asked whether this man or his parents had sinned. Jesus retorted that neither did (John 9:2–3).
At another time, the disciples were shocked when Jesus re-
marked that it is harder for a rich person to enter God's reign
than for a camel to pass through the eye of a needle (Mark
10:17–31). The disciples responded, "Then who can be
saved?" Their faulty logic was simple: if the rich, who receive God's approval through material blessings, cannot be
saved, then how can the poor, who lack God's approval
through material blessings, be saved? If the likely candidates
are not in God's reign, how can unlikely candidates enter?
Jesus opposed this logic outrightly. When the rich man left,
Jesus observed, "How hard it will be for those who have
riches to enter the reign of God!"[54]

The ingenuousness of the disciples' remarks underscores the prevalence of the view that the poor and the sick must be sinners. Jesus contested this religious ideology. He recognized that unjust structures would not change as long as the religious ideology supported the assumption that God rewarded and punished people economically on the basis of their religious life. Therefore he sought to replace the prevailing religious ideology that supported socioeconomic inequality with one that placed a God of justice at the center.

Jesus also opposed an ideology that regarded poverty as inevitable. When he blessed the poor, he did not do so because they voluntarily sought poverty, nor because they were resigned to poverty. He blessed them because with the dawning of God's reign the socioeconomic causes of their poverty were coming to an end. The God who had demanded justice through the ancient law codes (e.g., Ex. 22:22–27) and the prophets (e.g., Amos 2:6–8) intervened through a liberator who proclaimed and enacted a just reign. Because the reign of God brings liberation in its train, poverty *is* escapable, and the poor are blessed.

Jesus' blessing for the poor did not inhibit his love for oppressors. Jesus loved all people to the extent that he stood against all that made them less than human. The oppressors dehumanized themselves by refusing to imitate God's magnanimity (see Matt. 5:43–48); Jesus therefore opposed them for perpetrating injustice. The oppressed were dehumanized because they could not sustain a fully human life socially, economically, and religiously; Jesus therefore gave them the presence and promise of God's reign of justice. In other words, "Jesus' *universal* love takes different concrete forms, depending on the situation. He manifests his love of the oppressed by being *with* them, by offering them something that might restore their dignity and make them truly human. He manifests his love for the oppressors by being *against* them, by trying to strip away all that is making them less than human."[55]

The second group of poor for whom God has a preference is the evangelically poor. These are the poor who have chosen to renounce wealth, prestige, and power in order to be in complete solidarity with the poor.[56] The praxis of the evangelically poor includes calling the rich and the church in Latin America to conversion, forming base communities of the socioeconomic poor, and working within political organizations and trade unions to bring about liberation.

The evangelically poor respond concretely to Jesus by incorporating two dimensions of discipleship: effective action and suffering love. According to Sobrino, Jesus' ministry developed in two phases. In the first phase, Jesus used the effective action of miracles to demonstrate the presence of God's reign (Mark 1:1–8:26). A transition took place as Jesus began to be aware that injustice might win the battle with God's reign and that he would die.[57] Therefore, in the second phase, Jesus taught that, in the struggle for justice, power was to be supplanted by suffering, service by sacrifice. Sobrino suggests that, in the growing complexity of contemporary Latin America, "the two phases of love (as effective action and as accepted suffering) may coexist simultaneously, so that Christians continually seek effective power on behalf of human beings while being open to the realization that it may be snatched away from them."[58]

## Politics and Prophetic Critique

Because liberation theologians take an active interest in the political dimension, they are severely criticized by governments, Roman Catholic Church leaders in Latin America and Rome, and Protestant Church leaders. These theologians respond to the condemnation with three observations about the political dimension of contemporary Latin America that are illuminated by the ministry of Jesus.

First, liberation theologians observe that the Latin American church, by virtue of its size and influence, is and has always been a political power. It maintains intimate ties with the ruling class and adamantly defends the status quo. Thus the question is not one of nonintervention or neutrality. Rather, the question is, Where will the church put its political involvement—behind the perpetuation of the

present unjust situation which benefits a minority, or behind the liberation of the poor majority? On the basis of
Jesus' ministry, the answer is that the church must be involved politically on the side of the poor. Jesus not only
championed the cause of the poor; he also opposed collective powerful groups—lawyers, Pharisees, Sadducees—
for neglecting justice.

Second, liberation theologians note that the political dimension permeates every area of life. At the Puebla conference, the bishops described the political dimension as
"a constitutive dimension of human beings and a relevant
area of human societal life. It has an all-embracing aspect"
(PD:513). They further define politics as seeking "the
common good on both the national and international plane.
. . . In this broad sense politics is of interest to the Church"
(PD:521).[59]

This opinion characterizes Juan Luis Segundo's interpretation of Jesus' command to love. He admits that Jesus'
command can be understood interpersonally and apoliti-
cally. Still, he contends that love, "*effective love*, is the
commandment of Jesus, and anyone can see that such love
is conditioned by all the *systems* that affect human coexist-
ence, from the psychological and interpersonal to the social and international."[60] On this basis Segundo queries,
"When it comes to the Christian understanding of love,
therefore, what valid reason do we have for excluding from
consideration the field in which the most crucial decisions
affecting love's exercise will be made? Would it not be
much more logical to take Jesus' remarks, couched in apparently more interpersonal terms in line with his own era,
and translate them into political terms?"[61]

To support this extension of Jesus' command to the political realm, Segundo appeals to the observation of Vatican II
that many ills in antiquity could be alleviated by action in
one particular field, such as almsgiving in the economic
field or curing in the health field. Over two thousand years,
however, the factors conditioning the effectiveness of love
have changed. In particular, politics has become a powerful sphere which "brings together the threads of all the
other fields and weaves them together to serve the common welfare."[62] For example, the quality of education ex-

ceeds the competence of educators themselves. It depends
to a large extent on the balance between military and other
expenditures in a national budget, "and this is an emi-
nently political question." Jesus' command to love effectively and concretely, therefore, must address the political
dimension, where decisions directly affect even the sub-
sistence of the poor.

The third observation with which liberation theologians
support their political involvement is that the spiritual dimension is integrally related to the political. Once again,
they appeal to the Puebla document which denounces such
a dichotomy. "For Christianity is supposed to evangelize
the whole of human life, including the political dimension.
So the Church criticizes those who would restrict the
scope of faith to personal or family life; who would exclude
the professional, economic, social, and political orders as if
sin, love, prayer, and pardon had no relevance in them"
(PD:515). Without boundaries between the spiritual and
the political dimensions, movement between them is not
only possible but essential.

In addition to appealing to church documents, liberation
theologians appeal to the ministry of Jesus, in which the
religious and political spheres were inseparable. Jesus rejected a purely spiritual message that placed the reign of
God into the future and asked people to wait passively for
it. Instead, he placed the reign of God in the people's very
midst through proclamation, healings, and exorcisms (Luke
17:20–21). Jesus equally rejected a purely political role.
He "overcame temptations to political messianism, which
at the time manifested itself in three currents: prophetical,
in the appearance of the Messiah in the desert; sacerdotal,
in the manifestation of the Liberator in the Temple; and
political, in the revelation of the Messiah on the mountain
of God" (Matt. 4:1–11).[63] Rather than dichotomizing the
political and religious spheres, Jesus forged them together
to concretize a prophetic utopia that challenged all authority but God's and, consequently, led to his trial and death
at the hands of those authorities.

Liberation theologians, in the context of Latin American
oppression, have embraced a portrait of Jesus as prophet.[64]
This portrait lies in contrast to the church's Christology

which has often presented Jesus as Logos, Son of God, or "Christ," all of which are understood largely in apolitical ways. In these theologians' estimation, although "prophet" is a relatively neglected christological category, Jesus regarded himself as a prophet. He took the role of "a prophet mighty in deed and word before God and all the people" (Luke 24:19). Elsewhere, Jesus commented on his own predicament: "Prophets are not without honor, except in their hometown" (Mark 6:4). A few verses later, the people identified Jesus as John the Baptist raised from the dead, or Elijah, or a prophet "like one of the prophets of old" (Mark 6:14–15; see 8:28), underscoring Jesus' prophetic vocation.

Jesus is also paralleled with the prophet Elijah. For instance, as Elijah healed the son of a widow of Zarephath, so Jesus healed the son of a widow of Nain (Luke 7:11–17; 1 Kings 17:8–14). The people of Nain cried out, "A great prophet has risen among us!" The backdrop of Elijah's activity highlights Jesus' integration of the political and religious spheres, for "almost the entire cycle depicts Elijah taking a stand against the politics of Ahab."[65] On one occasion Elijah opposed Jehu's domestic policy because it oppressed the weak, such as Naboth, who lost his vineyard and his life to Ahab (1 Kings 21:1–24). This story struck deep roots in Israel's consciousness, no doubt helping the people to identify Jesus with Elijah as a champion of the powerless.

Jesus is also portrayed as the prophet Jeremiah, another prophet who combined politics and religion (Matt. 16:14). Jeremiah provided purely political counsel with the sanction that it came from God (e.g., Jer. 21:8–10), while on other occasions he demanded pure religion so that the people could escape dire political consequences (e.g., Jer. 22:3a, 5b).[66]

Like the prophets before him, Jesus called into question the religio-political authorities. He challenged the priests' authority by overturning the Temple's tables. He challenged the Pharisees' authority by disputing their oral tradition. He even challenged the authority and divinity of Caesar by arguing that taxes be paid to Caesar but one's whole self be given to God (Mark 12:13–17). In addition to his own challenges, Jesus mobilized the poor in such a way that they themselves threatened the religious and political authorities of first-century Palestine. By raising the dignity of the poor while simultaneously undermining the author- ity of the leaders, Jesus brought to light the socioeconomic conflicts latent in his society. His apparently religious proclamation of God's reign therefore took on an alarming political tone, for "someone who is systematically destroy- ing the *real* authority of the dominant group in a theoc- racy—even if, or rather precisely because, he is doing that in *religious* terms—becomes a fearful *political* adver- sary."[67]

Inevitably Jesus was put on trial. The two trials of Jesus exhibit the same fusion of religion and politics as the life of Jesus. Jesus was tried first before the Jewish leaders, where he was convicted of blasphemy, not because someone could not be the Messiah, but because Jesus, who had stood against divinely sanctioned authority—the Temple and tradition—could not possibly be the Messiah. The Jewish leaders then handed Jesus to Pilate, the Roman ruler, for a second trial, where he was convicted and sen- tenced to crucifixion.

The Jewish leaders accused Jesus before Pilate of incit- ing political rebellion: "He stirs up the people by teaching throughout all Judea, from Galilee where he began even to this place" (Luke 23:5). This indictment was not entirely true; Jesus had not opted with the Zealots to stir up the people against Rome. But on quite another level it was a valid charge. Jesus was not a political threat to Rome, but his popularity was a threat to the Jewish leaders. The irony of this charge about the politics of Jesus, at once true yet false, simply "demonstrates the conflict-ridden nature of every process of liberation undertaken when the structure of injustice has gained the upper hand. Under such condi- tions liberation can come about only through martyrdom and sacrifice on behalf of others and God's cause in the world."[68]

Jesus had known that his prophetic critique would lead to martyrdom, for that had been the fate of many prophets who had gone before him (Matt. 5:11–12). The prophets' view of a God who demanded justice as the true form of worship,[69] who required "mercy, not sacrifice,"[70] who called rulers to account for their injustice, had met with rejection. Having challenged the authority of the elite and sided with the powerless, Jesus had little left to do than to side with them in his death on the cross.

## NOTES

1. Thomas Skidmore and Peter Smith, *Modern Latin America* (New York: Oxford University Press, 1984), 46.

2. Ibid., 47.

3. "Besides, their [the middle class] role in changing society has been ambivalent, dependent as they are on the upper classes and vulnerable to the inflationary process and economic deterioration. The middle-class mentality—identified with the values of the upper class—is afraid of social changes from below and tends to support the status quo. Others, however, become aware of their common lot with the lower classes" (Esther and Mortimer Arias, *The Cry of My People: Out of Captivity in Latin America* [New York: Friendship Press, 1980], 20).

4. Ibid., 19.

5. Trevor Beeson and Jenny Pearce, *A Vision of Hope: The Churches and Change in Latin America* (Philadelphia: Fortress Press, 1984), 233.

6. On the ineffectiveness of the Alliance for Progress, see Beeson and Pearce, *A Vision of Hope*, 22, 233–234.

7. The Catholic Action movement employed this methodology and gave it this particular nomenclature.

8. Edward Cleary, *Crisis and Change: The Church in Latin America Today* (Maryknoll, N.Y.: Orbis Books, 1985), 22.

9. Leonardo Boff and Clodovis Boff, *Introducing Liberation Theology* (Maryknoll, N.Y.: Orbis Books, 1987), 24.

10. Two other important conclusions were made at Medellín. First, the bishops decreed that because of the unjust structures in Latin America, a situation of "institutionalized violence" exists (see Med. 2:16). Because of this already violent situation, the bishops conclude: "We should not be surprised therefore, that the 'temptation to violence' is surfacing in Latin America. One should not abuse the patience of a people that for years has borne a situation that would not be acceptable to any one with any de-

gree of awareness of human rights" (Med. 2:16). Second, the bishops sanctioned the role of the base communities as the "initial cell of the ecclesiastical structures and the focus of evangelization, and it currently serves as the most important source of human advancement and development" (Med. 15:10).

11. "The history of all hitherto existing society is the history of class struggles" (Karl Marx and Friedrich Engels, *The Communist Manifesto* [New York: Modern Reader Paperbacks, 1964], 2).

12. This understanding of praxis comes from Marx's eleventh thesis on Feuerbach: "The philosophers have only *interpreted* the world, in various ways; the point is to *change* it" (Karl Marx and Friedrich Engels, *Basic Writings on Politics and Philosophy* [Garden City, N.Y.: Doubleday & Co., 1959], 245). In a comment on Marx's notion of praxis, Steven Mackie ("Praxis as the Context for Interpretation: A Study of Latin American Liberation Theology," *Journal of Theology for Southern Africa* 24 [1978]: 32) writes, "Praxis is the basic/human power of transforming the environment by creative activity."

13. Gustavo Gutiérrez, "Statement by Gustavo Gutiérrez," in *Theology in the Americas*, ed. Torres and Eagleson, 310.

14. Gustavo Gutiérrez, *A Theology of Liberation: History, Politics, and Salvation*, rev. ed. (Maryknoll, N.Y.: Orbis Books, 1973), 11.

15. Ibid., 9–10.

16. Juan Luis Segundo, *The Historical Jesus of the Synoptics* (Maryknoll, N.Y.: Orbis Books, 1985), 1–12, 40–41. See also J. Severino Croatto, "The Political Dimension of Christ the Liberator," in *Faces of Jesus: Latin American Christologies*, ed. José Míguez Bonino (Maryknoll, N.Y.: Orbis Books, 1984), 112; and Mackie, "Praxis as the Context for Interpretation," 31–43.

17. Jon Sobrino, *Christology at the Crossroads* (Maryknoll, N.Y.: Orbis Books, 1978), 2–9.

18. For other examples, see Saúl Trinidad, "Christology, *Conquista*, Colonization," in *Faces of Jesus*, ed. Míguez Bonino, 49–65.

19. Their use of historical-critical methods ranges widely. Some use them sparingly: Elsa Tamez, *The Bible of the Oppressed* (Maryknoll, N.Y.: Orbis Books, 1982); Leonardo Boff, *Jesus Christ Liberator: A Critical Christology for Our Time* (Maryknoll, N.Y.: Orbis Books, 1978); and Hugo Echegaray, *The Practice of Jesus* (Maryknoll, N.Y.: Orbis Books, 1984). Sobrino (*Crossroads*, 35, 3) prefers to deal with the "intention" of Jesus rather than details of his words and deeds. Segundo (*Historical Jesus*, 45–70)

uses the historical-critical method throughout his analysis. He explains it in his introduction to part two. See the article by C. E. Gudorf, "Liberation Theology's Use of Scripture: A Response to First World Critics," *Interpretation* 41 (1987): 5–18.

20. According to Michael Cook, liberation theologians do not agree on which pole is prior. Boff and Sobrino begin with Jesus, applying their insights to Latin America. Gutiérrez, Assmann, and Segundo, who are interested primarily in method, seem to claim that one's image of God, and so of Jesus, will appear differently in different historical situations (Michael Cook, "Jesus from the Other Side of History: Christology in Latin America," *Theological Studies* 44 [1983]: 275).

21. On Latin American biblical interpretation, see David Batstone, *From Conquest to Struggle: Jesus of Nazareth in Latin America* (Albany, N.Y.: State University of New York Press, 1991), 139–164. Batstone also analyzes Latin American liberation interpretations of the life, death, and resurrection of Jesus.

22. Paulo Freire, *Education for Critical Consciousness* (New York: Seabury Press, 1973), 17.

23. Ibid., 17. See also Paulo Freire, *The Politics of Education: Culture, Power, and Liberation* (South Hadley, Mass.: Bergin & Garvey, 1985), 72–75.

24. Freire, *Education for Critical Consciousness*, 4.

25. Boff and Boff, *Introducing Liberation Theology*, 12.

26. Pablo Richard, *Death of Christendoms, Birth of the Church* (Maryknoll, N.Y.: Orbis Books, 1987), 146.

27. See Gutiérrez, *A Theology of Liberation*, xxxviii–xxxix; 24–25.

28. Paulo Freire, *Pedagogy of the Oppressed* (New York: Penguin Books, 1970), 28.

29. See Segundo, *Historical Jesus*, 126–127.

30. Boff, *Liberator*, 280–281.

31. Echegaray, *Practice of Jesus*, 81.

32. Mortimer Arias, *Announcing the Reign of God: Evangelization and the Subversive Memory of Jesus* (Philadelphia: Fortress Press, 1984), 39.

33. Sobrino, *Crossroads*, 358. No doubt this oppression of the sick was physical and social, that is, including ostracism from society, particularly where sin was regarded as the cause of sickness.

34. See Sobrino, *Crossroads*, 46–50; and Boff, *Liberator*, 54.

35. Leonardo Boff, *Desde el Lugar del Pobre*, 2nd ed. (Bogotá: Ediciones Paulinas, 1986), 45. Translation ours.

36. José Míguez Bonino, *Room to Be People* (Philadelphia: Fortress Press, 1979), 41.

37. "God's reign is at hand and already dawning, though it has not yet reached its culmination. It is not merely an extension of human potentialities; it breaks in as grace. Neither is it merely a transformation of the inner person. It is also a restructuring of the visible, tangible relationships existing between human beings. It is authentic liberation at every level of human existence" (Sobrino, *Crossroads*, 44).

38. Boff, *Liberator*, 282.

39. Segundo, *Historical Jesus*, 155.

40. Boff, *Liberator*, 291.

41. Sobrino, *Crossroads*, 65.

42. "To say that the coming of the Kingdom must be welcomed in history is in no way to deny that for the Christian the fullness of communion with God is to be realized beyond history. And belief in this future dimension of the Reign of God should not diminish a Christian's willingness to make a commitment within history. We have to take into account these two aspects of the Kingdom as we work out our Christian lives. It is not easy. We always tend to overemphasize one or the other, depending on the circumstances of the moment in the life of the church. *What is uniquely Christian is to hold onto both dimensions*" (Gustavo Gutiérrez, "Latin America's Pain Is Bearing Fruit," *Latinamerica Press* [May 26, 1983], 5). Italics ours.

43. José Míguez Bonino, *Doing Theology in a Revolutionary Situation* (Philadelphia: Fortress Press, 1975), 139.

44. Míguez Bonino, *Room to Be People*, 55.

45. Míguez Bonino, *Doing Theology*, 143.

46. Orlando Costas, *Christ Outside the Gate: Mission Beyond Christendom* (Maryknoll, N.Y.: Orbis Books, 1982), 14.

47. Segundo, *Historical Jesus*, 141. Segundo also utilizes the ideas of Freire when he states that the poor who are the objects of God's reign must learn to become the subjects of God's reign.

48. Sobrino, *Crossroads*, 52.

49. Ibid., 211.

50. Segundo, *Historical Jesus*, 131.

51. These designations for the two groups of poor come from Boff and Boff, *Introducing Liberation Theology*, 46–49.

52. The bishops at Puebla recognized that the plight of the socioeconomically poor is perpetuated by social, economic, and political conditions in society. "Analyzing this situation more deeply, we discover that this poverty is not a passing phase. Instead it is the product of economic, social, and political situations and structures" (PD:30).

53. In other words, they are not the *spiritually* poor. Liberation theologians naturally tend to prefer Luke's version to Matthew's (Matt. 5:3). See Echegaray, *Practice of Jesus*, 111 n. 16.

54. The note of reversal is especially evident when Jesus surprisingly proclaims, "Truly I tell you, the tax collectors and the prostitutes are going into the kingdom of God ahead of you" (Matt. 21:31b). On the parallel that exists between this passage and the blessing of the poor, see Segundo, *Historical Jesus*, 116.

55. Sobrino, *Crossroads*, 214. Boff writes, "Thus Jesus and his message divide people, and that is of the essence of the kingdom. People enter it by breaking with this world and changing it, not by prolonging its existing structure. Jesus was for all. But in the concrete he was for the poor insofar as he was one of them and shouldered their cause; he was for the Pharisees insofar as he unmasked their vaunted self-sufficiency; and he was for the rich insofar as he denounced the mechanisms they used to maintain injustice and worship mammon. Finally, he died so that we might know that not everything is permitted in this world" (Boff, *Liberator*, 288).

56. See the Puebla document, pars. 1148–1150.

57. Sobrino, *Crossroads*, 115–118, 125–127, 359–362.

58. Ibid., 136.

59. Medellín echoes this statement. "The exercise of political authority and its decisions have as their only end the common good" (Med. 1:16).

60. Segundo, *Historical Jesus*, 81.

61. Ibid., 83.

62. Ibid.

63. Boff, *Liberator*, 60. See also Segundo Galilea, "Jesus' Attitude Toward Politics: Some Working Hypotheses," in *Faces of Jesus*, ed. Míguez Bonino, 98. Liberation theologians unanimously reject aligning Jesus with Zealot nationalism.

64. Segundo, *Historical Jesus*, 77–79, 134–149; Ignacio Ellacuría, "The Political Nature of Jesus' Mission," in *Faces of Jesus*, ed. Míguez Bonino, 81–82; and Galilea, "Jesus' Attitude Toward Politics," 96–99.

65. Segundo, *Historical Jesus*, 78. Elijah's defeat of the prophets of Baal marked a political watershed for Ahab and Jezebel, for God's next command for Elijah was political: to anoint Hazael to be king over Syria and Jehu to be king over Israel (1 Kings 19:15–16).

66. Ibid., 79.

67. Ibid., 93; see also Sobrino, *Crossroads*, 210–211; and Croatto, "The Political Dimension of Christ the Liberator," 116.

68. Boff, *Liberator*, 290.

69. E.g., Amos 5:21–24; Micah 6:8.

70. Hos. 6:6, twice quoted by Matthew (Matt. 9:13; 12:7).

Chapter 3

# Jesus in Asia

## Issues Faced

### Asian Religiousness

Many of the "great scripture religions of the world" began
in Asia: Judaism, Christianity, and Islam in western Asia;
Hinduism, Buddhism-Jainism, and Zoroastrianism in southern Asia; and Confucianism, Taoism, and Shinto in eastern
Asia.[1] Although Christianity was founded in Asia (Palestine),
it "left Asia very early and forced its way back several centuries later as a stranger and 'intruder' which Asia consistently
refused to entertain."[2] For this reason, after four centuries of
missionary work, Christianity remains a tiny minority of approximately 2 to 3 percent of the Asian population.[3] In
China and India lives 60 percent of the Asian population,
but the percentage of Christians is minimal, probably less
than 1 percent in China and less than 4 percent in India.[4]

The liability of Christianity's minority status is com-
pounded by its association with Asia's colonial past. Western
missionaries accompanied the trading vessels coming to the
East, as can be seen in this description of Vasco da Gama's
arrival in India in 1498: "The captain-general's ship flew at
its mast a flag on which was painted a large cross of Christ
and also carried cannon, symbols of the new power entering
the East."[5] Missionaries' symbiosis with colonial govern-

ments enabled them to hold a privileged status. Asian converts to Christianity reflected this social standing, since
many came from the middle class and the ruling elite. Because Christianity derived its support from the colonial governments and powerful nationals, the gulf between the
institutional church and the poor majority widened.[6]

Asian religions have experienced a resurgence which results, in particular, from a new emphasis on justice. No
longer is it possible to categorize Christianity as historical
and life-affirming and Asia's religions as ahistorical and life-
negating. Rather, Asian religions contribute to justice
movements by emphasizing a common humanity called together to confront common human problems; by affirming
the dignity of the individual; and by rejecting historical fatalism in favor of collective activism that draws on religious
resources. Christianity as a minority religion, then, faces
not only the question of truth claims but also the existence
of powerful and relevant religious traditions. More than
ever before, Christianity must ask what contribution it can
make when Asian religions are meeting more effectively
the spiritual and social needs of the masses of Asians.[7]

### Asian Poverty

The second prominent issue that Asian theology must address is poverty. With a few exceptions, such as Japan and
South Korea, most Asian nations are immersed in poverty.
For example, in 1982 the Catholic Church in India determined that, out of a population of 690 million, some 597
million Indians live on or below the poverty line.[8] The report estimated that 70 percent of the Indian population
lacks vitamins and minerals for healthy growth and food for
a daily existence (less than 1,500–2,000 calories a day).
Such malnutrition perpetuates an inescapable cycle of
"low income/low consumption/lower capacities for work/
lower income."[9]

The cause most frequently cited by theologians for
Asia's poverty is colonialism. Before colonialism, Asia sustained a "subsistence-level" but "self-sufficient" econ-
omy.[10] As in Latin America, colonialism in Asia led to the
production of goods for export to other nations and to the

neglect of basic food production.[11] Although colonialism officially ended in Asia, neo-colonialism continues in its stead. With neo-colonialism, a small ruling elite inherited the power possessed by the colonials. In effect, then, there was never a distribution of power. "Our independence movement terminated in a transfer of power without a social revolution. A westernized elite with economic interests integrated into the interests of the outgoing colonial power became the successor. . . . It has been to their advantage to keep practically everything unchanged."[12] The result of neo-colonialism is evident in India where approximately one tenth of the population owns over half of the property and accounts for one third of India's total consumption.[13]

Economic inequality is reinforced by detrimental legacies from the pre-colonial period, such as social divisions based on sex, caste, or tribe. These inequalities frequently mount up on top of each other. For instance, a woman belonging to the Scheduled Caste (the *harijans*, or the untouchables) accumulates inequalities because of her gender and her caste.

## Sources and Method

The starting point for Asian theology is the Asian reality. This "reality becomes a theological source—*locus theologicus*—for its reflection, interpretation and formulation. In a way it is the most fundamental and important of all its sources—*loci theologici*. If there is no reality, if there is not this source, there will be no theology or no raison d'etre for it."[14] This Asian reality encompasses three aspects: the social reality of the Asian people, the religious reality, and the socioeconomic reality. The Bible, as a source for Asian theology, is the primary conversation partner with each of these realities.

Some Asian theologians begin with the *social reality* of the Asian people. For these theologians, the Asian people provide the fertile soil for theology. C. S. Song underscores the link between theology and the people: "Humanity to theology is something like water to fish. Fish die when taken out of water. Theology dies when divorced from hu-

man life and history."[15] In particular, Asian theologians reflect theologically on the people's folktales, stories, and
other artistic expressions. For instance, some Korean theologians reflect on social biographies of the *minjung*; the English translation of *minjung* comes closest to "the mass of
the people" or just "the people." Social biographies of the
minjung, who are workers, students, poor women farmers,
intellectuals, or the urban poor, reveal the present social
reality. Social biographies give rise to artistic forms when
the stories are enacted, such as the Korean mask dance, a
dramatic portrayal in which the minjung ridicule their oppressors. The plot is a simple one in which the protagonists, the minjung, poke fun at their oppressive religious
and political rulers, the antagonists. Through the mask
dance, the minjung "express a critical transcendence over
this world" by acting out its absurdity. In the mask dance
the minjung "not only see correctly the reality of the
world, which neither the rulers nor leaders can see because of their obsession with or separation from the world,
but also envision another reality over against and beyond
this one which neither the rulers nor leaders can see
either."[16]

Theologians like Song put such stories at the center of
their sociological and theological reflections: "the persons
who toil and labor, who hold anguish and hope in their
hearts, who long for an emancipated life in a world of conflict and strife. It is they who will tell us true stories of their
faith. . . . Theologians should read such stories and draw
theological meaning out of them."[17]

The Bible at this level is placed in conversation with social biography. Song uses the Bible to mirror social biography in a "people hermeneutic," in which he juxtaposes
popular Asian expressions and the Bible.[18] The Buddhist lotus and the Christian cross, for instance, both emerge from
the biographies of common people.[19] As the cross has been
the focus of Christian devotion, so the image of Buddha
seated cross-legged on the lotus has brought serenity to
countless people. On the surface these images are different. The lotus springs peacefully from fertile water and exists harmoniously with the earth as a symbol of gentleness.
The cross is lifted defiantly from the barren earth as a sym-

bol of brutality. Yet they are similar in many respects. The lotus and the cross are attempts to answer the basic question of human suffering: "Asian Buddhists enter human suffering through the lotus, and Christians through the cross."[20] Both symbols belong not to theologians but to people in their daily struggles. They represent two storytellers who lived among common people. And they reinforce the protest of power: Buddha against Hinduism's oppressive caste system and Jesus against the wealthy and the Pharisees.

*Asian religions* comprise the second aspect of the Asian reality. The scriptures of these religions, such as the Upanishads of Hinduism, the Analects of Confucius, or the Koran of Islam, are key ingredients in the mixture of Asian theology. When the Bible is juxtaposed with these scriptures, the question of relative merit naturally arises.[21] For instance, should Jesus be understood according to traditional biblical categories, such as "Messiah" or "Son of God"? Or should Jesus be understood according to the categories of other scriptures? There are countless examples of the latter throughout Asia. In Northeast Asia, where Buddhism dominates, Jesus is portrayed as a bodhisattva who postpones his own enlightenment in order to suffer with human beings in their quest for enlightenment.[22] In Southeast Asia, where Islam dominates, Jesus is portrayed as a guru who demonstrates to his disciples a life of union with God that is at once prophetic and mystical.[23] In south central Asia, where Hinduism dominates, Jesus' life is "altogether a picture of ideal Hindu life,"[24] and he is incarnated as an avatar, a Hindu savior figure.[25]

The ease with which Jesus has been assimilated to the great religious traditions of Asia has prompted caution among Asian theologians. To prevent the wholesale absorption of Jesus into Asian religions, they espouse in theory the Western distinction between the Jesus of history and the Christ of faith.[26] Most Asian theologians underscore that the mystical or risen Christ should share the same qualities as the historical Jesus.[27] This approach to Jesus can be diagrammed as a circle. At its center stands the incarnation. Emerging from the incarnation are diverse Christologies that interpret the incarnation by means of Asia's traditions, including Jesus as bodhisattva, guru, and avatar. But in theory these Christologies cannot be created ad infinitum, for at the circumference of the circle lies the recognition that the Christ who meets Asia's needs must be continuous with the incarnate Jesus.[28]

The third major aspect of the Asian reality is *socioeconomic*. To analyze this dimension, some Asian theologians adopt the use of Marxist social analysis from Latin American liberation theology. Marxism provides the framework for understanding class division in Asia, the poverty of the many and the opulence of the few, and the alienation of the workers from "both the means and the fruits of production."[29] Still, they do not implement Marxist social analysis as wholeheartedly as their Latin American counterparts. One reservation about its usefulness is their distrust of Western ideologies, and Marxism comes from the West. Another is that Marx separates the socioeconomic factor from people's religiosity. Because of this, Marxism is not comprehensive enough to address the entirety of the Asian reality.[30]

Their insistence on the "entirety" of the Asian reality has a direct impact on their use of the Bible. Asian biblical interpreters incorporate the socioeconomic aspect of Latin American liberation theology and Marxism as only one aspect alongside the personal and religious dimensions of the Asian reality. Asian biblical interpretation entails, at its best, a holistic approach to the Bible that reaches the social, religious, and socioeconomic dimensions of the Asian reality. The Bible "resounds with the Word of God in the Scriptures of other religions as well as . . . permeating actions for justice and peace."[31]

## Main Emphases

### Cosmic Christ

At the World Council of Churches meeting in New Delhi, India, in 1961 two theologians from different continents espoused a cosmic Christology. Joseph Sittler, on the basis of Colossians 1:15–20, commended "a cosmic Christology" which extends redemption from humanity to nature. By means of this cosmic Christology, he confronted his own North American context, with the capacity of its nuclear arsenal to destroy the natural world which Christ redeemed.[32]

Paul D. Devanandan espoused a cosmic Christology by which he extended Christ's presence to Asian religions. On the basis of Ephesians 1:9–10, he observed that "the whole creation, . . . every aspect of what we associate with earthly existence, will be brought eventually under the direct sway of God."[33] If the creation will be gathered in Christ, reasoned Devanandan, so too will other religions. By means of this cosmic Christology, he addressed his own Indian context, with its "surging new life manifest in other religions."[34] Devanandan observed among non-Christians the "deep, inner stirrings of the human spirit" which he was compelled to attribute to the Holy Spirit. A cosmic Christology provided the foundation for affirming God's presence in these stirrings.

Sittler and Devanandan furnished the basic characteristics of the cosmic Christ that many Asian theologians embrace. Christ's presence leaves its impression on all of nature. Christ's presence is also to be found in all religious experience.[35] The biblical foundation of this interpretation rests primarily with Colossians 1:15–20, in which Christ is shown to be universally accessible to humankind because his presence permeates all of creation. Three foci of this passage relate to Christ's universal presence in non-Christian religions.

First, according to Colossians 1, the cosmos has its origin, present sustenance, and fulfillment in Christ. Christ is the origin of creation: "All things have been created through him and for him" (Col. 1:16b). Christ is the sustainer of the creation: "and in him all things hold together" (Col. 1:17b). Christ is the goal of creation: "and through him God was pleased to reconcile to himself all things" (Col. 1:20a). This perception of Christ has implications for Christianity's relationship to other religions. Prior to any religious confession, people exist "in Christ" because they are part of the creation of which Christ is the origin. Although people may not confess Christ consciously, they are nevertheless sustained by Christ and are in relationship with him by virtue of being in the creation. Finally, since the cosmos is in the process of being fulfilled in Christ, people of all religions will find their final destiny "in Christ."

The second focus of Colossians 1 is cosmic unity. The concept of unity pervades Colossians 1:15–20 through the reiteration of the words "all things." "All things," every disparate part of creation, are unified in Christ before they can be distinguished from each other. Unity in Christ precedes any division, because the cosmic Christ contains them all. Therefore there remains no exception to the universal fulfillment of "all things" in Christ. Similarly, humankind is united by cosmic solidarity in Christ before it can be divided by religious confession. No religion, then, can mitigate the cosmic unity established in the creation by Christ. All religious dialogue must take place in the light of this recognition that "all things," including Christians and adherents of other religions, are held together by the cosmic Christ who unifies the creation.

The third focus of Colossians 1 is the universal accessibility of God to the creation through the mediation of Christ. Christ is "the image of the invisible God," the means by which the creation can perceive its Creator (Col. 1:15). This enlightenment manifests itself as a shared "conceptual framework" between Christianity and other religions: "Many Christian truths, abstracted from their original context, are found as unspoken presuppositions in what we may call the conceptual framework of non-Christian religious practice."[36]

Raimundo Panikkar, in *The Unknown Christ of Hinduism*, explores this conceptual framework. His goal is to discern the unity between Christianity and Hinduism without mitigating the differences between them. He discovers their meeting point at the deepest experience of mystery which both religions share. This mystery is neither "a principle unknown to Hinduism" nor "a dimension of the divine unknown to Christianity" but "that unknown *reality*, which Christians call Christ, discovered in the heart of Hinduism, not as a stranger to it, but as its very *principle of life*, as the light which illumines every Man who comes into the World."[37]

One experiences this mystery as a mediation between the divine (absolute) and the created (relative) world.[38] In Hinduism, this divine absolute is known as Brahman. The mediator between absolute Brahman and the created world is Isvara, who is Brahman in his aspect as personal God and Creator.[39] Isvara corresponds to the cosmic Christ, who is divine and the mediator between the divine and created spheres. This meeting point between Hinduism and Christianity leads Panikkar ultimately to say: "That from which this World comes forth and to which it returns and by which it is sustained, that is Isvara, the Christ."[40]

The minority status of Christianity in Asia has not, then, led to a minor presentation of Christ. On the contrary, the scope of Christ's presence is cosmic. Christ is not limited to Palestine or even to the church and two millennia of Christendom. As Panikkar testifies, "A Christ who could not be present in Hinduism, or a Christ who was not with every least sufferer, a Christ who did not have his tabernacle in the sun, a Christ who did not represent the cosmotheandric reality with one Spirit seeing and recreating all hearts and renewing the face of the earth, surely would not be my Christ, nor, I suspect, would he be the Christ of the Christians."[41]

## Liberation as Humanization

"Asia's Struggle for Full Humanity" was the focus of the 1979 EATWOT conference that met in Wennappuwa, Sri Lanka. The words "a full humanity" encapsulate the goal of liberation envisaged by Asian theology: that all people live fully human lives. Because people comprise the center of Asian liberation, "humanization" is often substituted for "liberation." Economic and political structures, cultural values and institutions, are relevant as they impede the liberative process toward humanization. Therefore Jesus the liberator in Asia is actually Jesus the humanizer. Jesus' proclamation of the reign of God is the proclamation of humanization, a new humanity characterized by "total human development, i.e., concerned both for the life of sin/ grace and for human dignity, human rights, human sufferings, human life, concern for both the world to come and for this world and its human concerns."[42]

The dominant image of the new humanity is Jesus' sitting at a table with the marginalized of society. By eating with social outcasts, Jesus demonstrated tangibly that they belonged to Jewish society and, even more, that they had a right to commune in God's presence during the prayers that preceded and followed the meal. This new humanity encircles the one who is "a glutton and a drunkard, a friend of tax collectors and sinners" (Matt. 11:19; Mark 2:15–17).[43]

At a more basic level is the dehumanization of destructive values that are internalized. For example, the untouchable within the caste system begins to believe that he or she *deserves* to be untouchable. The goal of liberation as humanization is to destroy negative cultural institutions and internalized values and to create responsible people.

Jesus was also cognizant of the dehumanizing cultural values and institutions that prevented the full establishment of the new humanity. In his teaching he opposed these oppressive institutions. He placed Torah at the disposal of humans by healing on the Sabbath (Mark 2:23–3:6). He placed the Temple at the disposal of all people by reestablishing its Court of the Gentiles as a place of prayer "for all the nations" (Mark 11:17). He placed the meal table at the disposal of the poorest and most marginalized of Israel (Mark 2:13–17). The three great institutions of Judaism—Torah, Temple, table—Jesus made accessible to the least in human society. In short, he placed the reign of God at the disposal of "the tax collectors and the prostitutes" (Matt. 21:31).[44]

Jesus also recognized that the attainment of full humanity requires repentance, regardless of socioeconomic condition. Fully human people must be full of mercy, like those depicted in Matthew's beatitudes (Matt. 5:1–12), and full of love for others that is expressed in tangible acts of service (Luke 6:35; 17:32–33; Matt. 7:21; 5:43–48; 6:14; Mark 10:42–45).[45] From this demand to love mercifully, even the poor are not exempt. For they become human only as they decide to work for the humanization of others: "The poor also, no less than the rich, have to put the reign of God before everything else. . . . No radical

change, personal or social, is possible so long as the enslaved love their own fetters. The Kingdom of God will belong to the poor only if they are also poor in spirit; i.e.,
open to the future."[46] The ideal of the new humanity is that
the oppressed, awakened to their new situation, will throw
off the shackles of internalized cultural norms and work for
liberation through organized struggle.[47]

Asian theologians emphasize that complete humanization requires the transformation of individuals into responsible members of the new humanity. Responsibility may
take on different forms in Asia, such as self-sacrifice or social revolution. On the one hand, Song espouses people's
politics, the power of the people in their self-sacrifice. An
example of people's politics is his *The Tears of Lady Meng*,
whose subtitle is "A Parable of People's Political Theology."[48] In this story, Emperor Shi Huang-Ti kills Lady
Meng's husband and buries him in the Great Wall of China.
As she searches for his body, her tears crumble the wall
where he is buried, thus exposing his body. The effect of
her tears demonstrates "the power of the people's tears."
In the meantime, the emperor wants to marry Lady Meng.
She demands that the emperor meet several requests, including building a funeral pyre in memory of her husband.
The story ends as Lady Meng throws herself off the pyre
into the river, where "the little pieces of Lady Meng's
body changed into little silver fish, in which the soul of the
faithful Meng Chiang lives for ever." This story of people's
politics mirrors the self-sacrifice of the politics of the cross.
"The politics of the cross has taken form in resistance, in
revolt, in revolution. But above all, it has inspired a great
many persons to believe in self-sacrifice as the most powerful weapon against self-serving political power."[49]

On the other hand, some Asian theologians opt for social
revolution to confront dehumanization caused by unjust
structures. Edicio de la Torre, a Filipino liberation theologian, criticizes talk of liberation as humanization. "There is
a tendency, however, for the theological meaning of liberation to be understood as 'human liberation' either in a very
personalistic sense (from sin, selfishness, any restrictions to
creativity) or in a very general a-historic sense. The precise
anti-colonial, political and class content is lost in the dra-

matic vision of a total liberation of all men in Christ."[50] Instead of humanization, he calls for social reform that unites
nationalism, scientific analysis of oppressive structures,
and revolutionary practice.[51] Social reform aims at the root
problem, which is an unjust socioeconomic structure from
which the Filipino people must be liberated. A significant
part of the church's role in liberation is to accompany the
poor as the "Servant of the Revolution," resisting all temptations "to lead the liberation process or even formulate a
distinct program."[52]

On the whole, however, theologians who live as a Christian minority in Asia interpret liberation as humanization
and the reign of God as a new humanity that anticipates the
humanization of the entire cosmos. Jesus' eating with acknowledged sinners constitutes "a partial anticipation of
the New Humanity in which all the children of God will
gather around to sit at table with him in total love and self-
giving."[53] In the context of massive social, political, economic, and cultural forces that virtually overshadow the
Christian church, these theologians opt for Jesus' opposition to all dehumanizing structures of oppression in the
context of a table community gathered in love.

This statement brings us full circle to the image of the
new humanity: Jesus' sitting at table with sinners. At Jesus'
final meal of this sort, when he offered the bread and wine
to his followers, we see clearly where the Asian understanding of liberation leads the Asian church. Although the
"Eucharist has become an institution of salvation in which
'the chosen' participate *on behalf of* the rest of humanity
but not *with* them, originally it was the last of Jesus' many
meals with the marginalized of Jewish society."[54] The
church must return to Jesus' understanding of this meal; it
must follow the scandalous eating habits of Jesus. It must
be prepared to share prayers and meals with the oppressed, even if this scandalizes its own ecclesial authorities, just as Jesus scandalized his.

### Pain-Love

"Asians do not have to look for suffering; it comes to
them. They do not have to wait for it; it strikes them out of

the blue. They cannot choose one kind of suffering as against another kind of suffering; suffering chooses them. In short, for them to be is to suffer."[55] Asians suffered in the past on account of tyrannous rulers and colonial expansionists, and they suffer today on account of an expanding population and decreasing resources which combine to produce growing numbers of underfed, malnourished, and ill persons.

Buddhism has addressed suffering, with its central claim that all of life is suffering. "This, monks, is the Noble Truth of Suffering (*dukkha*): Birth is suffering, old age is suffering, illness is suffering, death is suffering; and to be united with what is unloved, to be separated from what is loved is suffering; not to obtain what is longed for is suffering."[56] The path to enlightenment is encapsulated in Buddhism's Four Noble Truths: the Noble Truth of Suffering (all of life is suffering); the Noble Truth of the Origin of Suffering (with suffering comes desire); the Noble Truth of the Extinction of Suffering (to eliminate suffering, eliminate desire); and the Noble Eightfold Path that leads to the Extinction of Suffering. Enlightenment begins when one recognizes that suffering is the essence of life.

For Asian Christian theology, God addresses the experience of suffering through a "gravity-bound" love that draws God into human history and into the historical lives of human persons.[57] The sign of "gravity-bound" love is God's suffering with humanity. This is not God's suffering "on behalf of" in order to solve the conundrum of human suffering; rather, God suffers "with" humankind. "Here vicariousness is replaced by identification. The crucified God is the God who identifies all the way with us in our suffering and death. He suffers with us and dies with us."[58] God's love for humanity and God's suffering with humanity coalesce in the term "pain-love."[59] This suffering God feels pain-love; that is, God loves people to the extent of feeling their pain, as a mother feels pain in childbirth for the child whom she loves.

Jesus was the pain-love of God in his earthly life. He consistently refused to succumb to the temptations of power (Matt. 4:1–11; Luke 4:1–13) or to be hailed by the people as a kingly or political ruler (John 6). Instead, he consciously adopted the alternative of suffering (Mark 8:32; 9:31–32; 10:32–45). In Galilee, Jesus "felt that one by one the griefs of all the people in the world were coming to rest on his shoulders. The sorrows began to weigh on his back with an onerous crunch, like the heavy cross that he himself would have to carry sometime in the future."[60]

Jesus began to realize that he would have "to meet death in its most harrowing form. He had to go through every misery and pain that men and women go through, because otherwise he could not truly share in the misery and pain of humankind, and because otherwise he couldn't face us to say: 'Look, I am at your side. I have suffered like you. Your misery—I understand it; I went through it all myself.' "[61] The burdens he had carried throughout his life fell on him with a final crashing weight. On the cross, there could be no mistake that he was now one with the suffering masses. And, as in life, so in death and beyond death, he remained the "Eternal Companion" of those who suffer.[62]

After the resurrection, the disciples realized the import of Jesus as a suffering messiah. If all of life is suffering, then suffering is the one experience that unites all people together, regardless of status or class. Therefore the disciples "realize that a messiah with a gold crown on his head might save a nation but cannot redeem suffering humanity. And it is humanity in suffering that longs to be taken into the bosom of God laid open in the suffering of Jesus the messiah."[63]

In the resurrected community of Jesus, the church, there can be no talk of love without pain. In the Asian context, "If no transformation of love into suffering takes place, then your love for others is not genuine. It is not full-hearted love but half-hearted love. The distance between love and suffering is very short indeed."[64] With this depth of identification with suffering, the church embodies the pain-love of Jesus. His singular pain-love becomes communal compassion, "together-loving and together-suffering."[65]

### Toward A Holistic Christology for Asia

Asian contextual theologians have subjected the Christologies of the cosmic Christ, Jesus as liberator, and Jesus

as the pain-love of God to critique. These critiques in turn
have furnished the building blocks of a more holistic Christology that encompasses Asia's poverty and religiosity.

The Asian critique of Jesus as the cosmic Christ is that it
fails to take the historical Jesus seriously. In order to establish mystery as the deepest unifying point of encounter between Hinduism and Christianity, Panikkar downplays the
significance of the historical Jesus. For Panikkar, the "major obstacle appears when Christianity further identifies,
with the necessary qualifications, Christ with Jesus, the son
of Mary. It is precisely this identity that characterizes the
Christian belief. The Hindu can only respect, without sharing in, this 'theohistorical' aspect of Christianity."[66]

The relationship between the cosmic Christ and the historical Jesus which Panikkar disregards has been a thorny
problem even for those theologians who have attempted to
conjoin the two. The dichotomy of "Cosmic Christ or Man
of History" was an important topic at a theological sympo-
sium in India in 1974.[67] Yet, eight years later, the report of
D. Preman Niles as the secretary of the Christian Conference of Asia was riddled with ambiguity. Jesus is said not to
"exhaust the totality of the Cosmic Christ." His positive
relation to the cosmic Christ is left unexplained.[68] Later,
Lakshman Wickremesinghe devoted an entire article in the
*CTC Bulletin* to this topic, yet he too employed ambiguous
language. The historical Jesus is "something novel" which
"unveiled" the cosmic Christ in history.[69]

This inability to connect the cosmic Christ with the historical Jesus may be the most damaging liability of this
Christology, because such a Christology consequently disregards the actual historical experience of Asia. Asia has
benefited from Christianity, not when the cosmic Christ was
discovered, but when the historical Jesus provided a social
model of justice for leaders from a variety of religious traditions, including Mahatma Gandhi and a past president of India, Radhakrishnan. "It is not the 'unknown Christ' to whom
Christian witness points in India, but the Jesus Christ who
has already been named, known, recognized and even followed by millions at the cross roads of Indian life."[70]

The strength of the portrait of Jesus as liberator is that it
confronts Asian poverty, along with the concomitant values

and institutions that prevent change. But this portrait of Jesus is vulnerable in two respects. First, from a pragmatic perspective, if there is to be an *effective* struggle for liberation, it cannot be the sole effort of Christians in Asia. Their impact would be negligible.

Second, while emphasizing the liberative aspect of Christianity, many liberation theologians have neglected growing movements for justice within religions other than Christianity. Aloysius Pieris observes, "But these liberation theologians are hardly ready to grant that Asian religions, too, have the kind of prophetic-political resources that a Christian minority must appropriate."[71] By dubbing Christianity a liberative religion without acknowledging liberative dimensions in other religions, theologians risk exacerbating the isolationism that has all too often characterized Christianity in the past, even if now Christianity takes the side of the oppressed rather than the elite.

The portrayal of Jesus as pain-love emerges from the pulse of Buddhism: the inevitability of suffering in daily life. It also meets people in the midst of their poverty and daily struggles. In these respects, Jesus as the pain-love of God addresses Asia's poverty and religiosity. Its central weakness, however, is that this Christology provides no concrete means of alleviating the sort of daily suffering that is preventable, such as structures that cause poverty or the self-denigration that so often results from oppression. On the contrary, this personal companionship can lead to acquiescence in the face of oppression. According to Tsutomu Shoji, it has functioned in this way historically: "But this sort of understanding of the Christian Gospel was largely confined to the psychological and personal level, and did not open the eyes of Christians to the social realities which had brought misery to the people."[72]

Despite their relevance for Asia, these Christologies do not confront both issues that face Asia: poverty and religiosity. Jesus as pain-love fails to address the causes of poverty. The cosmic Christ fails to address the causes and effects of poverty. Jesus as liberator fails to address Asia's religiosity.

The tendency of Christologies to address either poverty or religiosity, but not both, reflects a debate in which Asian contextual theologians have been engaged. This debate erupted in 1979 at the EATWOT conference in Sri Lanka when those who viewed Asia through the lens of socio-economic factors met in confrontation with those who viewed Asia through the lens of religiocultural factors. The conference organizers facilitated the division by assigning separate papers on each set of factors: "Towards an Asian Theology of Liberation: Some Religio-Cultural Guidelines," by Aloysius Pieris, and "Socio-Economic and Political Reality in Asia," by K. Matthew Kurian. Throughout the conference, participants referred to the priority of one set of factors over the other. For instance, the Filipino delegation admitted that the Asian context is characterized by its "'Third World-ness' (with its thrust towards sociopolitical and total human liberation of the poor) and its 'Asianness' (the peculiar Asian character, whatever that happens to be in our different situations respectively)."[73] However, they gave primacy to Asia's "Third Worldness."

Many Asian contextual theologians, however, recognize the need to address both poverty and religiosity. At a significant joint gathering of the Society for Biblical Studies and the Indian Christian Theological Association in 1974, J. R. Chandran was the spokesperson for many participants when he argued for two liberations: from injustice and for dialogue.[74] At the first EATWOT gathering in 1976, D. S. Amalorpavadass contended that the two main realities facing India are religious traditions and the modern concern for development.[75] Two years after the 1979 EATWOT meeting in Sri Lanka, at an Asian ecumenical conference, Lakshman Wickremesinghe combined religiosity and poverty when he presented Jesus in relation to outcastes (i.e., socioeconomic), religious adherents other than Christians (i.e., religiocultural), and the disciples.[76] Two of the four categories with which D. Preman Niles summarized the emphases of the 1983 Christian Conference of Asia Workshop on Christology were interreligious dialogue and the struggle for justice.[77] Godwin R. Singh's appeal for a holistic Christology in 1987, although written as the editor of an Indian journal for an Indian audience, corroborated D. P. Niles's assessment of Asian Christology. Singh contended that India, "with its rich inheritance of cultural diversity and pluralistic heritage, and with its

teeming masses, struggling for justice, peace and liberation from social and economic oppression, demands a new
reorientation and fresh response to the Christological
question."[78]

Asia is not, therefore, bereft of theologians who attempt
to bridge the gap between socioeconomic and religiocultural factors. Two theologians in particular develop Christologies that confront Asian poverty and religiosity. One is
the Indian lawyer-theologian, M. M. Thomas who, as early
as 1968, following the World Council of Churches meeting
in Uppsala, rejected this dichotomy. He endorsed enthusi-
astically the WCC's Christology because it took seriously
sociopolitical factors, yet he criticized it for ignoring Asian
religions besides Christianity, which were themselves ex-
periencing renewal through their involvement in sociopolitical struggles.[79] The other is Aloysius Pieris, a Sri Lankan
priest and theologian who is engaged in Buddhist-Christian
dialogue. Even at the 1979 EATWOT conference, where
the debate about poverty and religiosity became most
heated, Pieris prefaced his paper with the inseparability of
both sets of factors: "There is in our cultural ethos 'a yet
undiscovered point' at which poverty and religiosity seem
to coalesce in order to procreate the Asian character of this
continent."[80] In his paper, he argued for the priority of the
religiocultural factors only because the organizers compelled him to represent that point of view.

In different ways, both Thomas and Pieris construct holistic Christologies that conjoin Asian religiosity and poverty. Both also place Christology within the context of a
viable Asian ecclesiology and apply their Christologies to
Asia beyond the church, where it provides the contours of
a new Asian society.

## Christology

Because M. M. Thomas's entry into theology was
"through politics and the concern for political and social
justice,"[81] he has developed what he designates a "Christ-
centred humanism," that is, a Christology whose validity is
based less on its doctrinal orthodoxy than on its contribution to the human "quest for a better quality of life and for

social justice."[82] This Christology recognizes the presence of Christ in all struggles for justice, whether Christian or not. Equally, it discerns the presence of Christ in any spirituality, whether Christian or not, that inspires struggles for justice. Christ is present in these struggles as the cosmic lord of history.[83]

One can appreciate Thomas's emphasis on Christ as the cosmic lord *of history* when it is compared with Panikkar's "Unknown Christ." Both Christologies address the issue of Asia's religiosity. For Panikkar, encounter occurs at the level of mystery rather than in historical endeavor. Unlike Panikkar's, Thomas's Christology does not deny the importance of history in order to provide a common basis for all religions. Rather, the cosmic lord of history becomes the meeting point of religions as they struggle for justice. Christ is present not so much in ahistorical mystery as in the human quest for a better life. Therefore, for Thomas, the cosmic lord of history and the historical Jesus, who labored among the poor, are one and the same, sharing an identical purpose.

Thomas recognizes that this striving toward justice is not limited to Christians and that renascent Asian religions, now more than ever, provide a spiritual basis for social justice.[84] Therefore Thomas discerns Christ's universal presence wherever religions provide the spiritual impetus for the struggle for justice. He infers from Colossians 1 and Ephesians 1 that, if Christ unifies the creation, providing its origin and future, then Christ is present in any spirituality that moves the creation toward its goal of justice for all people. Christ, the cosmic lord of history, is "the Source, the Judge and the Redeemer of the human spirituality" that is at work in "movements of human liberation."[85] In this respect, Thomas's Christology places the view of Jesus as liberator that characterizes much of Asian liberation theology alongside the liberative dimensions of other religions.

Pieris's commitment to these issues results in a distinctly different Christology from that of Thomas. Pieris links Asia's poverty and religiosity in Jesus' "double baptism" into "the Jordan of Asian religions and the Calvary of Asian poverty."[86] The word "baptism" describes these two "prophetic gestures" by which Jesus is immersed in the Asian reality.[87]

When Jesus was baptized in the Jordan by John, he rejected the powerful religiosities of his day and chose instead two religiosities of the powerless. Jesus rejected the
"narrow ideology of the Zealot movement, the sectarian
puritanism of the Essenes, the Pharisaic spirituality of
self-righteousness, and the aristocratic 'leisure-class' spirituality of the Sadducees."[88] In contrast to these, Jesus was
baptized into John the Baptist's religiosity of "prophetic
asceticism." John's prophetic asceticism renounced the
world. "We are told that he lived 'with nature' rather than
'in society'; his diet and his dress—things picked up from
the desert—were symbolic of this brand of hermetical asceticism." Also at the Jordan, Jesus was baptized into the
religiosity of the rural poor who were attracted to John's
message. They too had their own religiosity, and theirs was
more positive than John's. Jesus accepted these two religiosities and was baptized into both in the Jordan. "It was,
therefore, at the Jordan when Jesus stood before the Baptizer and among the baptized, that the two streams of spirituality found a point of confluence. Jesus, himself about to
pass through a wilderness-experience of hermetical asceticism, comes to John—not to baptize others, but to be baptized, thus identifying himself with the 'religious poor' of
the countryside."[89]

In time, the religiosity of the poor exerted more of an
influence on Jesus, and his religiosity became more positive than John's. For instance, "To John's curses on self-
righteous religious bigots and political leaders, Jesus would
add the blessings and promises offered to the marginalized
poor and the ostracized sinner. The Baptizer preached bad
news about the coming judgment, but Jesus . . . had good
news to give about imminent liberation."[90] Still, Jesus' baptism into the Jordan of John's religiosity and that of the
rural, religious poor prepared him for his second baptism
on the Calvary of poverty.

Just as Jesus rejected the religiosity of the powerful and
followed the religiosity of the poor, so he denounced mammon and the accumulation of wealth which operates as a
cosmic power to cause injustice.[91] Even more, he conscientized the poor as to their "unique liberative role in the to-
tally new order God is about to usher in."[92]

Both actions of Jesus—his denunciation of mammon and his conscientization of the poor—threatened the wealthy and powerful who responded in rage and with death threats. In the end, they brought in the colonizers from Rome who nailed Jesus to the cross, "a cross that the money-polluted religiosity of his day planted on Calvary with the aid of a colonial power (Luke 23:1–23). This is where the journey, begun at Jordan, ended."[93]

What can two Christologies as different as these have in common? One emphasizes Christ's cosmic presence and the other Jesus' historical example. Nevertheless an important point of contact connects their Christologies: both emerge from a specifically Asian context. As a result, both Christologies incorporate the two most significant factors of Asian society: poverty and religiosity. And it is these contextual factors, more than identical biblical bases or common creedal formulations, that lead Thomas and Pieris to espouse nearly identical paths for the church and for society.

## Ecclesiology

For both Thomas and Pieris, Christology leads to ecclesiology. In fact, it might be more precise to say that for these two theologians, Christology shapes a particular praxis in which the Christian church must be engaged.

According to Thomas, because Christ is the cosmic lord *of history*, the Christian church has no alternative but to encounter Christ's presence, not in its own religiosity, but in a larger history that includes all religions. As Thomas writes, "But since we believe . . . Christ holds all things together *now* (Col. 1) and will sum up all things in himself in the *end* (Eph. 1), should we not make greater efforts to discern how Christ is at work in other faiths, generally in their traditional patterns and more particularly in their renewal movements?"[94] This encounter with other religions does not occur on the level of doctrine or religious experience but in "renewal movements" for justice. The church discerns Christ's presence as lord of history when it unites "with adherents of all religions and secular ideologies in the Asian people's struggle to realize full humanity."[95]

Christianity and other religions meet the cosmic lord of history when they, with him, strive to bring justice to human history. For this reason, Thomas's colleague, S. J. Samartha, has suggested, "Co-operation in the struggle against injustice could also mean sharing the pilgrimage to the mountain of peace."[96]

However, this ecclesiology does not suggest that the church become involved indiscriminately in all liberation movements. Christ is the source of all liberation only when the agents of liberation conform to his model of suffering servanthood. The particular standard of judgment that the church brings to its discernment of Christ's presence is the cross of Christ. The cross ultimately stands over against all movements that do not conform to suffering servanthood and the love of the cross.[97]

Pieris is less reluctant than Thomas to indict the church for its faulty praxis. He contends that there is a harmful disjuncture between Jesus and the church because the church in Asia has failed to be immersed with Jesus in his double baptism. It is characterized neither by its cooperation with Asian religions nor by its involvement among the Asian poor. Pieris describes it as a church *in* Asia but not a church *of* Asia. The reason for this non-Asian character of the church is that it is caught between the Western cultural pattern of its colonizers and its own Asian context. The church's usual solution is to spend its energy and resources on programs of inculturation to become more a church *of* Asia. Pieris disagrees with this solution and contends that inculturation cannot be achieved through calculation or organization. "Inculturation is something that happens naturally. It can never be induced artificially. . . . That is to say, inculturation is the by-product of an involvement with a people."[98] This involvement proceeds in the same way as Jesus' double baptism in the Jordan of Asian religions and on the Calvary of Asian poverty.

To begin with, a church *of* Asia must be baptized with Jesus in the Jordan of Asian religions. This baptism requires working alongside other Asian religions for mutual collaboration on Asian issues and problems. With such collaboration, the church becomes more than a Christian community; it is a place where Christians and adherents of other religions gather together. But this community must also be baptized with Jesus on the Calvary of Asian poverty. Just as Jesus' spirituality was refined by being among the poor, so this community must also be shaped by the religiosity of the poor. In this way, the church *of* Asia which is doubly baptized will be a community "of Christians and non-Christians who form basic human communes with the poor, sharing the common patrimony of a religiousness that their (voluntary or forced) poverty generates."[99]

This church *of* Asia is a goal rather than a reality. Similarly, for Pieris, an adequate Asian Christology is a goal rather than a reality because "the church must be given time to step into the baptismal waters of Asian religion and to pass through passion and death on the cross of Asian poverty. Until the ecclesiological revolution is complete, there will be no Asian Christology. Instead, we shall have to be satisfied with mere 'christological reflections.'"[100]

What fuses the ecclesiologies of Thomas and Pieris together is that they extend the church's involvement beyond the boundary of institutional Christian confession on the basis of ecumenical Christologies, that is, Christologies that respond to Asia's religiocultural and socioeconomic quest for full humanity. In the same way that Jesus was baptized into the Jordan of Asian religiosity (Pieris) and his presence pervades all spiritualities that struggle for justice (Thomas), so the church must be in partnership with communities from other religious traditions. The purpose of this cooperation, for Pieris and Thomas, is the alleviation of poverty and the establishment of justice. It is to this end that Christ as the cosmic lord labors in history. It is to this end that Jesus was baptized on the Calvary of Asian poverty.

## New Society

Any vestige of ecclesial sequestering that the Christian church might permit itself disintegrates in the visions of a new society that Pieris and Thomas propose. The focal point of Thomas's new society is the cosmic lord of history, around whom religiosity and justice unite. In this new society, Christ is at the center, surrounded by three interrelated, concentric circles.[101] The narrowest circle is "the eucharistic community of the church, itself a unity of diverse peoples acknowledging the *Person* of Jesus as the Messiah." This is the circle of the Christian church in Asia, united by confession regardless of race or country. The second circle is a larger interfaith dialogue of people who acknowledge "the *pattern* of suffering servanthood as exemplified by the crucified Jesus." Mahatma Gandhi is an example of someone in this circle. Gandhi was deeply influenced by the example of Jesus' life and teachings. He patterned his life, in part, on Jesus' life of servanthood and nonviolent resistance. The third circle is a still larger communion of people involved in secular struggles for new societies and a world community *"informed by* the agape [love] of the cross."[102] This circle includes those who enter the struggle for justice without a consciousness of or commitment to Christ. An example of someone in this circle is the Buddhist monk who burned himself to death to draw attention to political repression.

This model suggests that the church is integrally related to the world through its cooperation with the two outer circles. Even more, this model suggests that Christ, as the lord of all histories, Christian and secular, permeates all three of the concentric circles; Christ is no less present in the outer than the inner circle.

Thomas's Christology extends Jesus' presence far beyond the borders of individual religious experience and the collective confession of the Christian church. If Christ is present only in mystery or Christian confession, then he exists as a bystander who watches as Asia's religions act to alleviate Asia's poverty. But Christ is not a spectator in Asia. For Thomas, Christ is present in "the main stream of national life"[103] because he is the cosmic lord of history.

Pieris's vision of a new society emerges from Jesus' double baptism into Asian poverty and religiosity. This new society will take the form of a religious socialism that bonds individual spirituality and collective activism. The individual spiritual dimension of the new society emphasizes the gnostic side of spirituality, with "gnostic" meaning "salvific knowledge."[104] It will incorporate "techniques of psychological introspection proper to Asian traditions."[105]

Also in the new society, Marxist tools of class analysis, with their emphasis on socioeconomic mechanisms, will complement individual spirituality. "For the evolution of the new society and the emergence of the new person contribute one indivisible process: which is to say that Marxist class analysis and gnostic self-analysis form a pincer movement in the liberation of Asian peoples living in the twofold context of religion and poverty."[106] One Asian leader who exemplified the combination of these two aspects, in Pieris's opinion, is Mahatma Gandhi, who "advocated a symbiosis of spirituality and activism. . . . The Indian sage made Hinduism socially meaningful."[107]

These coordinate visions of a new society, like the Christologies that undergird them, respond to the ecumenical insistence that full humanity must encompass both the religiocultural and socioeconomic arenas of life. The concentric circles of M. M. Thomas and the religious socialism of Aloysius Pieris are concrete models of a society in which Christ's influence is felt far beyond the church, whether by presence (Thomas) or by example (Pieris). In these visions, the traditional concerns of historic Christian orthodoxy have been somewhat supplanted by peculiarly Asian concerns, for it is Mahatma Gandhi, a Hindu, not a Christian, who embodies for Pieris and Thomas life in the new community.

In the West, where Christianity is the majority religion, there has been little need to look for Christ in the struggle for justice beyond the church's boundaries. But in Asia, where Christianity is a small minority religion, the struggle for justice normally occurs beyond the church's boundaries. In this Asian context, the Christologies of Pieris and Thomas are an exhortation to the church, not to isolate itself in a Christian enclave, but to become immersed in the two basic realities of Asia: its religiosity and its poverty.

## NOTES

1. Samuel Rayan, "Reconceiving Theology in the Asian Context," in *Doing Theology in a Divided World*, ed. Fabella and Torres, 126.

2. Aloysius Pieris, *An Asian Theology of Liberation* (Maryknoll, N.Y.: Orbis Books, 1988), 74.

3. This percentage includes the Philippines and South Korea, where Christians are 90 percent and 45 percent respectively of the populations. These two countries raise the percentage of Christians in Asia quantitatively.

4. Parig Digan, *Churches in Contestation: Asian Christian Social Protest* (Maryknoll, N.Y.: Orbis Books, 1984), 30.

5. Quoted in Hans-Ruedi Weber, *Asia and the Ecumenical Movement, 1895–1961* (London: SCM Press, 1966), 18.

6. See C. Lakshman Wickremesinghe, "Alienated Church and Signs of the Times," in *Living Theology in Asia*, ed. John C. England (Maryknoll, N.Y.: Orbis Books, 1982), 184.

7. M. M. Thomas, *Risking Christ for Christ's Sake: Towards an Ecumenical Theology of Pluralism* (Geneva: WCC Publications, 1987), 82; see 77–91 on S. J. Samartha and Paul D. Devanandan.

8. NBCLC, "The Indian Church in the Struggle for a New Society," *Indian Missiological Review* 4 (1982): 17.

9. K. Matthew Kurian, "Socio-Economic and Political Reality in Asia," in *Asia's Struggle for Full Humanity: Towards a Relevant Theology*, Papers from the Asian Theological Conference, January 7–20, 1979, Wennappuwa, Sri Lanka, ed. Virginia Fabella (Maryknoll, N.Y.: Orbis Books, 1980), 68–69.

10. Rayan, "Reconceiving Theology in the Asian Context," 127.

11. Ibid., 128. See the discussion in chapter 1 on dependency in Latin America.

12. Asian Report Group, "Toward a Relevant Theology in Asia," in *Irruption of the Third World: Challenge to Theology*, Papers from the Fifth International Conference of the Ecumenical Association of Third World Theologians, August 17–29, 1981, New Delhi, India, ed. Virginia Fabella and Sergio Torres (Maryknoll, N.Y.: Orbis Books, 1983), 63.

13. NBCLC, "The Indian Church in the Struggle for a New Society," 19.

14. D. S. Amalorpavadass, "New Theological Approaches in Asia," *Verbum SVD* 21 (3/4, 1980): 289–290.

15. C. S. Song, *Tell Us Our Names* (Maryknoll, N.Y.: Orbis Books, 1984), 10.

16. Hyun Young-Hak, "A Theological Look at the Mask Dance in Korea," in *Minjung Theology: People as the Subjects of History*,

ed. Commission on Theological Concerns of the Christian Conference of Asia (Maryknoll, N.Y.: Orbis Books, 1981), 50.

17. C. S. Song, *Theology from the Womb of Asia* (Maryknoll, N.Y.: Orbis Books, 1986), 168.

18. C. S. Song, *Jesus, the Crucified People* (New York: Crossroad, 1990), 12–14.

19. C. S. Song, *Third Eye Theology: Theology in Formation in Asian Settings* (Maryknoll, N.Y.: Orbis Books, 1979), 101–123.

20. Ibid., 123. See also the articles by Peter K. H. Lee, who places Asian and Christian concepts side by side for mutual illumination, in order to effect dialogue with each other. He often writes with a non-Christian: with Wing Yuk, "Ta-T'ung and the Kingdom of God," *Ching Feng* 31 (1988): 225–244; and with Shih Heng-Ching, "Karma and Christ," *Ching Feng* 31 (1988): 24–47; "Nothingness and Fulfillment: From Laozi's Concept of *Wu* to Jesus' Theology on the Kingdom of God," *Ching Feng* 29 (1986), 106–128; and "Rereading Ecclesiastes in the Light of Su Ting-P'o's Poetry," *Ching Feng* 30 (1987): 214–236.

21. This debate is still unresolved, as this evaluation of non-Christian scriptures, based on EATWOT's New Delhi statement and a 1974 Research Seminar on Non-Biblical Scriptures, evinces: non-Christian scriptures are "basic guidelines for the encounter with God and are *in a way somewhat* 'normative' for the communities to whom they primarily belong" (G. Gispert-Sauch, "Inspection and Extra Biblical Scriptures: Some Tentative Propositions," *Indian Theological Studies* 20 [1983]: 26). There exists a continuing dialogue on the role of non-Christian scriptures (e.g., Hindu Upanishads, Analects of Confucius) in Asian Christian theology. See, e.g., papers from the 1974 *Research Seminar on Non-Biblical Scriptures*, ed. D. S. Amalorpavadass (Bangalore: NBCLC, 1975).

22. Song, *Theology from the Womb of Asia*, 137. See also ibid., 133–141; and idem *Third Eye Theology*, 117–123.

23. See J. Bastiaens, E. v. d. Peet, E. Megant (under the direction of P. G. van Hooijdonk), "Jesus as Guru—A Christology in the Context of Java (Indonesia)," *Exchange* 13, no. 39 (1984): 33–57. This study is based on J. B. Banawiratma's doctoral thesis, *JESUS SANG GURU, Pertemuan Kejawen dengan Injil* (Yogya, 1977).

24. Quoted by M. M. Thomas, *The Acknowleged Christ of the Indian Renaissance* (London: SCM Press, 1969), 61. See ibid.,

56–81; and R. H. S. Boyd, *An Introduction to Indian Christian Theology*, rev. ed. (Madras: Christian Literature Society, 1975), 26–39. Thomas summarizes the view of Keshub Chunder Sen (1838–1884), who interpreted the Trinity as Sat, Cit, Ananda (being, intelligence, bliss). Sen founded an influential movement, the Brahmo Samaj of India, "introducing elements from many religions to form an eclectic church" (Thomas, *Acknowledged Christ*, 329).

25. Boyd refers to Chakkarai (1880–1958), who belonged to a well-known trio of South Indian theologians, with A. J. Appasamy (born 1891) and P. Chenchiah (1886–1959). Chakkarai was part of the "Rethinking Christianity" group. India also has a history of Hindu portraits of Jesus—quite apart from the Indian Christian ones—such as that of Mahatma Gandhi (1868–1948), who understood Jesus to be the embodiment of *satyagrahi*, the principle of resistance to evil through voluntary suffering (Boyd, *Introduction*, 165–185). Three books cover amply the fascinating history of Indian portraits of Jesus: Thomas includes Hindu and Christian leaders who were influenced by Jesus Christ in *Acknowledged Christ*; Boyd, *Introduction*; and S. J. Samartha, *The Hindu Response to the Unbound Christ* (Bangalore: CISRS; and Madras: Christian Literature Society, 1974).

26. L. Legrand refers, for instance, to M. Kähler's *Der sogenannte historische Jesus und der geschichtliche biblische Christus*, published in 1892 (Leipzig), "Christological Issues in the New Testament," *Indian Journal of Theology* 24 (1975): 75–76.

27. At symposia in two entirely different regions of Asia this distinction was discussed: at the Northeast Asia Association of Theological Schools' Inaugural Assembly in Japan (*Northeast Asia Journal of Theology* 2 [1969] includes major papers and summary) and at a 1974 meeting in India, where two of the four foci concerned "Cosmic Christ or Man in History" and "Christ of Mystical Union or the Prophetic Christ" (*Indian Journal of Theology* 24 [1975] includes major papers and summary).

28. See Matthew Vellanickal, "The Hermeneutical Problem in Christology Today," *Biblebhashyam* 6 (1980): 5–17.

29. Sebastian Kappen, *Jesus and Freedom* (Maryknoll, N.Y.: Orbis Books, 1977), 34.

30. J. C. Duraisingh and K. C. Abraham, "Reflections from an Asian Perspective," in *Irruption of the Third World*, ed. Fabella

and Torres, 211. On the Western bias of Marxism, see Pieris, *An Asian Theology*, 91–92. Still, the contributions of Latin American liberation theology named by Asian theologians are several: its use of social analysis; its recognition of God's preference for the poor; its emphasis on the primacy of praxis over theory; and its focus on liberation.

31. D. S. Amalorpavadass, "The Bible in Self-Renewal and Church Renewal for Service to Society," in *On Interpreting the Bible*, Voices from the Third World (EATWOT, 1987), 65.

32. Joseph Sittler, "Called to Unity," *Ecumenical Review* 14 (1962): 177–87. See the earlier work of Allan D. Galloway, *The Cosmic Christ* (New York: Harper & Brothers, 1951).

33. Paul D. Devanandan, "Called to Witness," *Ecumenical Review* 14 (1962): 155–156.

34. Ibid., 160.

35. For a definition of the cosmic Christ, see the report in *Indian Journal of Theology* 24 (1975): 180; and C. Lakshman Wickremesinghe, "The Cosmic Christ and Its Relation to Mission Today—Some Notes for Discussion," *CTC Bulletin* 5 (1984): 39. See the analysis of H. Bürkle, "The Debate of the 'Cosmic Christ' as Example of an Ecumenically Oriented Theology," in *Indian Voices in Today's Theological Debate*, ed. H. Bürkle and W. M. W. Roth (Lucknow: Lucknow with ISPCK, Christian Literature Society, 1972), 198–214.

36. Devanandan, "Called to Witness," 161–162.

37. Raimundo Panikkar, *The Unknown Christ of Hinduism: Towards an Ecumenical Christophany*, rev. and enl. ed. (Maryknoll, N.Y.: Orbis Books, 1981), 19–20. Panikkar makes frequent reference to John 1:9. In fact, John 1:1–18 is a passage, alongside Colossians 1, that provides a basis for the cosmic Christ. Christ is the agent of creation: "In the beginning was the Word . . . that was made" (John 1:1–3). Christ is the unifying principle of the cosmos, just as the logos is in Stoicism. The logos is also "the true light, which enlightens everyone" (John 1:9) prior to religious confession.

38. Ibid., 37.

39. Ibid., 164–165. To establish the correspondence between Hinduism and Christianity, Panikkar begins with a foundational text from Brahma-Sutra (I,1,2): "Brahman is that from which the origin, etcetera, of this World proceeds" (ibid., 107).

40. Ibid., 162.

41. Ibid., 20.

42. Abesamis, "Doing Theological Reflection in a Philippine Context," 122. This emphasis on comprehensive salvation for humanity emerges from both the Old and the New Testament. In the Old Testament, God provides for Israel through "spiritual deliverance but also total well-being, such as land, abundant harvest, security" (Tano, *Theology in the Philippine Setting*, 45). Matthew Vellanickal writes that "the liberation envisaged here is a total liberation and that it should not be reduced to a mere political or social one" ("Jesus the Poor and His Gospel to the Poor," *Biblebhashyam* 9 [1983]: 54).

43. Kappen, *Jesus and Freedom*, 100–104. For a précis of Kappen's interpretation, see idem, "The Man Jesus: Rupture and Communion," *Religion and Society* 23 (1976): 66–76.

44. Kappen, *Jesus and Freedom*, 119–132.

45. Ibid., 62–63.

46. Ibid., 92.

47. Felix Wilfred describes three types of awakening that the oppressed experience: "1. awareness of their right to have access to the basic necessities of life; 2. awareness concerns *samata*, equality; 3. awareness that they are not masters of their own destiny" (Wilfred, "The Liberation Process in India and the Church's Participation," *Indian Theological Studies* 25 [1988]: 304).

48. C. S. Song, *The Tears of Lady Meng: A Parable of People's Political Theology*, Risk Book Series (Geneva: WCC Publications, 1981). See also Steven Mackie, "People Power and Lady Meng," *The Modern Churchman* 32 (1991): 1–10.

49. Song, *Tell Us Our Names*, 180.

50. Edicio de la Torre, *Touching Ground, Taking Root: Theological and Political Reflections on the Philippines Struggle* (London: Catholic Institute for International Relations, 1986), 99.

51. Ibid., 100–101.

52. Ibid., 102. See also Wilfred, "The Liberation Process in India," 314–317.

53. Kappen, *Jesus and Freedom*, 101.

54. C.S. Song, *The Compassionate God* (Maryknoll, N.Y.: Orbis Books, 1982), 122.

55. Ibid., 163.

56. H. Wolfgang Schumann, *Buddhism: An Outline of Its Teachings and Schools* (London: Rider & Co., 1973), 39.

57. Song, *Tell Us Our Names*, 30.

58. Song, *Third Eye Theology*, 165.

59. For the phrase "pain-love," Song is indebted to Kazo Kitamori, who wrote the book *Theology of the Pain of God* (Richmond: John Knox Press, 1965). Writing in Japan in the 1940s, Kitamori believed that the Bible revealed a God in pain for the sinfulness of humanity and in pain for relinquishing an only child. He also found pain to be prevalent in Japanese tragedy, where the basic principle is *tsurasa*, which is the pain caused when a person suffers and dies, or makes a beloved one suffer and die, for the health and life of others (ibid., 134). *Tsurasa* explains in dramatic form God's pain-love in sending God's child, Jesus Christ, into human history to suffer and die for humanity.

Even though Song is influenced by Kitamori, Song does criticize him for ending with God's pain at the cross and thereby overlooking the resurrection. Song claims that Kitamori's theology "cannot in fact accommodate resurrection; it does not have room for it. . . . If pain and wrath are absolute and constitute the essence of God's being, how can they be overcome?" Song continues with the proclamation: "For resurrection is God's declaration of the end of pain and suffering. It is the eschatological victory over the power of pain" (Song, *Third Eye Theology*, 62).

For another interpretation of Kitamori's theology of pain-love, see Kosuke Koyama, *Waterbuffalo Theology* (London: SCM Press, 1974), 116–125.

60. Endo, *A Life of Jesus*, 51–52.

61. Ibid., 125. Asian feminist theologians, too, view the cross as the pain-love of God. "It is the very person on the cross that suffers like us, who was rendered as nobody that illuminates the tragic human existence and speaks to countless women in Asia. . . . We see Jesus as the God who takes human form and suffers and weeps with us" (Kwok Pui Lan, "God Weeps with Our Pain," *East Asia Journal of Theology* 2 [1984]: 230).

62. This is Endo's expression for who Jesus is throughout his book, *A Life of Jesus*.

63. Song, *The Compassionate God*, 116.

64. Song, *Theology from the Womb of Asia*, 111.

65. Ibid., 144.

66. Ibid., 56–57. See 28–29, 48–49, 52, 82–83, 164–65.

67. See *Indian Journal of Theology* 24 (1975).

68. D. Preman Niles, "A Continuing Ecumenical Journey—

Report of the Secretary for Theological Concerns, CCA January 1983," *CTC Bulletin* 4 (1983): 63.

69. Wickremesinghe, "The Cosmic Christ and Its Relation to Mission Today," 45.

70. S. J. Samartha, "Indian Realities and the Wholeness of Christ," *Indian Missiological Review* 4 (1982), 268. As the use of the word "acknowledged" in the title indicates, this lesson is explicit throughout Thomas's *Acknowledged Christ*.

71. Pieris, *An Asian Theology*, 61.

72. Tsutomu Shoji, "The Church's Struggle for Freedom of Belief—An Aspect of Christian Mission," in *Living Theology in Asia*, ed. England, 56.

73. Carlos Abesamis, "Faith and Life Reflections from the Grassroots in the Philippines," in *Asia's Struggle for Full Humanity*, ed. Fabella, 134.

74. J. R. Chandran, "Jesus: Freedom Fighter or Prince of Peace?" *Indian Journal of Theology* 24 (1975): 96–103.

75. D. S. Amalorpavadass, "The Indian Universe of a New Theology," in *The Emergent Gospel*, ed. Torres and Fabella, 137–156.

76. C. Lakshman Wickremesinghe, "Living in Christ with People," in *A Call to Vulnerable Discipleship*, CCA Seventh Assembly (1981), 38.

77. Niles, "A Continuing Ecumenical Journey," 63–64.

78. Godwin R. Singh, "Editorial: Christology in the Indian Context," *National Christian Council Review* 107 (1987): 2.

79. M. M. Thomas, "Uppsala 1968 and the Contemporary Theological Situation," *Scottish Journal of Theology* 23 (1970): 49.

80. Aloysius Pieris, "Towards an Asian Theology of Liberation," in *Asia's Struggle for Full Humanity*, ed. Fabella, 76. Again, he writes: "These are two inseparable realities which in their interpenetration constitute what might be designated as the Asian context and which is the matrix of any theology that is truly Asian" (ibid., 75–76).

81. M. M. Thomas, "The Absoluteness of Jesus Christ and Christ-centred Syncretism," *Ecumenical Review* 37 (1985): 390–391.

82. M. M. Thomas, *Towards a Theology of Contemporary Ecumenism* (Madras: Christian Literature Society, 1978), 311.

83. For this Christology, Thomas is indebted to Devanandan, as Thomas demonstrates in his *Risking Christ*, 85–105.

84. M. M. Thomas, *Salvation and Humanisation* (Madras:

Christian Literature Society, 1971), 21; and idem, *Risking Christ*, 12–15, 82, 101.

85. M. M. Thomas, "The Meaning of Salvation Today—A Personal Statement," *International Review of Mission* 62 (1973): 163.

86. Pieris, *An Asian Theology*, 63.

87. For Pieris, a prophetic gesture is "a prophetic word and deed" which is "self-authenticating. The prophet speaks and acts in God's name and with God's authority" (*An Asian Theology*, 47). Both prophetic gestures, in the Jordan and on Calvary, revealed Jesus' prophetic authority. "At the first baptism he was acknowledged as the beloved Son. At the second baptism the evangelist heard even the colonial power that killed him proclaim that he was truly a son of God (Mark 15:39)" (ibid., 49).

88. Ibid., 46.

89. Ibid.

90. Ibid., 48.

91. Aloysius Pieris, *Love Meets Wisdom: A Christian Experience of Buddhism*, Faith Meets Faith Series (Maryknoll, N.Y.: Orbis Books, 1988), 90.

92. Pieris, *An Asian Theology*, 49.

93. Ibid.

94. Thomas, *Towards a Theology of Contemporary Ecumenism*, 306.

95. Thomas, *Risking Christ*, 118; see M. M. Thomas, *The Christian Response to the Asian Revolution* (London: SCM Press, 1964), 95–125; idem, *Acknowledged Christ*, 301; and idem, "Theological Aspects of the Relationships Between Social Action Groups and Churches," *Religion and Society* 31 (1984): 17–23.

96. Samartha, "Indian Realities," 271.

97. Thomas cautions, "Revolutions for justice get lost in the fury of self-righteousness; they devour their offspring and become new sources of oppression. . . . The mission of the Church in this context is to be present within the creative liberation movements . . . as to be able to communicate the genuine gospel of liberation—from the vicious circle of sin and alienation, law and self-righteousness, frustration and death into the new realm of Christ's New Humanity where there is forgiveness and reconciliation, grace and justification, renewal and eternal life. It is this message that will liberate the liberation movements from the false spiritual structures of meaning based on idolatrous worship

of schemes of self-redemption, and thus redeem their creative impulses from self-destructive tendencies, enabling them to achieve their inner rationale of human emancipation" (Thomas, "The Meaning of Salvation Today," 164–165).

98. Pieris, *An Asian Theology*, 38.

99. Ibid., 125.

100. Ibid., 63.

101. Thomas, *Risking Christ*, 119.

102. Ibid.

103. Thomas, *Christian Response*, 106.

104. Pieris, *Love Meets Wisdom*, 9. This emphasis is primarily Buddhist in orientation.

105. Ibid., 40.

106. Ibid.

107. Aloysius Pieris, "Ecumenism and Asia's Search for Christ," *The Month* 239 (1978): 7. He discusses briefly two versions of religious socialism in Asia: clannic and monastic. See Pieris, *An Asian Theology*, 43–44; and idem, *Love Meets Wisdom*, 93–94.

Chapter 4

# Jesus in Africa

## Issue Faced

When European colonizers came to sub-Sahara Africa,[1] beginning in the fifteenth century, they succeeded in replacing the African way of life with European political, economic, social, and religious institutions. No area of African life was left untouched. While traveling in several cities and towns of Kenya, we were amazed at the preponderance of British traces left over from colonial days. At our first meal we sat down to steak and kidney pie. In many offices, tea with cream and sugar is served at midmorning. Even the electrical outlets and teapots were the same as those we had used in England. Colonialism has left a thorough imprint on Africa. In particular, the political, economic, and religiocultural legacies of colonialism confront African theologians.

During five centuries of colonialism, European settlers consolidated *political* power in Africa. To sustain political stability, they educated a small, select group of Africans to be useful participants in the colonial system as interpreters, civil servants, and teachers in mission schools. Gradually, this chosen group became an African elite separated from their own people and further divided by class consciousness.[2]

Independence came quickly to most of sub-Sahara Africa. Between 1957, when Ghana became the first country to gain its independence, and the mid-1960s, over thirty new African nations were formed. In 1960 alone, seventeen new countries emerged from colonial rule. For the most part, the colonialists departed en masse, leaving behind a vacuum of power and training.[3] As a result, the African elite, groomed by the colonialists, assumed the vacant positions of leadership. As in Asia, the political bureaucracy after colonialism remains largely unchanged in many African nations. This is the political climate of neo-colonialism.

From the midst of the African elite came forth African leaders, such as Kenyatta of Kenya, Nyerere of Tanzania, and Kaunda of Zambia, who embodied the best of African leadership. More often, however, neo-colonial African leaders and those who replaced them—frequently through military coups—have shown less competence in leadership. For example, Idi Amin of Uganda killed an estimated 300,000 of his people, and Bokassa of the Central African Republic spent $20 million to install himself as emperor. Because of leaders like these, the political situation in Africa remains relatively unstable.

Political divisions within Africa are heightened by tribalism, which "remains perhaps the most potent force in day to day African life."[4] Through favoring members of its own tribe, tribalism controls educational and employment opportunities. Tribalism is, then, a key factor in economic, social, and political African life. At its worst, tribalism exacerbates violence and political power struggles.

South Africa is a country whose unique situation within Africa is apparent in that a white minority practices racism against a black majority. In 1910, after two and a half centuries of struggle, the Europeans wrested control of the land from the Africans, who "became by and large a voteless and landless majority in the land of their birth."[5] Thus, in 1948, when the National Party came to power on the platform of apartheid, racial discrimination was already well on its way. Since 1948, apartheid, with its laws and policies that discriminate against people of color, has been systematically legislated into every sphere of life.[6] Only very recently, under international pressure and the leadership of Prime Minister de Klerk, has South Africa begun to dismantle apartheid.

*Economically*, many of the countries of sub-Sahara Africa share seemingly insurmountable poverty. The statistics of impoverishment are startling: over twenty of the world's poorest countries are in Africa; five million children die yearly in Africa and another five million are crippled by malnutrition and hunger; the World Bank estimates that more than half of the African population eat fewer calories each day than are officially estimated to be necessary for survival.[7]

Many economists trace Africa's economic woes to the cash-crop economies of the colonizers. Instead of edible food products for the population, coffee, tea, cocoa, sugar, cotton, and other export crops were planted, usually one or two in a country. The result is twofold: the population lacks enough food to eat, and dependence on the earnings from one or two export crops can render a country economically destitute if the price of that crop plummets. Like Latin America, Africa has an "external orientation" instead of "nutritional self-reliance."[8] A related economic problem is that Africa restricts its trade to the First World rather than within Africa itself. Kenyatta attempted to reverse this trend with a coalition of three African countries—Kenya, Tanzania, and Uganda—into the East African Community for trade, transport, and overall cooperation, but his dream collapsed in 1977, a year before his death. Then, of course, there are the perennial African problems—drought, inadequate agricultural technology, and deforestation. These obstacles are exacerbated by the African elite who control the vast percentage of wealth and who profit from dependence on foreign trade and capital.[9]

"This might well be the most terrible failure of the whole Church in Africa—that it meets people only in their best clothes. . . . Such Christianity becomes something to be put on at certain times and in particular circumstances, and has nothing to do with other areas of life."[10] The phenomenon this quote refers to is the *religiocultural* split within the African soul between Western Christianity and traditional African culture, a split which Desmond Tutu describes as "religious schizophrenia."[11]

As in the economic and political realm, so too in the religiocultural realm Western ideas and practices displaced African ones. In their zeal to present the gospel, missionaries often tended to denigrate African culture. A holistic African approach to life was divided by Western dualistic thinking, with its distinctions between sacred and secular, individual and corporate, and material and spiritual. African music and dance were replaced by hymns and liturgy in European languages.

For African liberation theologian Jean-Marc Éla, the Eucharist is the quintessential symbol of the Western domination of African Christianity. He focuses his critique on the Roman Catholic Church's insistence that European elements be used as the "matter" of the Eucharist in every locale rather than authorizing local food products, such as millet bread and nut beer, which already have economic and religious significance for the people. "For Masses celebrated among the blacks, then, the church has determined . . . that the bread and wine of whites is to be used! . . . We must admit, then, that through the eucharistic matter the church is imposing Western culture and its symbolic structure on us. Thus the case of the Eucharist reveals the domination at the heart of the faith as lived in Africa."[12]

As a result, many Roman Catholic leaders in Africa call for inculturation, and the All Africa Conference of Churches (AACC) calls for Africanization—terms that describe the need for an African church which is truly African in liturgy, leadership, organization, and theology. In order to accomplish this, in 1974 the AACC called for a moratorium on the sending of missionary personnel and funds. The rationale behind the moratorium was to allow the African church the opportunity to develop its autonomy from foreign aid and control.[13] Although the moratorium was criticized by many Africans and non-Africans, it poignantly illustrates the conundrum of Western domination which the church still faces in an "independent" Africa.

## Sources and Method

The term "African theology" is fraught with conflicting questions. First, does African theology refer to African Christian theology or to any theology done in Africa, including African traditional religion or Islam? The most accepted understanding is that African theology is African

Christian theology. Second, does the term "African theology" give the impression that one theology dominates Africa? If so, the assumption is incorrect, since African theologians themselves delineate three theologies in Africa: African, South African black, and African liberation. It is important to remember that the term "African theology" refers to a particular brand of theology that specifically incorporates traditional African culture, not to South African black or African liberation theologies.

To complicate matters even further, African theology and South African black theology, the two oldest and most developed, frequently oppose and criticize each other. African theology is an inculturation theology whose goal is to integrate Christianity into the life and culture of African people. South African black theology relates the gospel message of liberation to its oppressive context of apartheid. The debate between these two theologies is exemplified in the writings of Manas Buthelezi, a South African theologian, and Kwesi Dickson, an African theologian.

Buthelezi criticizes African theology for its ethnographic approach to theology, which he claims neglects today's African person in its emphasis on the traditional African worldview and culture. He opts instead for an anthropological theology that focuses on the person and "the throbbings of the life situation in which people find themselves."[14] In response, Dickson wonders why Buthelezi ignores African culture which greatly influences daily life in Africa. For Dickson, socioeconomic and political freedom is important, but cultural freedom is essential, for it "defines, more fundamentally, the humanity of a people."[15] In an attempt to contribute constructively to the debate, the Pan-African Conference of Third World theologians stated that "methodology must start from African worldviews" (which differ radically for independent Africa and South Africa), "examine the impact of Christianity and evaluate *the varieties of African responses.*"[16]

## African Theology

African theology is the "most researched brand" of theology in Africa.[17] The first conference devoted to African

theology was the Consultation of African Theologians at
Ibadan in 1966, sponsored by the AACC. African theology
can be understood as bringing Christianity and African culture to bear on each other. In the words adopted by the
1969 AACC Assembly at Abidjan, African theology is "a
theology which is based on the Biblical Faith and speaks to
the African 'soul.'"[18]

African theologians unanimously cite three sources for
theology: African Independent Churches, African traditional religion, and the Bible. These sources are used in a
comparative method in which the African sources and the
Bible are compared with each other to discover similarities
and differences.[19]

One source for African theology is the African Independent Churches. These churches are African in leadership
and constituency and in music, liturgy, and spirit. African
characteristics predominate in these churches: a charis-
matic and prophetic leader; an emphasis on community;
worship with drums, dance, and indigenous music; and
faith healing, including exorcisms.[20] These churches provide a model of truly indigenous African Christianity. The
studies of African Independent Churches by theologians
and anthropologists tend to be descriptive.[21] Therefore
they do not contribute as constructively to African theology as do African traditional religion and the Bible.

The second source for African theology is African traditional religion, which is "practised by a great host of Africans. Where it is not overtly practised, its presuppositions
nevertheless influence the life and thought of even those
Africans who have accepted Christianity."[22] At the foundation of African traditional religion is a community worldview composed of a creator God, humanity, and ancestors.
"Past, present, and future generations comprise *one community*."[23]

God is the Supreme Being, the creator God of all life.
God creates human beings who are always to be in community. One African story says that creation first appeared as a
"community of men, women, children and animals."[24] Being a human is possible only when one is in community, or,
to use an African proverb, "I am because we are." Ancestors are members of the community who continue to be

active and to regulate its affairs. In return, human beings acknowledge the ancestors' role in the community through prayers and ritual acts, such as pouring out drink offerings on the ground for them. Relationships between humanity, God, and the ancestors are ideally to be in a peaceful balance with each other. This strong sense of community complements other traditional African beliefs, including a holistic understanding that integrates the living and the nonliving as well as the spiritual and physical worlds. African traditional religion permeates all of life in Africa and provides the nucleus of African theology.

The third source for African theology is the Bible. African theologians have discerned two points of resonance between the Bible and Africa. First, "a kindred atmosphere" connects African traditional religion and the Old Testament.[25] Key elements of association include religion's pervasiveness in all activities of life, the preponderance of rituals and rites; the importance of oral tradition; and the centrality of solidarity and group loyalty.[26]

A second point of resonance exists between the mediators within the African community and Jesus' mediatorial role in the New Testament. In Africa, mediators must fulfill two requirements: they must be members of a human community and able to exercise influence in the divine sphere on behalf of their community. For this reason, African theologians cite biblical texts that reinforce Jesus' membership in the human community, such as his submission to rites of passage. Equally they turn to various passages that accentuate his influence in the ancestral sphere, such as his being "firstborn among the dead."

African theologians are drawn to two biblical books, in particular, because they emphasize Jesus' humanity and his mediatorial role between the human and divine spheres: John and Hebrews. The Gospel of John's portrayal of Jesus as the Word become flesh (John 1:14), coupled with his role as "the way, and the truth, and the life" (John 14:6) and the source of abundant life (John 10:10), meets the African demand for membership in the human community and mediation.[27] Hebrews is another biblical resource for Christology because of its presentation of Jesus as earthly brother and heavenly priest. Jesus undergoes the

rites of passage that establish his membership in the human
community; he then becomes a heavenly high priest who
mediates on behalf of humankind (Heb. 2:11, 17–18;
4:14–16; 5:7–10).[28]

However, the Bible did not arrive on African soil in a
cultural vacuum. As we noted, missionaries communicated
it in the context of colonialism. Consequently, African
theologians attempt to glean the essence of the Bible from
its Western surplus. They are compelled to ask, "How is it
possible to sort out the Gospel of Christ from the European
interpretation of Christianity?"[29]

The answer to this question has two simple parts. First,
Africans must be free to put *their own questions* to the Bible, for this implies that the African experience of life is a
valid resource for theology. Second, Africans must be free
to supply *their own answers* to these questions. "The African realises that, laudable as the missionary endeavours are
in Africa, . . . the answer to the question who Jesus is was,
from the start, supplied by missionaries in their own conceptual and value-laden categories."[30]

Although African theologians use the comparative
method with these sources, there are two approaches to
the question, "What is the relation between the revelation
in Christ and African religion?"[31] Some theologians, like
John Pobee, consider the African sources only after they
have studied a concept in the Bible. Pobee explains: "Put
simply, the question is how to couch Christian theology in
genuinely African terms and categories without losing an
iota of authentic and essential Christianity."[32] For instance,
only after he has established the biblical meaning of sin
does he turn to Akan thought for corresponding perspectives. These equivalents constitute for Pobee a theology
that is both African and Christian.[33]

Others, like Charles Nyamiti, begin the theological process by studying an African topic and then comparing the
findings with the Bible and Christian tradition. He investi-
gates the concept of African personality and discovers that
it consists in "fullness of life or vital maturity."[34] From this
point of departure, he constructs an African theology of
the incarnation.[35]

However, despite these two approaches to the comparative method, a unifying commitment underlies all African theology: to reappropriate African culture and religion as a significant source for understanding Jesus Christ. Whether they begin with the Bible or an African concept, African portraits of Jesus are painted with the hues and texture of African traditional religion.

## South African Black Theology

South African black theology officially began in 1971 when the University Christian Movement (UCM) sponsored a Black Theology Project for the purpose of dialoguing with James Cone's theology.[36] Papers from the project were collected and published in South Africa, only to be banned immediately, as were several organizers of the event.[37] Because of the effect of the bannings which left resources scarce, there was a lull of several years until 1977 when Allan Boesak's *Farewell to Innocence*, "the first major scholarly publication on South African Black Theology," was published.[38] Since that time, the volume of writings has increased dramatically, and organizations such as the Institute of Contextual Theology with its Black Theology Task Force have been founded.

Black theology in South Africa "stands with one leg in Africa and the other in Black America" which gives it a "double advantage."[39] With Africa, South African blacks share an African cultural inheritance. With Black America, they share the experience of oppression and disinheritance. The sources for South African black theology reflect this double stance.

The experience of blackness is the starting point of black theology in South Africa. Most theologians diagnose their society's basic problem as apartheid's racist ideology, so that race is the primary cause of oppression.[40] Blackness first and foremost refers to a skin color, and that particular skin color has meant enslavement and oppression by people with white skin color.[41] To be black in South Africa, Buthelezi explains, "daily determines where I live, with whom I can associate and share my daily experience of life. Life, as it were, unfolds itself to me daily within the limits and range of black situational possibilities. The word of God

addresses me within the reality of the situation of my blackness. I can only go to black churches and the only pastor who
normally can minister to me is a black like myself."[42]

The source that has greatly influenced the centrality of
blackness in this theology is the Black Consciousness
movement which arose in the mid-1960s to provide leadership to the black community. The movement urged
blacks to purge their inner slave mentality and to embrace
as beautiful and human their blackness, the very aspect of
themselves that is considered negative by whites.[43] More
than just individual pride, however, Black Consciousness
called blacks to rally together and "to operate as a group to
rid themselves of the shackles that bind them to perpetual
service."[44]

Black Consciousness has been called "the nerve centre
of Black Theology" because it has "challenged black theologians to take seriously the particularity of black experience."[45] Black Consciousness and black theology share the
goal of liberation from apartheid; they are like "soulmates
walking together in the ongoing struggle of black liberation . . . like the hands of a potter who is trying to mould
something symbolic and yet concrete in terms of the vision
of the future."[46]

Black South African theologians discovered this unity of
blackness and liberation in the writings of black theology in
North America, especially those of James Cone. Cone's
books had a profound impact in the initial stages of South
African black theology, even though the government soon
banned two of his early books. For Cone, blackness is identified with both liberation and oppression. Blacks are oppressed; yet it is with blacks that God sides and on behalf of
blacks that God works for liberation. "God's revelation is
black and all talk about liberation must be black talk."[47]
These sorts of affirmations were a refreshing resource for
black theology in South Africa.

To reclaim an *African* notion of blackness, some South African theologians, but by no means all, incorporate African
cultural inheritance as a third source.[48] For these theologians, recapturing dimensions of African culture from the
rubbles of colonial destruction is integral to the liberation
process. They press "back to the roots of broken African

civilization, and examine the traditional African forms of worship, marriage, sacrifice, etc., and discover why these things were meaningful and wholesome to the traditional African community."[49] In addition, they are beginning to research African Independent Churches as early expressions of contextualization and as protest movements against the theological domination of the mainline white churches.[50] This reclamation is essential, according to these theologians, for fostering black self-respect and consciousness.

In conjunction with Black Consciousness, James Cone, and African culture, the Bible becomes an indispensable source for South African black theology. South African biblical interpretation is indebted to its black North American and Latin American counterparts, for whom praxis is central. T. A. Mofokeng reveals this debt when he writes, "During and in the praxis of liberation occasions of crisis that necessitate reflection arise. . . . During the process of this reflection the process of liberation also throws light on the Scriptures making the Word of God perceptible. There is, in other words, a fruitful dialectical movement or interplay between the text (Scripture) and the context which is the liberation project."[51]

In this reflection, the exodus has become the centerpiece of South African black theology. It is the paradigm of holistic liberation and parallels the experience of South African blacks who live under Afrikaner domination and who hope to regain access to their ancestral land. Nearly all leading South African black theologians[52] regard the exodus as the central liberating act of God prior to Jesus Christ. Jesus fulfills the liberation begun in the exodus, bringing holistic salvation to the oppressed.

Despite its dominance, two reactions to an exodus-based theology have been proposed. Mofokeng accepts the centrality of the exodus but does not think it should be utilized to rescue the entire canon of scripture for black people. Instead, fidelity to the black tradition requires utilizing only those texts which meet the exigencies of the black struggle. This selective process has always characterized black interpretation, despite the concerted opposition of the missionaries.[53] I. Mosala rejects the exodus altogether as the key to unlocking the Bible's relevance for South African blacks. He contends that isolating a universal, abstract word of God, such as "God's preference for the poor" or "God's liberating act," is irrelevant to working-class blacks. The starting point of their experience is "struggle," and this struggle must be the key to interpreting the Bible. Liberative biblical interpretation should be an attempt to uncover the struggles between cultures, gender, class, and race that lie under the surface of the Bible.[54] The fact, however, that Mofokeng and Mosala construct their hermeneutical alternatives in response to the "exodus" axis reveals how central the exodus is to South African black theology.

From its starting point of blackness, then, black theology in South Africa reflects upon liberative aspects from the Black Consciousness movement, James Cone's theology, the Bible, and the African cultural inheritance. Reflection on these sources culminates in a challenge for the black church to "reject its distorted white image and its theological formulations which support the status quo" and to become a "servant of liberation."[55] Theologians exhort the black church to carry out widespread demonstrations of civil disobedience, to cooperate in campaigns, such as consumer boycotts, and to coordinate its efforts with the popular political organizations. These actions are designed to contribute to a new social order for blacks and whites which will incorporate the best of African values—"solidarity, respect for life, humanity, and community."[56]

## African Liberation Theology

The newcomer to theology in Africa is African liberation theology. The initial impetus for this theology came in a declaration at the 1977 EATWOT meeting in Accra, Ghana: "Because oppression is found not only in culture but also political and economic structures and the dominant mass media, African theology must also be *liberation* theology."[57] In response, several theologians from independent Africa have begun to construct an African liberation theology.

Their analysis of the African context leads them to critique neo-colonialism in all its manifestations. In response to their findings, they call the church in Africa to a liberative praxis. It must take sides with the oppressed and work for their liberation. In addition, it must judge those in power as to their liberative or nonliberative leadership. "Theology must inform and lead the church to be sharply critical of any alienating tendency. . . . It is the Christian community's task to witness to the shortcomings of any social or political programme."[58]

In keeping with the African value of wholeness in all things, these theologians seek socioeconomic liberation as well as cultural liberation. Culture, for them, is not an idyllic precolonialist past or African song and dance. Rather, culture is the life and times that Africans are living today. "Today's tragedies, internal lacerations, and challenges are the place where a culture is being born out of a people's struggle to rediscover its memory and regain its dignity."[59]

## Main Emphases

Three dimensions of African culture, the first two of which we have already noted, provide the seedbed of African Christologies. First, Africans view life holistically. An African Christ should effect a holistic salvation to meet the physical, spiritual, political, and social needs of Africans. Second, African communities value mediators highly. African Christologies should incorporate this role of mediator, particularly between the human and the divine sphere. Third, Africans have tended to concretize their ideals and aspirations in key historical figures who lead communities. They naturally identify Jesus with such African figures rather than with abstract concepts, such as *logos*.[60]

### Kinship Within the Community

The essential christological question that African theologians, as *Christians*, ask is, Can the incarnation be indigenized within Africa without distorting or truncating its meaning? The essential christological question that African theologians, as *Africans*, ask is, "Why should an Akan [or any African] relate to Jesus of Nazareth, who does not belong to his clan, family, tribe, and nation?"[61] This question is acute, since Christ is often identified, not with African realities, but with the ideals of missionaries and colonizers.

The point of contact between the doctrine of the incarnation and African values is community solidarity. The incarnation cannot be understood simply as the mystery of Word made flesh; it is God become human. And human, in the African sense, as we have seen, is to be in community. Consequently, Jesus the incarnate one can be at home on African soil only if he becomes "a bundle of interpersonal relations welding the human subject to the human community and to the totality of the cosmos."[62]

We have seen that African community includes God, ancestors, and human beings. The status and actions of the individual are regulated by social relationships. The kinship system is a vast network that connects everyone in a tribe or clan or family, so that each individual is a mother, brother, daughter, cousin, and so forth, to everyone else. When two strangers meet in a village, one of their first duties is to sort out their relationship so that they may act according to accepted behavioral patterns. For example, if they are aunt and niece, then the niece will accord greater respect to the aunt.[63]

Jesus' incarnation requires that he enter this vast web of kinship ties.[64] The New Testament itself provides the kinship relationships that define Jesus as a human being in community. He is, of course, son of the creator God (John 3:16; Rom. 8:3). He is the elder brother of human beings: "the firstborn within a large family" (Rom. 8:29). And he is also the elder brother of the ancestors: "the firstborn from the dead" (Col. 1:18).

### Firstborn Among the Living

A popular interpretation of Jesus in Africa is that of an elder brother. Christians in Angola sing, "Jesus Christ is our Elder Brother / He is an African!"[65] This interpretation is natural in the light of the kinship responsibilities of the elder brother. He defends the younger siblings in their quarrels with other families and mediates between the younger siblings and parents in important matters such as marriage. He even bears responsibility for the actions of younger siblings. It is no wonder, then, that he sacrifices himself on account of their wrongs, like the suffering servant of Isaiah 53 or the high priest of Hebrews 8–10.[66]

This priest in Hebrews is a brother whose solidarity with his family leads to salvation:

> For the one who sanctifies and those who are sanctified all have one Father. For this reason Jesus is not ashamed to call them brothers and sisters. . . . Therefore he had to become like his brothers and sisters in every respect, so that he might be a merciful and faithful high priest. . . . Because he himself was tested by what he suffered, he is able to help those who are being tested. (Heb. 2:11, 17–18)

This portrait of Jesus introduces a significant point of identification between Jesus and his African brothers and sisters: sharing in the rites of passage by which an individual enters into the life of the community. This is what is required of Jesus' full humanity in an African context.

Although rites of passage differ markedly from tribe to tribe, they all function to incorporate individuals into communal existence. The rites at birth, particularly the proper disposal of the umbilical cord, symbolize that the child is now related to the community and not just to the mother who birthed it. Rites usually associated with puberty symbolize rebirth into adulthood in the community; solitude and seclusion are followed by reentry and celebration. Marriage unites families rather than individuals, and procreation extends the life of both families. Death is entrance into a new sphere of existence, and detailed rites ensure comfort for the ancestors in their new villages.[67]

Jesus, as elder brother, developed as a mature member of his community through rites of passage. Genealogies clarify his tribal affiliation (Matt. 1:1–18; Luke 3:23–38). Attended to at birth with the required offerings and period of maternal purity (Luke 1–2), he went on to join in solidarity with his people at his baptism. Following a period of seclusion in the wilderness, he entered public life, healing and teaching among his brothers and sisters. His life ended in the final rite of passage, death on the cross, which symbolized completeness rather than shame. "He died on the cross because he was a perfect, complete, entire, mature and responsible Man."[68]

As elder brother who undergoes communal rites of passage and cares for his younger brothers and sisters, Jesus can find a place in the kinship ties of Africa.

Our Brother Christ is walking through Africa,
through the copper mines of Zambia and the forests of Zaire;
Our Brother Christ is walking through Africa,
Alleluja.[69]

Yet this interpretation, on its own, accentuates the human component of the incarnation without incorporating the divine element. But while it was "as an ordinary man that Jesus died . . . the great Christian *differentia* comes obviously from the fact of the Resurrection by which the Christian faith stands or falls."[70] The centrality of the resurrection raises the further possibility that Jesus is firstborn both of the living and of the ancestors or living dead.

### Firstborn Among the Dead

By virtue of his death and resurrection, Jesus now belongs to the world of the ancestors. His relationship to the living has changed; he is no longer merely elder brother but ancestor, and among these he is firstborn as well.

Only those Africans who meet certain requirements enter the sphere of the ancestors. They must live well, not be party to sorcery, quarreling, and anger; they must also die well at an old age; and they must have produced children to whom they can convey the life force.[71] The living are responsible for preparing them for their journey to the ancestral home. Once the dead have arrived in this sphere, the living must communicate with them in corporate gatherings; must remember them with offerings and prayers at significant events; and, as long as someone is alive who knows them, must be mindful of their presence. In short, the living must accord their ancestors due respect to receive blessings from them.[72]

According to African traditional religion, God's life exists in abundance among the ancestors; they are a reservoir that brims with the life force, or *élan vital*, from which the living derive the resources of life's wholeness and goodness. In the same way, Jesus is like a vine that mediates fullness of life, the *élan vital*, to the branches (John 15:4–7).[73] All the blessings of the creator God are mediated through Jesus, the ancestor: living water (John 4:14), living bread (John 6:51), abundant life (John 10:10).

In an equally important role as ancestor, Jesus mediates between the living and the creator God by bringing people, their prayers, offerings, and aspirations, to God. This is precisely how Africans understand Jesus' words, "I am the way, and the truth, and the life. No one comes to the Father except through me" (John 14:6). Jesus is the gate of the sheepfold (John 10:9), for only those "to whom the Son chooses to reveal" God know their creator (Luke 10:22).

Like other ancestors, Jesus provides an exemplary model of behavior: "For I have set you an example, that you also should do as I have done to you" (John 13:15). He serves the needs of others, restores their dignity by defending the weak (women, children), identifies himself with sinners, and heals the sick. He confirms positive African values. "Hospitality and family spirit, solicitude for parents and orphans, and the unfortunate are, in him, taken up and perfected."[74] Jesus is the model of the best of African behavior.

Finally, Jesus provides a watchful presence over the community. Refusing to leave them desolate (John 14:18), Jesus promises to be with them always (Matt. 28:20). He stands allied with them until the community of the living enters the community of the ancestors.

Jesus, then, fulfills the roles that Africans attribute to the ancestors: mediator of God's blessings, mediator of human prayers, exemplary model of behavior, and provider of watchful care. Yet, a question still remains: How can Jesus belong to the ancestors of a particular African tribe when he lived as a Jew in Palestine? The answer to this question is based on the resurrection.

At the resurrection, Jesus accomplished the "future the ancestors sought to guarantee."[75] "In him the mediatory words and actions of our ancestors culminate and are fulfilled."[76] At his resurrection, he achieved what no other liv-

ing being has achieved and, as a result, became elder
brother. At his resurrection, he achieved what no ancestor
has achieved and, as a result, became Proto-Ancestor.[77]

Jesus' precedence among the ancestors has a direct impact upon the living, who share in community with them.
First, Jesus holds authority over malevolent spirits and dis-
satisfied ancestors so that Africans need fear them no
longer. Second, Jesus mediates the *élan vital* to the living,
for he is the second Adam, a "life-giving spirit" (1 Cor.
15:45).[78] Finally, his resurrection and present reign over
the entire cosmos transcends national, tribal, clan, and familial solidarity.[79] African believers are related to all humanity, with whom they receive the life force from the
firstborn of all creation.[80]

According to Nyamiti, Jesus' role as ancestor illuminates
not only his relationship to Africa and humankind but also
his place in "the inner life of God (Trinity)." There is an
ancestral kinship among the persons of the Trinity: "the
Father is the Ancestor of the Son, the Son is the Descen-
dant of the Father." They live out their ancestral kinship
through the mediation of the Spirit. This ancestral relationship extends beyond the Trinity. "The Incarnation and
Christ's redemptive ministry . . . are the extensions of the
trinitarian communication to the man Jesus and, through
Him, to the rest of creation." The portrait of Jesus as ancestor, therefore, unifies African communities, the human
community, the divine community, and the human with
the divine community.[81]

## Key Figures of the Community

Salvation in traditional African religion is wholeness
within this life. It entails social equilibrium—harmony
with the living and the dead. It also entails personal
equilibrium—inner harmony that produces physical well-
being.[82] It occurs here and now in the blessings of friendship, plentiful offspring, and a long life. For Jesus to become a savior to Africans, he must do more than procure
for them an eternal destiny. He must control the forces
from which Africans themselves struggle to be saved here
and now, whether that be infertility or malevolent spirits.

Two figures within African communities have as their responsibility to accomplish this sort of salvation: the tribal
chief and the healer or "witch doctor."

## Chief

The chief is the guardian of African community, the one
person who embodies the religious and political aspirations
of the tribe.[83] The chief must be a courageous, heroic figure, able to triumph over enemies in the terrestrial and
spiritual worlds. Honorific titles accrue to the chief: hurri-
cane, pillar, serpent's folds—the curling and strangling
power of the python.[84]

The chief derives strength from his position at the intersection of the terrestrial realm and the spiritual realm,
where healers, sorcerers, manipulators of nature, and others, exist.[85] The chief's authority in this sphere derives
from the ancestors. Among the Akan tribe, for example,
the chief gains intimate access to the ancestors through a
ritual of initiation when the chief is lowered and raised
three times on the chair of his most renowned ancestor.
Once installed, the chief is "more than just a head of state.
He is, in a sense, an ancestor himself. From that moment
everybody must call him Nana (grandfather)."[86]

At this intersection the chief is the mediator between all
the constituents of the community: the tribe, the ancestors,
and even those unborn. Further, the community derives its
identity and coherence from the chief. Such solidarity
between tribe and chief matches that which exists between
the church and Christ—its head and mediator of life. As
the tribe is identified with the chief, so the church is identified with Christ (1 Cor. 12:27). As the chief mediates blessings from the ancestors, so Christ mediates blessings to the
church. Christ is "the head . . . from whom the whole
body, joined and knit together by every ligament with
which it is equipped, as each part is working properly, pro-
motes the body's growth in building itself up in love" (Eph.
4:15–16).

There is another dimension to this mediatorial role.
When communal misfortunes occur and the social equilibrium becomes imbalanced, the chief must subordinate his

own well-being to the needs of the community.[87] This requires doing all he can to allay the tensions that disrupt the
community. In other words, mediation becomes reconciliation. Jesus' ultimate act of mediation as reconciliation as
chief took the form of complete self-subordination to the
community. On the cross, Jesus reconciled the world to God
(2 Cor. 5:18) and created one new humanity free from hos-
tility (Eph. 2:11–16). Jesus is lord or "chief" precisely because he humbled himself in life and in death (Phil. 2:5–7).
Therefore the entire cosmos, which is itself a web of relationships that exists under, on, and above the earth, will
confess that Jesus Christ is "chief" (Phil. 2:8–11).[88]

A variation of this view presents Jesus as spokesperson
for the chief.[89] African chiefs tend to have subchiefs and
officials who mediate between them and the people, particularly through skill in public speaking. Many Africans
naturally regard God as the great chief, an identification
that opens the way to understand Jesus as the great
chief's spokesperson. This figure is as the chief in all
public matters and is, still, obedient to the chief. Pobee
suggests that this relationship is similar to the Fourth
Gospel's portrait of the Logos, "being at one and the
same time divine and yet subordinate to God."[90] The position of the spokesperson is closely akin to the portrayal
of Jesus as high priest in the Letter to the Hebrews. Jesus
is at once human, learning obedience through what he
suffers, and more than human, a priest in the order of
Melchizedek who has passed through the heavens (Heb.
4:14; 5:5–10).

### Healer

Another figure within African society who attempts to
effect salvation is the healer, or "witch doctor."[91] The
healer functions to bring salvation or wholeness to every
aspect of community life. "He plays a part in the political,
social and economic spheres: he confers authority on the
village chief, encourages fertility, blesses every undertak-
ing. He is undoubtedly the most powerful, influential and
complex figure in Congolese society. That is why the word
[healer] may be translated priest, chemist, doctor, magi-

cian, prophet and visionary."[92] This final list suggests significant parallels between Jesus and the healer in the arenas of healing, exorcism, and clairvoyance.

The healing by the healer, unlike scientific medicine, is holistic. It requires determining the spiritual cause in the true inner being which has revealed itself in a physical ailment. Equally, the healer looks for a social cause, perhaps in communal tensions and aggressiveness.[93] Once the ailment is diagnosed, the healer prescribes remedies that range from sacrifices to dances to restoration of social relationships. Often healing requires the use of the particular fetishes, or sacred devices, of the healer.

The Gospels are replete with accounts of Jesus' healing that share the healer's holistic approach. Like the healer, Jesus acknowledges a relationship between the spirit and the body of those whom he heals. Along with physical healing, Jesus absolves the unhealthy of guilt ("Your sins are forgiven" to the paralytic [Mark 2:5]), commends them for their faith ("Your faith has made you well" to Bartimaeus, a blind beggar [Mark 10:52]), and restores them to responsibility ("Go . . . and from now on do not sin again" to the adulterous woman [John 8:11]).

Also like the healer, Jesus places healing within the context of social reintegration into the community. In other words, he reestablishes equilibrium to the community by returning those who are healed to normalcy. Jesus asks healed lepers to present themselves to the priests, the preservers of cultic regulations (Mark 1:44; Luke 17:14). He returns the Gerasene demoniac to his village with the words, "Go home to your friends, and tell them how much the Lord has done for you" (Mark 5:19). He permits Peter's mother-in-law to take up her role as host immediately upon her healing (Mark 1:31). To this can be added innumerable examples of Jesus' eating with outcasts and so-called sinners—an action by which he restores them to the central activity of communal life. Social reintegration is also implicit in many miracle stories about those who have been ostracized for cultic reasons on account of their sickness, such as the woman with a flow of blood. The simple words "Go in peace" are redolent of social wholeness and restored health (Mark 5:34).[94]

Finally, some of Jesus' methods of healing are akin to those of the healer. He applies saliva (Mark 8:23) or a mixture of saliva and dirt (John 9:6) to the unhealthy body part; he spits on his finger, then touches the tongue of a deaf-mute (Mark 7:33); and he makes noises that can be interpreted variously as a sigh or a snort or a groan. In these ways his method of healing conforms to the healer of Africa, whose holistic healing, characterized by the unity of spiritual and physical healing, reintegrates the healed person into the life of the community.[95]

Jesus also shares with the healer mysterious, perhaps clairvoyant, knowledge. The healer claims to know the secrets of a person's heart and to be able to foretell the future.[96] Similarly, Jesus is able to feel power leaving his body through his clothing (Mark 5:28–32). He knows that the man at the pool of Bethsaida was handicapped for many years (John 5:6), that Lazarus was dead before Jesus reached Bethany (John 11:11), and that Judas is about to betray him (Matt. 26:20–25). He can even predict the downfall of Jerusalem (Mark 13:1–8).

The healer exercises power over the spirit world by interposing himself or herself between the ordinary person and sorcerers or ghosts (spirits that have been shut out of the sphere where the ancestors reside). Only the healer can destroy these malevolent beings. Similarly, Jesus' exorcisms demonstrate his authority over the spirit world. When the Seventy return from their mission, they exclaim, "Lord, in your name even the demons submit to us!" Jesus replies, "I watched Satan fall from heaven like a flash of lightning" (Luke 10:17–18). Later, he retorts to would-be opponents, "But if it is by the finger of God that I cast out the demons, then the kingdom of God has come to you" (Luke 11:20).

The healer and Jesus both exhibit power for holistic healing, a knowledge of mysteries, and the capacity to mediate between the human world and the spirit world. It is conceivable that the healer possesses these extraordinary skills to help the suffering because he or she has been subjected to suffering, to treat the marginalized because he or she has been marginalized through some physiological, psychological, or social aberrance. A parallel could easily be drawn between Jesus and the healer in this respect. Jesus was known as a friend of outcasts and sinners. He was a relatively poor Galilean, on the social fringes of Judaism. And at death, his marred visage suggested Isaiah 53 to some of his followers. In addition, Africans believe that the healer can divine witches and sorcerers because they themselves utilize sorcery.[97] This evaluation of the healer suggests the response that Jesus evoked among some of his contemporaries: "He casts out demons by Beelzebul, the ruler of the demons" (Luke 11:15). Jesus' ambiguity and marginalized status comport well with those of the healer.

## Liberation

### Holistic Dimension

Africans seek liberation from deleterious structures. For South Africans, these are the structures of apartheid. For other Africans, these are the destructive legacies of colonialism that divided and decimated African social and political stability.[98] Yet the more immediate cause of Africa's problems lies in the arena of domestic politics. All Africans must be liberated to participate more fully in the social and political spheres to improve the welfare of their nations and the continent as a whole.[99]

Yet liberation in Africa extends far beyond oppressive structures to include all that oppresses communities and individuals. In studies of African Independent Churches, John Mbiti and Marthinus Daneel unearth a holistic Christology of *Christus Victor* that meets the African need "to see, to know, and to experience Jesus Christ as the victor over the powers and forces from which Africa knows no means of deliverance," including spirits, sorcery, anxiety, sickness, and death.[100] This holistic liberation Christology has been concretized in the lives of black prophets,[101] most of whom founded African Independent Churches through a combination of religious and political leadership. Douglas Waruta summarizes the "essential elements" of prophetic leadership: "the quest for spiritual/physical liberation from external domination. For the followers of these independent churches, the prophet is their spiritual and political leader and liberator."[102] As examples, he cites the Kinjikitile of the Maji Maji revolt against the Germans in Tanganyika, the Mau Mau movement in Kenya, and the recent "Holy Spirit Movement" led by self-declared prophetess Alice Lakwena in Uganda.

South African black theologians underscore the holistic nature of liberation in order to undermine the white South African church's promulgation of oppressive dichotomies. Black theologians refuse a Christ who could be preached while black people were violently displaced from their own land. They refuse to accept that God can be worshiped spiritually in the context of systematic racial oppression. For black South African theologians, therefore, Jesus cannot be "the romantic preacher who declared a message of submission oriented solely to the future"[103] but a liberator whose life embodies a salvation that is consistent with the holistic African worldview. "It is liberation from sin in all its manifestations of alienation from God and neighbor. It is liberation from economic exploitation, dehumanization, and oppression. It is liberation from meaninglessness and self-alienation, from poverty and suffering. It is liberation toward a meaningful human existence seeking freedom and human fulfillment."[104]

Prior to Jesus, God accomplished holistic liberation at the exodus. The exodus constituted physical salvation in that the Hebrews had to be protected from enemies in chariots, fed when hungry, given water when thirsty. It was political in that a group of slaves escaped bondage.[105] It was religious in that they were led to Sinai, where they joined with God in covenant. It was social in that they were to be compassionate to the widow, the orphan, and the alien, for they had been slaves and aliens in Egypt (Ex. 22:21–24; 23:9; Deut. 10:18–20). This liberation was total: political, religious, material, and social.[106]

Jesus' incarnation signaled God's refusal to address only the spiritual realm of life even more forcefully than the exodus. Here human frailty and divine glory united, bridging the gap between spiritual and physical. Jesus was born in the poverty of a manger, completely emptied of all that humans deem glorious. He spent his energy as a slave (Phil. 2:5–7), serving the poor, liberating them from their poverty by means of his own poverty: "For you know the generous act of our Lord Jesus Christ, that though he was rich, yet for your sakes he became poor, so that by his poverty you might become rich" (2 Cor. 8:9). He chose the company of sinners and prostitutes, the "scum of society," leaving behind the ninety-nine well-behaved sheep "to go out and look for the smelly troublesome old ram."[107]

## A New History for South Africa

South African theologians explore the contemporary implications of a Christology of liberation more thoroughly than do independent African theologians. They are particularly aware of the history—past, future, and present—that Jesus creates for black South Africans.

In the exodus, God transformed the Hebrew people from objects of oppression into subjects with a unique consciousness free from the tyranny of their Egyptian oppressors. With this new consciousness came the recognition that they had their own history apart from the Egyptians. They saw the exodus not as an event in isolation but a new creation; Exodus 1 is a continuation of the history in Genesis 1.[108] God controlled all of nature, turning a river to blood, turning day into night, commanding lice and locusts to do God's bidding.

This reclamation of the creation brought with it the reclamation of their ancestral history. The Hebrews claimed that the God who heard their cry is the God of Abraham and Sarah, Rebekah and Isaac, Jacob and Rachel and Leah, and Joseph. Therefore they could claim a prior history, beginning with creation, mediated through the ancestors, and culminating in the exodus. This was not history dominated by the ideology of Egypt but history told by liberated Hebrew slaves.

Jesus spent his life restoring to the oppressed their lost histories and traditions. These were the sick whose blood and disease rendered them ritually impure; the demon-possessed who were not permitted to praise God in the synagogue; the prostitutes whose poverty had driven them to a profession forbidden by Torah and despised by society. To such as these Jesus granted a new history. Healed lepers made the prescribed offerings to the priests. Healed cripples could worship on the Sabbath. The blind, the lame, and the children followed Jesus directly into the Temple. Prostitutes would become the first to enter God's reign. Tax collectors received the honorific title "children of Abraham." All of these people, the sick and sinners who were once excluded from the traditions and history of their people, had their history and institutions returned to them and their health and human dignity restored by Jesus.

Like the new consciousness forged by the exodus, the Black Consciousness that God is creating in South Africa eschews a slave mentality. Their dignity, robbed by white South Africans, is bestowed by God. God is granting to the blacks of South Africa their own history, just as Jesus instilled among the outcasts a desire to reclaim their history and tradition. It is no longer a history told by Dutch and English oppressors about black heathen but a history about black martyrs who sought justice for their black brothers and sisters. It is not a history of exclusion and subjugation but of inclusion and liberation. It is the history of a people who know who they are in the presence of God.

The exodus, however, pointed not only to the past but also to the future, for it led to the promised land. This land was given in trust to the Hebrews, with the requirement that it become a source of reconciliation rather than division. In addition to laws that require justice for the poor in the land, the foremost symbol of reconciliation is the year of Jubilee: "You shall return, every one of you, to your property and every one of you to your family" (Lev. 25:10). Land can never finally be lost; it is an inalienable inheritance.

Jesus' point of departure for his ministry was the inauguration of the year of Jubilee (Luke 4:16–21).[109] For South African blacks in homelands and townships, the year of Jubilee represents far more than financial restoration. There is a vital union between the people and the land. The land is the locus of community: sacred places of initiation for generations, locations—rocks or trees or rivers—where the ancestors commune with the living. When the colonizers violently displaced the blacks and put them into foreign homelands, they stripped them of their history, of their consciousness, of their community. Jesus' proclamation of the year of Jubilee, in this context, is "a reconnection of the black umbilical cord of history."[110]

This new consciousness of their history and future requires of black South Africans a new understanding of suffering in the present. In black South Africa, on the Thursday night before Good Friday (i.e., the night of betrayal and harassment), black churches are full of people who give witness to their understanding of Jesus' capture, trial, and crossbearing. There is frequent perspiring, weeping, and fainting because of their intense identification with Jesus' experience; his experience is their experience. "In fact it is their own painful life story that they are reliving and narrating. Jesus of Nazareth is tortured, abused and humiliated and crucified in them."[111]

Black Consciousness requires, however, a distinction between this sort of innocent suffering and the suffering that Jesus endured. Black suffering has been systematic, braced by poor education, untreated disease, and the exploitation of black labor.[112] Their suffering does not lead beyond oppression. The suffering of Jesus, in contrast, was redemptive. He suffered in his struggle to liberate people from oppression. He *chose* to struggle with others in a way that engendered in them a solidarity that threatened the status quo (e.g., John 11:45–53).

There is, therefore, a vast chasm between "a fatalistic resignation to the structures of oppression" and "suffering in the course of an active struggle for liberation."[113] Black theologians have called blacks in South Africa not to suffer passively but to suffer redemptively for their black brothers and sisters. The transition from innocent to redemptive suffering is tantamount to a conversion. Boesak wonders whether the church is prepared to be converted, for it is often plagued by a colonial mentality, accepting Western theology and clinging to a pietistic, otherworldly religiosity that has no bearing on the present situation.[114] Yet in

1976 Buthelezi already discerned a hopeful shift: "The black people are now regarding their suffering as a step towards liberation instead of a pool of fate and self-pity. Right in the midst of the experience of suffering the black people have made themselves believe that they can do something about their own liberation. Black consciousness is an instance of how the black people have transmuted their present suffering into the medium of liberation towards self-esteem."[115] The release of Nelson Mandela from prison is a salutary instance of redemptive suffering. His freedom fired further hope for freedom among South African blacks, and his dignity after years of unjust imprisonment gained the attention of the entire world.

In many respects, the social and political climate in South Africa is changing as many of the regulations of apartheid are being dismantled. Yet the experience of independence among other African nations signals the need for caution and persistent aspiration for freedom. Laurenti Magesa of Tanzania recalls that the freedom struggles that brought about independence were interpreted as a new exodus. The attainment of political independence could not "be interpreted otherwise than that it was fundamentally the doing of God. He had heard 'the cry of His people' and He was telling the colonial Pharaohs of the day, through the events of the independence struggles, 'Let my people go, that they may serve me.'" This new exodus promised abundant life in the land of their African ancestors. Three decades after Africa's political independence, though, many Africans are asking the somewhat cynical question, Was it worth it? Magesa then recalls that the descendants of Abraham and Sarah, during their sojourn in the wilderness following the exodus and on the way to the promised land, asked exactly the same question and made the same complaint.[116] Yet Magesa remains hopeful. Jesus the liberator will use "the memory of the long, hard, brutal years of slavery and colonialism" to urge forward the construction of just structures. Through a holistic effort that includes courageous people in church and society, "Jesus Liberator will untiringly and unceasingly say no to hunger, torture, the muzzling of free speech, detention without trial, disregard of the common good and the incitement of inter-ethnic hatred for selfish political ends."[117]

## NOTES

1. This chapter will only consider theology in sub-Sahara Africa, which comprises forty-six countries south of the Sahara desert. The five Moslem countries to the north will not be included in the chapter because of their political, socioeconomic, and religious differences.

2. See Sam Kobia, "Elitism, Wealth and the Church," *AACC Bulletin* 11 (1978): 32–35. See also Jean-Marc Éla, *My Faith as an African* (Maryknoll, N.Y.: Orbis Books, 1988), 63.

3. Several statistics illustrate the vastness of the vacuum: "The Congo had but a single senior African civil servant. . . . Zaire, a country as large as the United States west of the Mississippi, had only a dozen university graduates among its 25 million people. Several countries, such as Guinea-Bissau and Cape Verde, had not one African doctor" (David Lamb, *The Africans* [New York: Vintage Press, 1987], 139).

4. Lamb, *The Africans*, 9.

5. Lebamang Sebidi, "Towards an Understanding of the Current Unrest in South Africa," in *Hammering Swords Into Ploughshares: Essays in Honor of Archbishop Mpilo Desmond Tutu*, ed. Buti Tlhagale and Itumeleng Mosala (Grand Rapids: Wm. B. Eerdmans Publishing Co., 1987), 256.

6. The statistics of apartheid's oppression of nonwhites are grim: 17.25 million Africans have been arrested between 1916 and 1981 for violations of pass law regulations; 3 million people were relocated under apartheid policies; in 1983/84 per capita expenditure on white pupils was R1184 versus R213 on African pupils; and in 1983 the average household income per month was R1390 for whites versus R204 for Africans. These statistics come from several sources: Sebidi, "Towards an Understanding," 262; Buti Tlhagale, "Nazism, Stalinist Russia and Apartheid—A Comparison," in *Hammering Swords*, ed. Tlhagale and Mosala, 274; and Dorothy Ramodibe, "Women and Men Building Together the Church in Africa," in *With Passion and Compas-*

*sion: Third World Women Doing Theology*, Reflections from the Women's Commission of the Ecumenical Association of Third World Theologians, ed. Virginia Fabella and Mercy Amba Oduyoye (Maryknoll, N.Y.: Orbis Books, 1989), 21.

7. Sanford Ungar, *Africa: The People and Politics of an Emerging Continent* (New York: Simon & Schuster, 1986), 442.

8. Éla, *My Faith*, 96.

9. In the face of widespread poverty among the masses, the elite depend increasingly on the military to keep dissent at a minimum. See Kobia, "Elitism, Wealth and the Church," 39. See also Jean-Marc Éla, *African Cry* (Maryknoll, N.Y.: Orbis Books, 1986), 68–73.

10. John V. Taylor, *The Primal Vision: Christian Presence Amid African Religion*, Christian Presence Series (London: SCM Press, 1963), 20.

11. Desmond M. Tutu, "Black Theology/African Theology— Soul Mates or Antagonists?" in *Black Theology: A Documentary History, 1966–1979*, ed. James H. Cone and Gayraud S. Wilmore (Maryknoll, N.Y.: Orbis Books, 1979), 484. See also J. C. Thomas, "What Is African Theology?" *Ghana Bulletin of Theology* 4 (1973): 15.

12. Éla, *African Cry*, 4–5.

13. See AACC, *The Struggle Continues*, Official Report of the Third Assembly of the All Africa Conference of Churches, Lusaka, Zambia, May 12–24, 1974 (Nairobi: AACC, 1975), 53. John Gatu, an AACC official, had previously issued calls for a moratorium in 1971 at the Mission Festival in Milwaukee and at the 1972 WCC Assembly at Bangkok. Burgess Carr, former General Secretary of the AACC, explained that the strategy had to do with *"restructuring relationships*, and renewing patterns of cooperation so as to ensure that self-reliance liberates us from the service of mammon" (Burgess Carr, "The Moratorium: The Search for Self-Reliance and Authenticity," *AACC Bulletin* 7 [1974], 44).

14. Manas Buthelezi, "Towards Indigenous Theology in South Africa," in *The Emergent Gospel*, ed. Torres and Fabella, 69.

15. Kwesi A. Dickson, *Theology in Africa* (Maryknoll, N.Y.: Orbis Books, 1984), 139. For a secondary source on this debate, see Matthew Schoffeleers, "Black and African Theology in Southern Africa: A Controversy Re-Examined," *Journal of Religion in Africa* 18 (1988): 99–123.

16. "Final Communiqué," in *African Theology en Route*, Papers from the Pan-African Conference of Third World Theologians, December 17–23, 1977, Accra, Ghana, ed. Kofi Appiah-Kubi and Sergio Torres (Maryknoll, N.Y.: Orbis Books, 1979), 191. Italics added. Though the debate continues, several theologians are discovering conversation points between the two theologies: Tutu, "Black Theology/African Theology—Soul Mates or Antagonists?" 483–491; and James H. Cone, "A Black American Perspective on the Future of African Theology," in *African Theology en Route*, ed. Appiah-Kubi and Torres, 176–186.

17. Justin S. Ukpong, *African Theologies Now—A Profile*, Spearhead No. 80 (Eldoret, Kenya: Gaba Publications, 1984), 4.

18. AACC, *Engagement*, Second AACC Assembly "Abidjan 69" (Nairobi: AACC, 1969), 114. African theology assumes that God's revelation is present in African culture to some degree. "African culture, far from being 'pagan' or satanic, therefore provides a genuine, if limited, knowledge of God" (John Parratt, *A Reader in African Christian Theology* (London: SPCK, 1987), 7). This was confirmed at the AACC Ibadan Conference: "We believe that God the Father of our Lord Jesus Christ, Creator of Heaven and earth, Lord of History, has been dealing with mankind at all times and in all parts of the world. It is with this conviction that we study the rich African heritage of our African peoples, and we have evidence that they know of Him and worship Him" (Kwesi A. Dickson and Paul Ellingworth, eds., *Biblical Revelation and African Beliefs* [London: Lutterworth Press, 1969], 16).

19. Two important articles on method in African theology are Charles Nyamiti, "A Critical Assessment on Some Issues in Today's African Theology," *African Christian Studies* 5 (March 1989): 5–18; and J. C. Thomas, "What Is African Theology?" 14–30.

20. A. R. Sprunger, "The Contribution of the African Independent Churches to a Relevant Theology for Africa," in *Relevant Theology For Africa*, ed. Hans-Jürgen Becker (Durban, Natal: Lutheran Publishing, 1973), 165. See also Kofi Appiah-Kubi, "Indigenous African Christian Churches: Signs of Authenticity," in *African Theology en Route*, ed. Appiah-Kubi and Torres, 118–120.

21. Studies of their Christology have been undertaken by Thomas G. Christensen, "The Gbaya Naming of Jesus: An Inquiry Into the Contextualization of Soteriological Themes

Among the Gbaya of Cameroon" (D.Min. thesis, Lutheran School of Theology, Chicago, 1984); Marthinus L. Daneel, "Towards a Theologia Africana? The Contribution of Independent Churches to African Theology," *Missionalia* 12.2 (1984): 64–89; John S. Mbiti, "Some African Concepts of Christology," in *Christ and the Younger Churches*, ed. C. F. Vicedom (London: SPCK, 1972), 51–62; Matthew Schoffeleers, "Folk Christology in Africa: The Dialectics of the Nganga Paradigm," *Journal of Religion in Africa* 19 (1989): 157–183; and Aylward Shorter, *Jesus and the Witchdoctor: An Approach to Healing and Wholeness* (Maryknoll, N.Y.: Orbis Books, 1985).

22. Dickson, *Theology in Africa*, 38.

23. Mercy Amba Oduyoye, "The Value of African Religious Beliefs and Practices for Christian Theology," in *African Theology en Route*, ed. Appiah-Kubi and Torres, 110.

24. Gabriel M. Setiloane, *African Theology: An Introduction* (Johannesburg: Skotaville, 1986), 9.

25. Dickson, *Theology in Africa*, 159.

26. Ibid., 148–158; Aylward Shorter, ed., *African Christian Spirituality* (London: Geoffrey Chapman, 1978), 10–11; and John Parratt, "African Theology and Biblical Hermeneutics," *Africa Theological Journal* 12 (1983): 88–94.

27. See François Kabasélé, "Le Christ comme ancêtre et aîné, in *Chemins de la christologie africaine*, ed. François Kabasélé et al., (Paris: Desclée, 1986), 132–141.

28. See Kwame Bediako, "Biblical Christologies in the Context of African Traditional Religions," in *Sharing Jesus in the Two Thirds World: Evangelical Christologies from the Contexts of Poverty, Powerlessness and Religious Pluralism*, ed. Vinay Samuel and Chris Sugden (Grand Rapids: Wm. B. Eerdmans Publishing Co., 1984), 100–101, 112–113; and Anselme T. Sanon, "Jésus, maître d'initiation," in *Chemins de la christologie africaine*, ed. Kabasélé et al., 143–166.

29. Kofi Appiah-Kubi, "Why African Theology?" *AACC Bulletin* 7 (1974), 5. See also J. C. Thomas, "What Is African Theology?" 29.

30. Ch. B. Okolo, "Christ, 'Emmanuel': An African Inquiry," *Bulletin de Theologie Africaine* 2.3 (1980): 17.

31. Dickson, *Theology in Africa*, 37.

32. John Pobee, *Toward an African Theology* (Nashville: Abingdon Press, 1979), 79.

33. Ibid., 108.

34. Charles Nyamiti, "African Christologies Today," in *Jesus in African Christianity: Experimentation and Diversity in African Christology*, ed. J. N. K. Mugambi and Laurenti Magesa (Nairobi: Initiatives, 1989), 19.

35. This is developed in two articles in consecutive volumes: Charles Nyamiti, "The Incarnation Viewed from the African Understanding of Person," *African Christian Studies* 6 (March 1990): 3–27, and *African Christian Studies* 6 (June 1990): 23–76.

36. For more on James Cone, see chapter 5 on black theology in North America.

37. The book was subsequently republished in the United States. See Basil Moore, ed., *The Challenge of Black Theology in South Africa* (Atlanta: John Knox Press, 1973).

38. Mokgethi Motlhabi, "Introduction," in *The Unquestionable Right to Be Free*, ed. Itumeleng J. Mosala and Buti Tlhagale (Maryknoll, N.Y.: Orbis Books, 1986), x; and Allan Boesak, *Farewell to Innocence: A Socio-Ethical Study on Black Theology and Black Power* (Maryknoll, N.Y.: Orbis Books, 1977).

39. Mokgethi Motlhabi, "The Historical Origins of Black Theology," in *The Unquestionable Right*, ed. Mosala and Tlhagale, 48.

40. See Lebamang Sebidi, "The Dynamics of the Black Struggle and Its Implications for Black Theology," in *The Unquestionable Right*, ed. Mosala and Tlhagale, 1–36. Obijole criticizes South African black theology in general and Boesak and Tutu in particular for failing to adopt a class-analysis paradigm as Latin American liberation theologians do. Obijole argues that racism is a capitalist category and that by "challenging racism without combating the very structure, namely capitalism that creates and nourishes it, he [Boesak] is only scratching the surface of the problem" (Olubayo Obijole, "South African Liberation Theologies of Boesak and Tutu—A Critical Evaluation," *Africa Theological Journal* 16, no. 3 [1987]: 208). Similarly, Boga comments that more South African blacks are participating in the capitalist system through the formation of a black middle class (Bonganjalo Goba, "A Black South African Perspective," in *Doing Theology in a Divided World*, ed. Fabella and Torres, 54). Thus, although race is the primary issue confronted by black theologians in South Africa, criticisms of this priority are increasing.

41. Ibid., 40.

42. Buthelezi, "Towards Indigenous Theology in South Africa," 74.

43. See the South African Student Organization's (SASO) definition of black consciousness in *The Challenge of Black Theology*, ed. Moore, 60–61.

44. Steve Biko, "Black Consciousness and the Quest for a True Humanity," *AACC Bulletin* 11, no. 1 (1978): 10.

45. Bonganjalo Goba, "The Black Consciousness Movement: Its Impact on Black Theology," in *The Unquestionable Right*, ed. Mosala and Tlhagale, 68. Black Consciousness "created a new theological climate in South Africa" (Simon Maimela, "Black Power and Black Theology in Southern Africa," *Scriptura* 12 [1984]: 45).

46. Goba, "The Black Consciousness Movement," 63.

47. Boesak, *Farewell to Innocence*, 125.

48. On the one hand, see Motlhabi, "The Historical Origins of Black Theology," 50–54. On the other hand, Obijole argues that traditional Africa was always a class society and that African traditions have no liberative components (Obijole, "South African Liberation Theologies of Boesak and Tutu," 209–210).

49. Nyameko Pityana, "What Is Black Consciousness?" in *The Challenge of Black Theology*, ed. Moore, 62.

50. See Motlhabi, "The Historical Origins of Black Theology," 50–52; and J. B. Ngubane, "Theological Roots of the African Independent Churches," in *The Unquestionable Right*, ed. Mosala and Tlhagale, 72–100.

51. Takatso A. Mofokeng, *The Crucified Among the Crossbearers: Towards a Black Christology* (Kampen: J. H. Kok, 1983), 21.

52. Allan Boesak, *Black and Reformed: Apartheid, Liberation and the Calvinist Tradition* (Maryknoll, N.Y.: Orbis Books, 1974), 71–74; Boesak, *Farewell to Innocence*, 17–18; Mofokeng, *Crossbearers*, 24–26, 30; E. K. Mosothoane, "The Use of Scripture in Black Theology," in *Scripture and the Use of Scripture*, ed. W. S. Vorster (Pretoria: University of South Africa Press, 1978), 29–31; and Desmond M. Tutu, *Hope and Suffering*, ed. John Webster (Grand Rapids: Wm. B. Eerdmans Publishing Co., 1983), 55–56, 81–84. For a comparison with white South African biblical interpretation, see J. A. Loader, "The Use of the Bible in Conventional South African Theology," in *Scripture and the Use of Scripture*, ed. Vorster, 1–5.

53. Takatso A. Mofokeng, "Black Christians, the Bible and Lib-

eration," in *Towards Freedom, Justice and Peace*, Voices from the Third World (EATWOT, 1987), 22.

54. Itumeleng J. Mosala, *Biblical Hermeneutics and Black Theology in South Africa* (Grand Rapids: Wm. B. Eerdmans Publishing Co., 1989), 13–42, 190–193. His approach utilizes a sociohistorical analysis of the Bible (pp. 31–32). Mosala illustrates this approach by interpreting Micah and Luke 1–2. Micah, for instance, contains prophetic oracles that reflect a struggle between three classes of people: rulers, middle class and working class.

55. Bonganjalo Goba, "Doing Theology in South Africa: A Black Christian Perspective," *Journal of Theology for Southern Africa* 31 (1980): 29.

56. Boesak, *Farewell to Innocence*, 152.

57. "Final Communiqué," 194.

58. Laurenti Magesa, "Towards a Theology of Liberation for Tanzania," in *Christianity in Independent Africa*, ed. Edward Fasholé-Luke et al. (Bloomington: Indiana University Press, 1978), 511.

59. Éla, *My Faith*, 170.

60. Nyamiti provides an important overview and critique of African Christologies in his "African Christologies Today." Robert Schreiter is editing a forthcoming volume (Orbis Books) that includes select articles from this volume and *Chemins de la christologie africaine*, in English translation. This new volume, then, will incoporate Christologies of Eastern Africa (*Jesus in African Christianity*) and Western Africa (*Chemins*).

61. Pobee, *Toward an African Theology*, 81. He himself is Akan, but the question is relevant for all other tribes. See Bediako, "Biblical Christologies," 99–100.

62. Alphonse N. Mushete, "The Figure of Jesus in African Theology," in *Christian Identity*, ed. Christian Duquoc and Casiano Floristán, Concilium 196 (Edinburgh: T. & T. Clark, 1988), 75–76.

63. John S. Mbiti, *African Religions and Philosophy* (Garden City, N.Y.: Doubleday & Co., 1970), 136.

64. Enyi B. Udoh ("Guest Paradigm: An Alternative Christological Approach in Africa," *Reformed World* 39 [1987]: 661–674) builds a Christology on this central notion of kinship.

65. Emilio J. M. de Carvalho, "What Do the Africans Say that Jesus Christ Is?" *Africa Theological Journal* 10 (1981), 24; 17.

The song continues that Jesus helps his siblings in the struggle for liberation in Zimbabwe, Namibia, and South Africa. See also J. W. Z. Kurewa, "Who Do You Say that I Am?" *International Review of Mission* 69 (1980): 183–184.

66. Kabasélé, "Le Christ comme ancêtre et aîné," 136.

67. For many specific examples, see Mbiti, *African Religions and Philosophy*, 143–216.

68. Mbiti, "Some African Concepts," 57.

69. This is a song sung in the United Methodist Church of Angola (Kurewa, "Who Do You Say That I Am?" 183).

70. Mbiti, "Some African Concepts," 57.

71. E. Bolaji Idowu (*African Traditional Religion: A Definition* [London: SCM Press, 1973], 187) suggests that childless and young, if they live good lives, are thought to become ancestors.

72. On ancestors in general, see Mbiti, *African Religions and Philosophy*, 107–118; Idowu, *African Traditional Religion*, 178–189; Kabasélé, "Le Christ comme ancêtre et aîné," 129–132; Pobee, *Toward an African Theology*, 46–47; and Charles Nyamiti, *Christ as Our Ancestor: Christology from an African Perspective* (Gweru, Zimbabwe: Mambo Press, 1984), 15–20, 23.

73. Kabasélé, "Le Christ comme ancêtre et aîné," 127–128.

74. Bénézet Bujo, "A Christocentric Ethic for Black Africa," *Theology Digest* 30 (1982), 144. See his *Afrikanische Theologie in ihrem gesellschaftlichen Kontext* (Düsseldorf: Patmos Verlag, 1986), 79–98.

75. Bujo, "Christocentric Ethic," 144.

76. Mushete, "Jesus in African Theology," 76.

77. Bujo, "Christocentric Ethic," 143. See also Nyamiti, *Christ as Our Ancestor*, 70; and E. J. Penoukou, "Réalité africaine et salut in Jésus-Christ," *Spiritus* 23 (1982): 374–392.

78. Damian Lwasa, "Traditional and Christian Community in Africa," in *African Christian Spirituality*, ed. Shorter, 143.

79. Bujo, "Christocentric Ethic," 144.

80. For criticisms of Christ as ancestor, see Aylward Shorter, "Ancestor Veneration Revisited," *African Ecclesiastical Review* 25 (1983): 197–203; François Kabasélé, "L'au-delà des modèles," in *Chemins de la christologie africaine*, ed. Kabasélé et al., 212–220; and Raymond Moloney, "African Christology," *Theological Studies* 48 (1987): 510–511.

81. Nyamiti, "African Christologies Today," 26, 25–27.

82. John S. Mbiti, "ὁ ωτὴρ ἡμῶν as an African Experience," in

*Christ and Spirit in the New Testament*, ed. Barnabas Lindars and Stephen S. Smalley (Cambridge: Cambridge University Press, 1973), 397–414; and Mercy Amba Oduyoye, *Hearing and Knowing: Theological Reflections on Christianity in Africa* (Maryknoll, N.Y.: Orbis Books, 1986), 97–108.

83. It is frequently difficult to distinguish between the chief and other key figures of the community, such as prophet, priest, and king. Nevertheless the chief provides perhaps the most familiar paradigm of Jesus' leadership. See, e.g., Douglas Waruta, "Who Is Jesus Christ for Africans Today? Prophet, Priest, Potentate," in *Jesus in African Christianity*, ed. Mugambi and Magesa, 40–59.

84. François Kabasélé, "Le Christ comme chef," in *Chemins de la christologie africaine*, ed. Kabasélé et al., 112–115.

85. Ibid., 117–120. See John 8:42.

86. Peter Sarpong, *The Sacred Stools in Akan* (Accra-Tema: Ghana Publishing, 1971), 537, quoted by Bediako, "Biblical Christologies," 105.

87. Kabasélé, "Le Christ comme chef," 118–119.

88. Ibid., 112. For criticism of the identification of Jesus Christ as chief, see Harry Sawyerr, *Creative Evangelism: Towards a New Christian Encounter with Africa* (London: Lutterworth Press, 1968), 72–73; and Kabasélé, "L'au-delà des modèles," 206–212.

89. For this discussion, see Pobee, *Toward an African Theology*, 94–98. This spokesperson is the Akan *Okyeame*. He clarifies further: "There are two types of *Okyeame*: (a) *Ahenkyeame*, who is also a chief, and that is hereditary; (b) a common linguist [spokesperson] who is appointed by the Chief because he was judged to be responsible and reliable and was generally capable of fulfilling the roles of an *Okyeame*" (ibid., 167 n. 21). Sawyerr gives other examples of the chiefs' mediaries: *Bangura* of the Temne of Sierra Leone; *Balogun* of the Yoruba; and *Lavale* (mouthpiece) of the Mende of Sierra Leone (Sawyerr, *Creative Evangelism*, 73).

90. Pobee, *Toward an African Theology*, 95.

91. R. Buana Kibongi, "Priesthood," in *Biblical Revelation and African Beliefs*, ed. Dickson and Ellingworth, 47–56. Over a decade ensued before the appearance of other studies on the *nganga*: Daneel, "Towards a Theologia Africana?" (1984); Shorter, *Jesus and the Witchdoctor* (1989); and Schoffeleers, "Folk Christology" (1989). Schoffeleers avers that the silence

with which Kibongi's article was met reflects the reluctance of missionaries and missionary churches to accept this possibility, since the healer was perceived to be the rival of the missionary. In African Independent Churches, where missionary influence is less apparent, prophet-healer leaders exhibit many characteristics that are similar to the healer (ibid., 158–159).

92. Kibongi, "Priesthood," 50. He is Congolese and writes from that perspective. More generally, see Schoffeleers, "Folk Christology," 160.

93. Schoffeleers, "Folk Christology," 161.

94. On social reintegration see Célé Kolié, "Jésus guérisseur?" in *Chemins de la christologie africaine*, ed. Kabasélé et al., 171–173.

95. Shorter (*Jesus and the Witchdoctor*, 10) also observes the similarities between Jesus and the itinerant healer-exorcists of Palestine.

96. Kibongi, "Priesthood," 50.

97. Schoffeleers, "Folk Christology," 161–162.

98. Carvalho, "What Do the Africans Say that Jesus Christ Is?" 17–18; Laurenti Magesa, "Christ the Liberator and Africa Today," in *Jesus in African Christianity*, ed. Mugambi and Magesa, 84–85.

99. Ibid., 85.

100. Mbiti, "Some African Concepts," 54–55.

101. Daneel, "Towards a Theologia Africana?" 82.

102. Waruta, "Who Is Jesus Christ for Africans Today? Prophet, Priest, Potentate," 47; see 46–48.

103. Boesak, *Black and Reformed*, 11.

104. Ibid., 74.

105. Tutu, *Hope and Suffering*, 55.

106. Ibid., 56–59. Like other liberation theologians, they cite the prophets for preserving the relationship between worship and justice (e.g., Isa. 1:15–17).

107. Desmond M. Tutu, *General Secretary's Report* (1984), 5, quoted by Simon Maimela, "Abp. Desmond Tutu—A Revolutionary Political Priest or a Man of Peace," in *Hammering Swords*, ed. Tlhagale and Mosala, 47.

108. Mofokeng, *Crossbearers*, 24–26, 30; and Tutu, *Hope and Suffering*, 53–55.

109. See Isa. 61:1–2; 58; 52:7; Ps. 107:20. See also Boesak, *Farewell to Innocence*, 24, 20–26.

110. Mofokeng, *Crossbearers*, 236, 230–237.

111. Ibid., 28. See also Gabriel M. Setiloane, "I Am an African," *Currents in Theology and Mission* 13.2 (1986): 78–80.

112. Manas Buthelezi, "Daring to Live for Christ," in *Third World Theologies*, ed. Anderson and Stransky, 179.

113. Manas Buthelezi, "Reconciliation and Liberation in Southern Africa," in *African Challenge*, ed. Kenneth Y. Best (Nairobi: AACC, 1975), 46.

114. Boesak, *Black and Reformed*, 71–75.

115. Buthelezi, "Daring to Live for Christ," 180.

116. Magesa, "Christ the Liberator and Africa Today," 84.

117. Ibid., 89.

Chapter 5

# Jesus
# in North America

## Issue Faced

Despite the disparity of their histories and the differences in their theologies, feminists and blacks together identify an ideology of domination that characterizes North American society. An ideology can be defined as a "basic system of goals and values, plus the means to achieve them."[1] The *goal* of the North American ideology of domination is to suppress and to control certain groups within society. This ideology is effective because it structures North American society into subject/object dualisms, such as white/black and male/female, and then accords positive and negative *values* to opposing sides of the dualism. The *means* of instituting this ideology have taken a variety of forms, including slavery and segregation for blacks and patriarchal structures for women.

A prevalent subject/object dualism in North America is the white/black dualism. Throughout the centuries, "black and white were constantly presented as antipodes, negative and positive poles on a continuum of goodness. Negroes stood as the antithesis of the character and properties of white people."[2] Racism is the term that describes white and black in a relationship of subject/object. Racism is "any attitude or activity which subordinates a person because of color, and then rationalizes that subordination by attributing to that person undesir-

able biological, psychological, social, or cultural characteristics."[3]

Perpetrators of the ideology of domination solidify sub-
ject/object dualisms with a story that the dominated group
sinned at a primeval stage. This "original" sin validates the
subjugation of the object. For blacks, there is the sin of
Ham. Because Noah's son, Ham, sees his father's naked-
ness, Ham's descendants are enslaved with the curse—
"lowest of slaves shall he be to his brothers" (Gen. 9:25).
Some rabbis and Christian interpreters assumed that the
curse blackened the skin of Ham's descendants. Stories
such as this reinforce the belief that the objects—in this
instance, black people—possess a weak nature with a
strong capacity toward evildoing. For this reason, blacks
are labeled as "lazy, cunning, lewd, impure, naturally infe-
rior, full of animality and matriarchal proclivities, incapable of life's higher thoughts and emotions."[4]

In North America, this racist ideology of domination was
institutionalized in slavery, which meant "being snatched
from your homeland and sailing to an unknown land in a
stinking ship, . . . being regarded as property, like horses,
cows, and household goods, . . . working fifteen to twenty
hours a day and being beaten for showing fatigue, . . . having the cost of replacing you calculated against the value of
your labor during a peak season, so that your owner could
decide whether to work you to death."[5]

Even though the institution of slavery legally ended in
1863 with the Emancipation Proclamation, racism continues. Today, racism is "a ghetto; it is poverty. . . . It is economic deprivation; it is red-lining which curtails the flow of
financial aid to the inner city where the Black population is
located. It is benign neglect; it is police brutality; it is infe-
rior education; it is blatant disregard for the health, welfare
and safety of the Black community. It is the denial of employment opportunities."[6]

Another instance of the subject/object dualism perpetuated by the ideology of domination in North America is the
male/female dualism. Many scholars believe that subject/
object dualisms originated with the male/female dualism;
Friedrich Engels called it the first oppressor-oppressed
relation.

As with blacks, there is, for women, a story of original sin
that validates their subjugation. There is the sin of Eve
(Gen. 3:13). Because of Eve's culpability in the Fall, "she
[woman] is now, within fallen history, subjected to the
male as her superior. This subjugation is not a sin against
her, but her punishment for her sin. It is the expression of
divine justice."[7] The application of Eve's sin to women jus-
tifies their being labeled as "shallow, fickle-minded, irra-
tional, carnal-minded, lacking all the true properties of
knowing and willing and doing."[8]

In North America, sexism takes concrete form in the institution of patriarchy: "the powers of the fathers: a familial-social, ideological, political system in which men—by
force, direct pressure, or through ritual, tradition, law, and
language, customs, etiquette, education, and division of labor—determine what part women shall or shall not play,
and in which the female is everywhere subsumed under
the male."[9] Patriarchy is pervasive from the inside of a
woman's own consciousness where there exists "an internalized patriarchal presence, which carries with it feelings
of guilt, inferiority and self-hatred"[10] to "outer space and
the future" where—if science fiction authors provide us
any clue—women will not "get far beyond the role of
space stewardess."[11]

In these two examples from North American society the
circular working of the ideology of domination is evident.
First, it divides the world into subject/object dualisms such
as white/black and male/female. Next, it provides rationale
for the subjugation of the object with stories of an original
sin. Then, it identifies the object with characteristics that
render it "the quintessence of evil."[12]

However, the neat division of sexism and racism is not
sufficient for black women who are dominated by both
"isms." They are oppressed by white and black men in the
male/female dualism; they are oppressed by white men
*and women* in the white/black dualism. Which is the
greater evil for black women—white supremacy (racism)
or male superiority (sexism)? Some white feminists answer
on behalf of black women that sexism is the greater evil.[13]

With their own approach to the question, black women
who do "womanist" theology[14] name the disparity between

the histories of black women and white women: "The difference is so radical that it may be said that White women
and Black women are in completely different realms. Slavery and segregation have created such a gulf between
these women, that White feminists' common assumption
that all women are in the same situation with respect to
sexism is difficult to understand when history so clearly
tells us a different story."[15] Similarly, they name the disparity between the priority issues of black and white women.
Whereas white women face "such priority issues as rape,
domestic violence, women's work, . . . inclusive language,
the gender of God," black women contend with "physical
survival and spiritual salvation of the family, . . . the re-
distribution of goods and services in the society, . . . en-
countering God as family, . . . ending white supremacy,
male supremacy, . . . and upper-class supremacy in all
American institutions."[16]

For this reason, a white woman's definition of patriarchy,
quoted above, is insufficient for black women. A womanist
theologian rewrites the definition of patriarchy from her
vantage point as a black woman: "the power of . . . [white
men and white women]: a familial-social, ideological, political system in which [white men and white women] . . . determine what part [black women] shall or shall not play,
and in which the [black female] is everywhere subsumed
under the [white female] and white male."[17]

## Sources and Method

### Feminist Theology

The roots of feminist theology lie in two movements for
the emancipation of women in the nineteenth and twentieth centuries. The first movement began under the leadership of two Christian women, Elizabeth Cady Stanton and
Lucretia Mott, who in 1848 organized the first meeting for
the rights of women in Seneca Falls, New York. Their efforts affected the secular sphere when, in 1920, women
obtained the right to vote. The second movement for the
liberation of women began as a secular movement in the
1960s with the publication of *The Feminine Mystique* by

Betty Friedan and the founding of the National Organization for Women (NOW). This movement in turn affected
the religious sphere and led directly to greater involvement and leadership by women in the church. Women
scholars in religion and women ministers pressed the question, "Does religion enforce and perpetuate sex-role ste-
reotypes and the power of men over women?"[18] To answer
this question, feminist theologians began to develop an ar-
ticulate methodology.

Feminist theology employs women's experience as the
woven cord that binds the theological process together.
Women's experience is the fabric of life as it is lived *by
women.* This experience, shut out of traditional theological
reflection, "explodes as a critical force, exposing classical
theology . . . as based on *male* experience rather than on
universal human experience."[19]

Whose experience is women's experience? Some feminist
theologians argue that "without denying or ignoring the
complex factors which interact to produce such differing expressions of women's lives, there remains an underlying
*unity of experience* forged by women's common physiological nature and by a shared history and present experience of
oppression and powerlessness."[20] Other women, particularly women of color, challenge this universalization, charg-
ing that it trivializes the vast difference in oppression
between white women and black women. Even as "universal" an experience as motherhood differs substantially because of racial, economic, and sociological conditions.[21]
Although the matter of whose experience is women's experience has not been settled, nonetheless women's experience remains "the basic source of content as well as a
criterion of truth."[22]

### Critique

The first task of feminist theology is to evaluate the
sources of theology—the Bible and tradition—according
to the criterion of women's experience. This analysis results in a *critique* of their implicit and explicit sexism.

Feminist theologians often approach the Bible with suspicion because it has functioned historically to subjugate

women. Their suspicion is based on the recognition that men dominated the culture in which the Bible was written; that men, perhaps without exception, wrote the Bible; that men ultimately selected the texts included in the Bible; that men, until very recently, translated the Bible; and that men have comprised the vast majority of its interpreters.

Their suspicion is also supported by many biblical examples of sexism: rules for the liberation of male and female slaves differ; women were excluded from the Israelite priesthood; Paul's letters contain commands for women to remain silent during worship; unfaithfulness is frequently symbolized by a prostitute; and the Gospels place Jesus and his male disciples at the center, displacing significant women to the periphery.

Along with the Bible, Christian tradition is also subjected to feminist critique because male theologians have written that women are in the image of God only as they are joined with a man (Augustine), that women are defective men (Aquinas), and that women must submit to men within the hierarchy of creation (Barth). Even a recent Roman Catholic Church document declares that maleness is required for the priesthood: "When Christ's role in the Eucharist is to be expressed sacramentally there would not be this 'natural resemblance' which must exist between Christ and *his* minister if the role of Christ were not taken by a *man*."[23]

Despite the palpable sexism of the Bible and tradition, most feminist theologians do not jettison them completely. Rather, they have developed a method to recover in them what is liberative for women.

### Recovery

The second task of feminist theology is to recover the lost history of women. This lost history is contained not only within the Bible and Christian tradition but also in ancient Near Eastern texts (e.g., Babylonian and Egyptian), where goddess worship persisted, and in the documents of countercultural Christian movements, such as Gnostics, the Montanists, the Shakers, and the Quakers, in which women had more significant leadership roles than in the traditional church. In all of these texts, feminist theologians claim to recover "fragments of our own experience that were not completely erased."[24] In this task of recovery, the critical principle that is operative is "the promotion of the full humanity of women. Whatever denies, diminishes, or distorts the full humanity of women, is therefore, appraised as not redemptive. . . . What does promote the full humanity of women is of the Holy."[25]

In order to recover the Bible as a source of liberation, feminist theologians develop several complementary methods. Rosemary Radford Ruether's method is to discern a prophetic-liberative axis that traces God's concern for the oppressed from the exodus through the prophets to Jesus.[26] Since women are the oppressed among the oppressed, the prophetic-liberative axis for feminists is a critique of a particular form of oppression: patriarchy.[27]

Another method is to place women at the center of the Bible even when they exist on the periphery of the biblical narrative. In *Texts of Terror*, Phyllis Trible places four abused women who were destroyed by patriarchal culture at the center: Hagar, who bears Abraham's child and then is expelled from his home, only to be commanded by God to return to this abusive household; the daughter of Jephthah, whom he murders to fulfill an unnecessary vow to God; an unnamed concubine who is handed over to strangers to be raped throughout the night; and Tamar, whom her stepbrother, Amnon, rapes and then rejects. This method protests sexism by preserving texts that embody patriarchal atrocities. Also at the center can be located women who have succeeded despite patriarchal culture: Deborah the prophet-judge; Mary the student of Jesus; and women leaders in the early church, represented by Phoebe the deacon, Priscilla who teaches Apollos, and Junia the apostle.[28]

Another method is to recover women's experience by looking *behind* patriarchal biblical texts to the historical circumstances that preceded them. For instance, Elisabeth Schüssler Fiorenza reconstructs a renewal movement spearheaded by Jesus in which women had full participation, although the Gospels provide only minor clues to its existence.[29] It is possible also to look behind Paul's letters to demonstrate that biblical prescriptions, though they appear to be oppressive, often yield liberating descriptions of the world of women behind the text. For example, Paul's command for women to wear veils (1 Cor. 11:2–16) is evidence that, in fact, some women refused to wear this sign of man's authority; otherwise, the command would be superfluous.[30] The historical world of women, therefore, is discernible despite patriarchal biblical texts.

Feminist theologians who employ these sophisticated methods believe that the past, despite its patriarchy, is a usable resource for liberation. Therefore they investigate a prophetic-liberative axis, place women at the center, and recover the liberative realities of women behind the patriarchal text. However, not all feminist theologians concur about the usability of patriarchal texts and symbols. Mary Daly answers "No!" to the question, "Is the past usable?" She rejects the texts and symbols of the past as irredeemably sexist: "If the symbol *can* be 'used' that way [oppressively] and in fact has a long history of being 'used' that way, isn't this an indication of some inherent deficiency in the symbol itself?" According to Daly, "women have the option of giving priority to what we find valid in our own experience without needing to look to the past for justification."[31] On the other hand, Anne Carr is more optimistic about the past. While she recognizes that many traditional symbols have oppressive effects on women, nevertheless she contends that these symbols can be recovered "by ethically and spiritually sensitive interpretation."[32] This is the task of revision.

## Revision

The third task of feminist theology, in addition to critique and recovery, is to revision traditional categories. For instance, theology traditionally constructs an image of God with male categories: "KINGAFAP (the King-God-Almighty-Father-Protector)."[33] Feminist theologians revision this image in the light of their own experience "of birth and gestation, nurturance, and compassion."[34] This revisioning does not merely replace or complement traditional categories about God. Rather, it heightens the complexity, deepens the mystery, and broadens the relevance of God for women and men.

Analogously, feminist theologians have also revisioned
and expanded the category of sin which has been particularly destructive to women. They contend, for two reasons,
that the traditional definition of sin as pride or will to
power in an individual is inadequate for men and especially
for women. First, sin for women tends not toward pride but
rather toward the "underdevelopment or negation of the
self."[35] Because of this, pride in oneself may be the very
antidote to women's frequent sin of self-deprecation. Second, the traditional definition considers sin only in an individual. This too is inadequate, for it ignores collusion in
sinful structures and social ideologies, such as the ideology
of domination. Men usually contribute to systemic social
sin as "monopolizers of power and privilege," whereas
women often contribute to social sin through their passivity.[36] Thus, feminist theologians expand sin to encompass
"the breaking of relationship with both God and with human beings that can take the form of weakness as well as
pride in its denial of the importance of human responsibility in both the personal and the political realms."[37]

The radical revisioning of Christianity will take place
within the nurturing liturgy and community of Women-
Church. Women-Church gathers wherever and whenever
women can separate to form a community sharing women's
experience and constructing an alternative to the forms
and symbols of patriarchal religion. Without this community, which is on an exodus from patriarchal religion,
women in churches suffer from "linguistic deprivation and
eucharistic famine. They can no longer nurture their souls
in alienating words that ignore or systematically deny their
existence. They are starved for the words of life, for symbolic forms that fully and wholeheartedly affirm their per-
sonhood and speak truth about the evils of sexism and the
possibilities of a future beyond patriarchy."[38]

## Black Theology

Black theology was conceived, birthed, and nurtured
in the black church. It began in the "invisible institution"
of black religion during slavery and came to the fore in the
black church during the civil rights movement. The group

largely responsible for its emergence was the National Conference of Black Churchmen (NCBC). In a statement published in the *New York Times* on July 31, 1966, they separated themselves from the nonviolent strategy of Martin Luther King, Jr., and aligned themselves with the Black Power movement. Several years later, in June 1969, this group of radical black clergy issued a statement defining black theology as "a theology of black liberation. It seeks to plumb the black condition in the light of God's revelation in Jesus Christ. . . . Black Theology is a theology of 'blackness.' It is the affirmation of black humanity that emancipates black people from white racism."[39]

As with feminist theology and women's experience, black experience is the starting point of black theology. Black experience "determines [the] theological agenda" of black theology.[40] Because black experience means suffering in a white racist context, when black theologians reflect on black experience, they "reflect upon the nature, the cause, and the justice of their suffering, since suffering prescribes the permanent predicament of the oppressed."[41] Suffering does not, however, circumscribe black experience. In response to suffering, black theologians are determined to construct a theology of black liberation. This task is a natural one, because, through the centuries, black religion has sung about, preached about, prayed for, and worked for the liberation of black people. Black theologians therefore are in continuity with their past when they discern liberation in their two primary sources, black religion and the Bible.

Black religion includes three elements: black religious leaders, spirituals, and African traditional religion. First, the lives and the writings of black religious leaders are valuable resources for acts and words of liberation. *Acts* of liberation were undertaken by leaders who organized slave rebellions, such as Nat Turner and Gabriel Prosser, and by those who guided slaves to freedom, such as Sojourner Truth and Harriet Tubman. More recently, *acts* of liberation were accomplished by Martin Luther King, Jr., and Malcolm X who combined the heritage of their respective religious traditions, Christianity and Islam, to promote justice for blacks. *Words* of liberation written by Henry High-

land Garnet and David Walker urged slaves to revolt
against their captors as the Israelites revolted against the
Egyptians.[42]

The spirituals are the second element in black religion.
Many of them are "black freedom songs which emphasize
black liberation as consistent with divine revelation."[43]
Their subject matter comes from stories of liberation in the
Bible, such as God's deliverance of the Israelites from
Egypt and Daniel from the lions' den. Even prior to emancipation, when spirituals could not explicitly refer to liberation, they often contained double meanings that merged
the black and biblical experiences. "Steal away to Jesus"
referred to heaven, but Harriet Tubman used it also as a
signal of freedom for slaves who would flee with her to the
north or to Canada. According to Frederick Douglass, "O
Canaan, Sweet Canaan" referred both to salvation in
heaven and to liberation from slavery in the promised land
of the north.[44] "Swing Low, Sweet Chariot" envisions
heavenly reunion as well as the experience of crossing the
Ohio River (the Jordan) from Kentucky as part of the journey along the Underground Railroad:

> I looked over Jordan, and what did I see,
> Coming for to carry me home?
> A band of angels coming after me,
> Coming for to carry me home.
>
> If you get there before I do,
> Coming for to carry me home;
> Tell all my friends I'm coming too,
> Coming for to carry me home.

African traditional religion is the third element of black
religion. With the African concept of religion as permeating
all of life—the past, the present, and the future—the slaves
undoubtedly brought with them to their new world an established religious framework.[45] When African traditional religion amalgamated with Christianity, it brought with it "the
creative employment of rhythm, singing, and dancing in the
celebration of life and the worship of the Creator."[46] For instance, African rhythm and melodies show up in the spirituals, and black preachers incorporated African folktales,

parables, riddles, and proverbs, as well as the "call-and-response" of African verbal tradition.[47] Slaves found in their African heritage with its "emotionality, spontaneity, and freedom" the instinctive ability to resist "absolute white-nization."[48] Thus, through its multifarious expressions, from its spirituals to its sermons to its sages, black religion is an essential source of liberation motifs for black theology.

The Bible functions in tandem with black religion as the other major source of black theology. It is considered reliable, not because of any doctrine about its objective value (e.g., inerrancy or inspiration), but because it has functioned for centuries in the black experience as a reflection of the struggle for liberation. While white oppressors used the Bible to condone slavery and segregation, blacks found biblical resources for the struggle against slavery, segregation, and the image of God as keeper of the white status quo. Several biblical passages—including the exodus from Egypt, the redemptive suffering of the servant in Isaiah 40–55, the deliverance of Daniel, Jesus among the poor and the oppressed in Palestine, and the poverty of the earliest Christians (Acts 2)—continue to provide assurance that God will deliver them from racist oppression.[49] It is not difficult for the sons and daughters of slaves to identify Egypt with America, or Pharaoh and the Egyptians with white slaveholders, or black leaders, such as Harriet Tubman and Martin Luther King, Jr., with Moses.[50]

This close identity between the persistent black struggle for liberation and the ongoing Israelite struggle against successive oppressors (Egypt, Assyria, Babylon, Persia, Greece, Rome) actually allows the two histories to collapse into each other in the sermons of black preachers and books by black theologians. For instance, Major Jones writes, "The Black Messiah suffers on the cross of our lynchings and rises out of our suffering to liberate us from suffering."[51] Albert Cleage, Jr., can proclaim, "Jesus was a black Messiah not in terms of his death on Calvary, but in terms of his dedication to the struggle of black people here on earth."[52] As we have seen, this identification of the black and biblical struggles is not novel; it is part and parcel of the liberative dimension of the spirituals.

The challenge of black theology is to remain faithful to

its origin within the black church.[53] Blacks have the fortune, unlike feminists, of an institution of their own which is predominantly free of white racism. This institution is the black church. Its importance in the development and continuation of black theology has been expressed in a paraphrase of John 1:1: "In the beginning was the black church, and the black church was with the black community, and the black church was the black community. The black church was in the beginning with the black people; all things were made through the black church, and without the black church was not anything made that was made. In the black church was life, and the life was the light of the black people. The black church still shines in the darkness, and the darkness has not overcome it."[54]

## Main Emphases

### *Liberation*

By the close of the 1960s, James Cone brought together Black Power, black liberation, and black theology in two books with portentous titles: *Black Theology and Black Power* and *A Black Theology of Liberation*. The late 1960s, with the rise of the women's liberation movement, were also the crucible for feminist theology. In the ensuing decades, blacks and feminists further develop the portrait of Jesus as a liberator from racism and sexism. Ruether, a pioneer of feminist liberation theology, suggests that "the Jesus of the synoptic Gospels can be recognized as a figure remarkably compatible with feminism. This is not to say, in an anachronistic sense, that 'Jesus was a feminist,' but rather that the criticism of religious and social hierarchy characteristic of the early portrait of Jesus is remarkably parallel to feminist criticism."[55] Cone characterizes the Bible as "the revelation of God in Christ as the liberator of the oppressed from social oppression and political struggle"[56] and claims that the "event of the kingdom today is the liberation struggle in the black community."[57]

Jesus did not create this vision of liberation out of nothing. There exists, according to black and feminist liberation theologians, a prophetic-liberative strain that begins with the exodus when God rescued the oppressed Hebrews from the powerful Egyptians. The prophetic-liberative dimension resonates throughout the Hebrew Bible in the prophets' demand for justice from the kings (e.g., Amos 8:6–8; Micah 6:8); in the concern of wisdom literature for the poor (e.g., Prov. 19:17; 23:10–11); and in the literature of the exile, in which prophets promise a second exodus when God will rescue the oppressed Israelites from the Babylonians (e.g., Isa. 41:1–2; Ezek. 36:26; Jer. 31:31–34).[58]

According to black and feminist liberation theologians, this prophetic-liberative dimension provides the foundation for Jesus' vision of the reign of God. For the former, Jesus' vision of God's reign directly challenges the stranglehold of racism; for the latter, Jesus' vision dismantles the wall of sexism.

### Black Liberation

Black theology understands the life, death, and resurrection of Jesus as experiences that recur in the contemporary black community. As we have seen, the black experience includes both suffering and liberation. Analogously, Jesus liberates the black people as the "Oppressed One," just as he did among the poor and the oppressed of Palestine.[59] Therefore Jesus' proclamation of his liberating deeds— the blind see, the lame walk, the lepers are healed, the deaf hear, the dead are raised, the poor have good news preached to them (Luke 7:18–22)—"is not pious talk. . . . It is a message about the ghetto. . . . In Christ, God enters human affairs and takes sides with the oppressed. Their suffering becomes his; their despair, divine despair."[60]

This identification of the biblical struggle and the modern black struggle for liberation is the legacy of a tradition in which spirituals meld past and present. With these songs, blacks bridge two thousand years to walk together with the Israelites in Egypt or with Jesus as he healed the blind and lame.[61] Biblical struggle becomes black struggle. Jesus' deliverance becomes black deliverance; Jesus' pain, black pain. It was, in fact, the slave experience that allowed them to parallel the solitary, silent suffering of Jesus with their own:

I must walk my lonesome valley
I got to walk it for myself,
Nobody else can walk it for me,
I got to walk it for myself.

. . . . . . . . . . .

Jesus walked his lonesome valley,
He had to walk it for himself,
Nobody else could walk it for him,
He had to walk it for himself.[62]

God's most complete identification with human suffering occurred at the crucifixion, where Jesus wept the silent weeping of slaves.

Oh, dey whupped him up de hill, up de hill, up de hill,
Oh, dey whupped him up de hill, an' he never said a
   mumbalin' word,
Oh, dey whupped him up de hill, an' he never said a
   mumbalin' word,
He jes' hung down his head an' he cried.[63]

But, in the black tradition, the cross is ineffectual without the resurrection, which demonstrates that suffering and death are not final and that God transforms suffering into liberation. Most important, the resurrection teaches that God sided with the Palestinian poor of Jesus' day because God's universal will is to side with the poor of every age. That is, Jesus' *particular* identity as one of the poor confirms God's *universal* will. The risen Christ, who was once the Oppressed One, continues to *act among the oppressed* to liberate them from racism.[64]

Because the risen Christ champions liberation, as did the historical Jesus, he can presently be found among black people, for who more than they symbolize suffering and unwarranted oppression in North America? The risen liberator Jesus continues his mission in the ghetto, where he "meets the blacks where they are and becomes one of them. We see him there with his black face and big black hands lounging on a streetcorner."[65]

For black theology, liberation does not end with the risen Jesus but with the expectation that the risen Christ will return in an act of final emancipation, when life will become what it ought to be. The present struggle for black liberation is grounded in Jesus Christ who promises liberation in the future ("not yet") and who works in history to fulfill that promise ("now").[66] "He is the ground of our present freedom to struggle and the source of our hope that the vision disclosed in our historical fight against oppression will be fully realized in God's future."[67] There exists a "home over yonder," vividly and artistically depicted in the spirituals, which is the daily bread that sustains the black people in their struggle against racism.[68]

### Feminist Liberation

Feminist liberation theology shares with its North American counterpart the conviction that "Jesus renews the prophetic vision whereby the Word of God does not validate the existing social and religious hierarchy but speaks on behalf of the marginalized and despised groups of society."[69] The central vision of Jesus was not the "holiness" of the Temple or the Torah, which was safeguarded through excluding certain groups of unclean people, but the "wholeness" of all people.[70] Therefore Jesus gathered around a festive table a "discipleship of equals": those whose low social status barred them from participation in Temple and Torah. Three groups in particular constituted the discipleship of equals. The destitute poor constituted one group; to them Jesus promised a share in God's future, for they had not yet received their inheritance, while the rich had already consumed theirs. The sick and demon-possessed constituted the second group. The woman with the flow of blood, for instance, was impoverished economically by countless, ineffective visits to doctors; she was permanently impure, according to Torah, so that she polluted all whom she touched (Lev. 15:19–31). By healing this woman, Jesus restored her dignity as a "daughter" of Israel (Mark 5:25–34). The third group in the discipleship of equals included tax collectors, sinners, and prostitutes, a motley group economically so destitute that they were compelled to engage in dishonorable professions.[71]

Liberation theologians across the globe recognize that Jesus' vision of God's reign required this sort of alternative praxis. Nevertheless, while feminist liberation theologians share a concern for the poor with other liberation theologians, they contest that women often represent the doubly oppressed because sexism heightens the effects of poverty: widows are the most destitute poor; women with perpetual menstrual bleeding are the most pathetic symbols of ritual impurity; and prostitutes are emblematic of the most unrighteous among the morally outcast.[72]

Feminist liberation theologians also emphasize the significant impact that women had on Jesus. Their relationship with him is encapsulated in Mark's Gospel, following the death of Jesus and the Roman centurion's confession, "Truly this man was God's Son!":

> There were also women looking on from a distance; among them were Mary Magdalene, and Mary the mother of James the younger and of Joses, and Salome. These used to *follow* him and *provided* for him when he was in Galilee; and there were many other women who had come up with him to Jerusalem. (Mark 15:40–41)

The word "follow" epitomizes the following of the disciple ("If any want to become my followers, let them deny themselves and take up their cross and follow me" [Mark 8:34]). These women, independent of men, demonstrated a willingness to be executed alongside Jesus by their persistent identification with him. The word "provide," or "serve," epitomizes the characteristic behavior of the disciple ("whoever wishes to become great among you must be your servant" [Mark 10:43]).[73] In other words, at the most crucial juncture of Jesus' life, his crucifixion, women—who embodied the ideal behavior of discipleship—provided the community, the web of relationships, among whom Jesus died.

The placement of this summary about women immediately after the confession of a *Roman* centurion is apropos, since a woman convinced Jesus to extend the discipleship of equals to include non-Jews. When a foreign woman, "a Gentile, of Syrophoenician origin," begged him to cast a demon out of her daughter, Jesus retorted, "Let the children [i.e., Israelites] be fed first, for it is not fair to take the children's food and throw it to the dogs." The woman's response, "Sir, even the dogs under the table eat the children's crumbs," convinced him to extend his power of exorcism beyond the borders of Israel. It is this foreign woman who adroitly challenged Jesus to extend his festive table, his discipleship of equals, to non-Israelites; she who sought wholeness for her daughter is the "foremother" of all Gentile Christians.[74]

In the light of the role that women played in shaping Jesus' inclusive vision of God's reign and embodying the "serving" and "following" ideals that epitomize discipleship, Jesus' explicit opposition to sexism is hardly surprising. In four specific ways Jesus dismantled sexism and patriarchy.

First, Jesus challenged patriarchal marriage by refusing to agree with his dialogue partners, the Pharisees, that a woman could be forced out of her husband's household by divorce (Mark 10:2–9). Jesus quoted Genesis 2:24: "For this reason a man shall leave his father and mother and be joined to his wife, and the two shall become one flesh." With this quotation he challenged patriarchal marriage, for in it the man leaves his own patriarchal household; the woman does not leave hers to perpetuate the man's lineage. In fact, the two become one, establishing a common life together. With this text, Jesus unmasked the Pharisees' assumption that a wife belongs to a husband's family.[75]

Second, Jesus challenged the traditional patriarchal family. He replaced it with a nonbiological household. When his family asked for him, Jesus rejected his biological family for his new family: "Who are my mother and my brothers? . . . Whoever does the will of God is my brother and sister and mother" (Mark 3:31–35). He also promised to those who had left their biological families many more "brothers and sisters, mothers and children" (Mark 10:30).[76]

Third, Jesus challenged patriarchy by prohibiting hierarchy within the household of disciples. The role of mother is present, but no one can take on the role of the father. Jesus said this cogently when he called God "father" and, at the same time, prohibited anyone in the community from being called father: "And call no one your father on earth, for you have one Father—the one in heaven. . . . The greatest

among you will be your servant" (Matt. 23:9, 11). This say-
ing "uses the 'father' name of God not as a legitimization
for existing patriarchal power structures . . . but as a critical subversion of all structures of domination. Neither the
'brothers' nor 'sisters' in the Christian community can
claim the 'authority of the father' because that would involve claiming authority and power reserved for God
alone."[77] Jesus' rejection of patriarchy in the community of
equals was complete when he gave priority to those who
are least in the traditional, patriarchal household: slaves
and children[78] (Mark 9:35–37; 10:42–45).

Fourth, Jesus challenged a patriarchal image of God.
He transformed the concept of God's fatherhood from authority to concern for the oppressed by presenting God as
a father with "the gracious goodness usually associated
with a mother."[79] Jesus also challenged a patriarchal image of God by conceiving of God as Wisdom (Sophia). In
the Jewish world of Jesus, Sophia was regarded as "Israel's God in the language . . . of the goddess. Sophia is
called sister, wife, mother, beloved, and teacher."[80] In
several instances Jesus referred directly to Sophia-God.
The image of a hen with her brood under her wings (Luke
13:34) and the invitation to the burdened and heavy
laden to rest (Matt. 11:28–30) were already associated
with Sophia in early Judaism.[81] Hence, the earliest followers understood "the mission of Jesus as that of the
prophet and child of Sophia sent to announce that God is
the God of the poor and heavy laden, of the outcasts and
those who suffer injustice. As a child of Sophia he stands
in a long line and succession of prophets sent to gather
the children of Israel to their gracious Sophia-God."[82]
Jesus was crucified because of the historical conflict that
his role as a liberating emissary of gracious Sophia caused
between him and other Jews.[83]

The life of Jesus, therefore, was an explicit affront on
sexism. He gathered oppressed women around him, extended the festive table to non-Jews because of conversations with women, replaced patriarchal households with a
household of equality, and envisioned God as divine Wisdom with motherly qualities. Little wonder, then, that
women stood with him at his crucifixion, even when men

scattered and hid, and that women were the first followers to visit the empty tomb early in the morning.

Nor is it difficult to understand why the risen Christ was understood in the earliest church, not simply as the messenger of Wisdom, but as Wisdom herself: "Christ Jesus, who became for us wisdom from God" (1 Cor. 1:30). This identification of Jesus as female Wisdom rather quickly lost ground in the early church to her male counterpart, the Word, Logos (John 1), just as women's varied roles of leadership were thwarted by the emergence of a dominance of ideology that gave sole leadership to men.[84]

Black and feminist liberation portraits share a vision of Jesus' life as the proclamation and enactment of God's reign, founded in the prophetic strand of the Hebrew Bible, according to which God sides with the oppressed in order to liberate them. For both groups, an important continuity connects the historical Jesus and the risen Christ. According to Cone, the risen Christ continues to side with the oppressed, presently in North America's ghettos. Similarly, for feminists, the emissary of Wisdom has become Wisdom herself.

At the same time, these theologians tend to differ on the meaning of Jesus' death. Black liberation theologians present Jesus as a cosufferer whose suffering liberates. Feminist theologians, in contrast, tend to de-emphasize Jesus' suffering because it reinforces the harmful vision of women as victims.

### Liberation as Reconciliation

The anticipation of a new humanity as the goal of liberation pervades liberation theologies.[85] But the best *method* for attaining that goal is not a matter of consensus. This issue divides theologians who are otherwise quite similar: those who regard Jesus as a liberator of the oppressed and those who regard him as the one who liberates through reconciling all people.

The portrait of Jesus as liberator from racism reflects the focus of the Black Power movement: to restore dignity and full humanity to black Americans. Liberation of blacks is the prerequisite to reconciliation with whites. The portrait of

Jesus as liberator proposed by civil rights leaders, such as Martin Luther King, Jr., is also an attempt "to relate the Christian gospel to the struggle for racial justice in American society."[86] But the method of the civil rights movement differed from the Black Power movement. Rather than focusing directly upon black dignity, civil rights leaders focused upon the relationship between black and white peoples. Liberation, love, and forgiveness are set within the context of the anticipated reconciliation between whites and blacks. In this context, Jesus is portrayed as one who accomplishes liberation through nonviolent reconciliation.

A similar distinction separates two feminist models of liberation. Ruether contends that the male/female (subject/object) dualism will be dismantled only *after* women are liberated. Letty Russell and others contend that this dualism will be dismantled only if women *in partnership with* men become subjects together. To draw a loose comparison, Ruether's conception of liberation corresponds to that of the Black Power movement and Russell's to the civil rights movement. For Ruether, Jesus liberates the oppressed who are quintessentially represented by women, while for Russell, Jesus liberates the oppressed by reconciling them with their oppressors.

For those feminist and black theologians who view liberation as reconciliation, Jesus represents the true humanity because he reconciles dualisms in his person and social practice. For instance, he commanded his followers to combine the wisdom of serpents and the innocence of doves (Matt. 10:16). Tough-minded wisdom is necessary to challenge segregation. Tenderhearted innocence is necessary to forestall the bitterness that results in violence. Wisdom and innocence unite when the oppressed resist both racism and violence in order to bring about reconciliation.[87]

Although Jesus was male, he lived as the true human being who embodied both female and male characteristics. In his relationship with God, he accepted what was regarded as a feminine posture: he submitted to God.[88] In his relationships with people, he exhibited "characteristics of love, compassion, and caring often considered to be cultural characteristics of women."[89] In his particular relationships with women, he "was a 'feminist' in the sense that he considered men and women equal." He conversed with, taught, and was touched, even kissed, by women.[90] By combining the male/female dualism in these ways, Jesus was "a whole person who brought that possibility to others."[91]

Jesus also merged opposites on the cross: conquered yet conquering ruler, the Suffering Servant yet Lord, passive victim yet high priest, the one who cannot save himself yet saves the creation. "The crucifixion, therefore, witnesses to a truth that feminism also affirms: dualisms, be they of dominance and submission, male and female, matter and spirit, have no place in a Christian understanding of a redeemed universe."[92]

The crucifixion, for Martin Luther King, Jr., symbolizes not so much the *merging* of the black/white dualism as the *overcoming* of white hatred by black forgiveness. In the final moments of his life, Jesus said, "Father, forgive them; for they do not know what they are doing" (Luke 23:34). With the words "forgive them," the cross becomes "the magnificent symbol of love conquering hate and of light overcoming darkness."[93] It is incumbent upon Jesus' followers to work and to suffer for reconciliation. "With Jesus on the cross, we must look lovingly at our oppressors and say, 'Father, forgive them; for they know not what they do.'"[94]

Reconciliation was achieved at the cross and resides permanently in the risen Christ. "The life of the risen Christ that pervades all things united the divided, and continues as an active force for reconciliation in the world. Feminism, with its strong drive to both preserve the integrity of all beings and yet nurture the interconnectedness of the world, is confirmed in the figure of the risen Christ."[95]

The resurrection also applies to the black/white dualism of racism. The risen Christ does come specifically to the black race as liberator, to confront all systems of evil that dehumanize them; in this sense, the risen Christ is black. At the same time, the risen Christ is also the universal lord who crosses all racial and national barriers and who desires to reconcile the black race with all other races.[96] In short, "the black Christ liberates and the universal Christ reconciles."[97]

The task of reconciliation is not, however, complete with the resurrection. God looks to people to become representatives of the true humanity through a partnership that embodies and anticipates reconciliation. But this process of reconciliation itself merges two poles of a paradox: suffering and hope. "It is a time for overcoming divisions and alienations, prejudices, hatred, and painful dualisms. The present is both a period of hopeful growth, as well as a bloodstained arena in which the forces of good labor toward their goal and sometimes painfully lose."[98]

In this struggle, Jesus' followers must aspire to love their enemies. On the personal level, the oppressed person's failure to love issues in dehumanizing hatred that makes the oppressed less than a true human because it "scars the soul and distorts the personality."[99] On the societal level, in response to reconciling love, expressed by nonviolent resistance to evil, oppressors will begin to relinquish their power: "To our most bitter opponents we say: 'We shall match your capacity to inflict suffering by our capacity to endure suffering. . . . Be ye assured that we will wear you down by our capacity to suffer. One day we shall win freedom, but not only for ourselves. We shall so appeal to your heart and conscience that we shall win *you* in the process, and our victory will be a double victory.'"[100]

### Iconoclastic Portraits: The Black Messiah and Christa

In 1967 a black caucus at a National Council of Churches conference defined Black Power as "an expression of the need for Black Authenticity in a white-dominated society, a society which has from its earliest beginnings displayed unadulterated racism. We affirm without fear of repudiation the meaningfulness of blackness."[101] The portrait of Jesus that arose within this powerful affirmation of blackness was a response to an inadequate American or white Christ whose teachings had been used to justify wars, segregation, and prejudice. Blacks had always felt ambivalence toward this Jesus: "We first met the American Christ on slave ships. We heard his name sung in hymns of praise while we died in our thousands, chained in stinking holds beneath the decks. . . . When we leaped from the decks to be seized by sharks we saw his name carved on the ship's solid sides. When our women were raped in the cabins they must have noticed the great and holy books on the shelves. . . . And the horrors continued on America's soil."[102]

At the same time, while the Black Power movement brought into question the whiteness of Jesus, the feminist movement provided a context for questioning his maleness: Can a male savior save women? One response to this question has been to universalize Christ, to argue that he was not Chinese or elderly or black, but could still save the Chinese, elderly, and blacks. Therefore, although Jesus was not a woman, he can save women. According to Mary Daly, however, the experience of women invalidates this response because the maleness of Jesus, unlike his ethnic origin or relative youth, has been used to exclude women from certain roles in the church. "Non-Semites or persons over, say thirty-three, have not been universally excluded from the priesthood on the basis that they do not belong to the same ethnic group or age group as Jesus. By contrast, the universal exclusion of women from the priesthood, and until recently from the ministry in most Protestant churches, has been justified on this basis."[103]

As a result of the North American subjugation of women and blacks, many have internalized a sense of inferiority and shame. Albert Cleage describes his first experience on a segregated railroad car: "When you climbed into that car you had to have some kind of sinking feeling that there must be something wrong with you. You knew the [white] man was right because it was his thing. It was his station. He was letting you ride. He had to be right."[104] Rita Nakashima Brock agrees: "The ideologies and institutions are used to subjugate and devalue the oppressed who begin to believe the system is true. When we feel wrong within a prescribed system that proscribes us, we are ashamed of ourselves."[105]

To ask blacks and women to identify with a white or male Christ is to require them to seek salvation in a representative of the system that oppresses them. For this reason, Cleage rejects the white Christ: "Black people cannot build dignity on their knees worshipping a white Christ. We must put down this white Jesus which the white man gave us in slavery and which has been tearing us to pieces."[106] He takes history seriously when he attempts to demonstrate that the historical Jesus was black. Unlike Cleage, Daly and Brock displace the historical Jesus with women's consciousness.

### Christa/Community

Daly rejects Christology as "Christolatry" for several reasons.[107] First, it fails to acknowledge that Jesus was a limited human being; therefore, to set him up as more than human, or divine, is idolatry. Second, his maleness in the context of sexist societies inevitably reinforces the superiority of men over women. Third, presenting Jesus as a model from the past to imitate turns him into a father figure. This misrepresents Jesus, a model breaker himself, who pointed people beyond their limitations toward further liberation.[108]

Brock supplements Daly's third critique of traditional Christology with her own critique of feminist Christologies. The liberation portrait (e.g., Ruether; Schüssler Fiorenza) and the reconciliation portrait (e.g., Russell; Wilson-Kastner; Mollenkott) are inadequate because Jesus as a liberator reflects a male preoccupation with heroes. Portrayed as a hero, Jesus unilaterally liberates people without their help, thus failing to embody the feminist commitment to mutual relationships.[109] These relationships, known as Christa/Community,[110] are the fountain of a Christology that is "not centered in Jesus, but in relationship and community. . . . He is brought into being through it and participates in the cocreation of it. . . . Hence what is truly christological, that is, truly revealing of divine incarnation and salvific power in human life, must reside in connectedness and not in single individuals."[111]

The relational nature of Jesus' power is evident in the Gospel miracle stories of exorcism and healing. The exorcism of Legion's demons (Mark 5:1–13), for instance, portrays Jesus in relationship. The demons that possess Legion represent the feminist concept of "the enemy within," the inferiority and shame that occur when the oppressed believe what the ideology of domination says about them. Below the demon noises, Jesus hears the anguished cry for deliverance; together, in relationship, Jesus and Legion remove the demons.[112] Similarly, Gospel healing stories present Jesus as one who responds in relationship to people who initiate conversations, touching, or anointing. Through these encounters, Jesus learns about the power that the weak bring to the community. "The point is not Jesus' sole possession of power, but the revelation of a new understanding of power that connects members of the community. The power reversal comes from those perceived as weak who reveal the divine way of power."[113]

The miracle of the resurrection is also a story of relationship because, without the community's "stubborn witness that oppressive powers will not have the last word," Jesus would not be remembered.[114] The resurrection is, then, "a powerful metaphor for connection, . . . a powerful image of the need for solidarity among and with victims of oppressive powers."[115]

This most radical feminist Christology answers no to the question, Can a male savior save women? Jesus does not liberate people on his own, nor does he reconcile people by himself. Rather, he shares in, but does not originate, the life flow of relationships in Christa/Community.

### The Black Messiah

In a collection of sermons under the title *The Black Messiah*, Cleage attempts to expose the "lie" of the white Christ by demonstrating the historical truth about Jesus: he was a black Jew. Jesus' Israelite ancestors were black. Abraham and Sarah were born in Chaldea, where people are nonwhite, and migrated to black Egypt, where Abraham even took Hagar, an Egyptian, as his second wife. From the period of Joseph to the exodus, approximately four hundred years, the Jews intermingled in Egypt, which deepened the black hue of their skin. Israel was, then, a Black Nation.[116]

Jesus came to this Black Nation when it was oppressed

by a white empire, Rome. Its character was marred by individual opportunism rather than solidarity, as "each individual was trying to secure his own little individual
benefits from his relationship with the Roman oppressor,
some little favor, some little special privilege. . . . Black
people no longer believed in themselves and black people
no longer loved each other. . . . They loved their oppressors and hated their brothers because their oppressors had
power and their brothers were powerless."[117]

Jesus' task was to rebuild the Black Nation. To this end,
he taught them an "internal ethic" of solidarity in Matthew
5:21–48. The need for forgiveness, purity, truthfulness,
giving up one's cloak, turning one's cheek, giving to the
poor—all of these were internal commands to members of
the Black Nation. In particular, Jesus commanded the
Black Nation to love the enemies amongst themselves so
that they could with one voice demand justice of the oppressor. In this way, individualism would be eliminated by
a solidarity which claimed that they, not their white oppressors, were a people of dignity, God's chosen.[118]

Jesus also had to rid the Black Nation of its interiorized
self-hatred, its denigration of blackness, and its desire to
identify with Rome. They had begun to believe what their
oppressors had taught them, that their oppression was their
own fault. To counteract their self-hatred, Jesus taught them
with parables. In one parable he told of an enemy who
sowed tares of individualism and hopelessness among the
wheat (Matt. 13:24–28). The question raised in the Black
Nation, "Sir, did you not sow good seed?" reveals the self-
blame that characterizes oppressed people. Jesus corrected
their thinking by placing the blame squarely in the camp of
the oppressor: "An enemy has done this."

Jesus knew that his attempt to rebuild the Black Nation
would meet with the opposition of collaborators, the Uncle
Toms and Aunt Jemimas who would identify with the oppressors rather than their own Black Nation.[119] They are
the scribes, the Pharisees, and the Sadducees, who gained
individual benefit from their uneasy alliance with Rome.
They questioned his authority, told his followers to be silent, and spread rumors about his mission that led eventually to the cross. In other words, the enemy used these

collaborators from the Black Nation to destroy their eman-
cipator.

Despite this opposition, Jesus dedicated the final week of
his life to rebuilding the Black Nation out of fragmented
individuals. Jesus entered Jerusalem triumphantly to restore the reign of David the king. He confronted the Uncle
Toms, the Pharisees and Sadducees, in the Temple. He
sidestepped the question put to him by the Pharisees, "By
what authority . . . ?" in other words: "Do you have the
white 'man's' approval?" He washed the disciples' feet to
demonstrate that his revolutionary disciples must rise
above their individualism for the sake of the nation. He
broke the bread and served the wine to reinforce that
members of the Black Nation must be willing to die for
freedom. And when the disciples unsheathed their swords
in the Garden of Gethsemane he told them to put them
away because it was too little too late; successful revolution
would involve the entire Black Nation. Finally, he knew he
had to die in Jerusalem, in public, to solidify the Black Nation with his martyrdom.[120]

The significance of the resurrection is not that Jesus'
body arose but that the Black Nation now carries on Jesus'
revolution. Jesus is immortal in the Black Power movement. "The immortality which Jesus has lies in the fact that
two thousand years later we . . . are trying to do the same
thing he tried to do with the Black Nation in Palestine. Today, in the midst of corruption, we are drawing people one
by one, two by two, into the Black Nation. This task and
the faith that it can be done, this is the Resurrection."[121]

It is impossible to distinguish between the historical
Jesus and the black experience in the sermons of Cleage.
Rome and North American whites are the oppressors. The
Jewish leaders are the black middle class who allow them-
selves to be coopted by the ideology of domination for per-
sonal gain. Jesus is the Black Messiah who rebuilds the
Black Nation based on the ideals of the Black Power move-
ment: self-love, solidarity, and a passion for emancipation.

No black theologian has accepted uncritically Cleage's
radical revisioning of the historical Jesus, yet all have responded to it with various levels of appreciation, from rejection to sympathy.[122] On the one hand, Allan Boesak of

South Africa dismisses the literal color of Jesus as irrelevant.[123] On the other hand, Cone accepts Cleage's portrait critically: "But as it happens, *Jesus was not white* in any sense of the word, literally or theologically. Therefore, Albert Cleage is not too far wrong when he describes Jesus as a black Jew; and he is certainly on solid theological grounds when he describes Christ as the Black Messiah," the liberator of the oppressed.[124]

## NOTES

1. Alfred Hennelly, *Theologies in Conflict: The Challenge of Juan Luis Segundo* (Maryknoll, N.Y.: Orbis Books, 1979), 123.

2. Henry Allen Bullock, *A History of Negro Education in the South from 1619 to the Present* (Cambridge, Mass.: Harvard University Press, 1967), 155–156, as quoted in Katie Cannon, *Black Womanist Ethics*, American Academy of Religion Academy Series, no. 60 (Atlanta: Scholars Press, 1988), 41.

3. Albert Pero, "On Being Black, Lutheran, and American in a Racist Society," in *Theology and the Black Experience: The Lutheran Heritage Interpreted by African-American Theologians*, ed. Albert Pero and Ambrose Moyo (Minneapolis: Augsburg Publishing House, 1988), 163.

4. Cannon, *Black Womanist Ethics*, 41.

5. James H. Cone, *The Spirituals and the Blues: An Interpretation* (New York: Seabury Press, 1972), 21.

6. Position Paper of the African Methodist Episcopal Church, "Liberation Movements: A Critical Assessment and a Reaffirmation," in *Black Theology: A Documentary History*, ed. Cone and Wilmore, 290.

7. Rosemary Radford Ruether, *Sexism and God-Talk: Toward a Feminist Theology* (Boston: Beacon Press, 1983), 97. In this quote, Ruether is paraphrasing Martin Luther's argument on the subjugation of women because of Eve's sin.

8. Rosemary Radford Ruether, *Liberation Theology: Human Hope Confronts Christian History and American Power* (New York: Paulist Press, 1972), 20.

9. Adrienne Rich, *Of Woman Born: Motherhood as Experience and Institution* (New York: W. W. Norton & Co., 1976), 40.

10. Mary Daly, *Beyond God the Father: Toward a Philosophy of Women's Liberation* (Boston: Beacon Press, 1973), 50.

11. Mary Daly, *Gyn/Ecology: The Metaethics of Radical Feminism* (Boston: Beacon Press, 1978), 1.

12. Frantz Fanon, *The Wretched of the Earth* (New York: Grove Press, 1963), 41.

13. For instance, Daly contends that racism focuses "attention upon some deformity *within* patriarchy." Her conclusion is that "giving priority to racial identification does not serve women's best interests" (Daly, *Beyond God the Father*, 56–57).

14. The term "womanist" was coined by Alice Walker to describe "the liberative efforts of Black women." She defines womanist as "a Black feminist or feminist of color. . . . Usually referring to outrageous, audacious, courageous or willful behavior. . . . Acting grown up. Being grown up" (Alice Walker, *In Search of My Mother's Garden* [New York: Harcourt Brace Jovanovich, 1983], xi, as quoted in Jacquelyn Grant, *White Women's Christ and Black Women's Jesus: Feminist Christology and Womanist Response*, American Academy of Religion Academy Series, no. 64 [Atlanta: Scholars Press, 1989], 204–205).

15. Grant, *White Women's Christ and Black Women's Jesus*, 195–196.

16. Delores Williams, "The Color of Feminism: Or Speaking the Black Woman's Tongue," *Journal of Religious Thought* 43 (1986): 54.

17. Ibid., 48. The bracketed phrases are Delores Williams's.

18. Carol P. Christ and Judith Plaskow, eds., *Womanspirit Rising: A Feminist Reader in Religion* (San Francisco: Harper & Row, 1979), 3.

19. Ruether, *Sexism and God-Talk*, 13.

20. Nicola Slee, "Parables and Women's Experience," *Modern Churchman* 26 (1984): 21–22, as quoted in Ann Loades, *Searching for Lost Coins: Explorations in Christianity and Feminism* (Allison Park, Pa.: Pickwick Publications, 1987), 18. Italics added.

21. See Susan Thistlethwaite's analysis of the differences in motherhood between black women and white women in *Sex, Race, and God: Christian Feminism in Black and White* (New York: Crossroad, 1989), 51–55.

22. Ruether, *Sexism and God-Talk*, 12.

23. Franjo Cardinal Seper, "Vatican Declaration," *Origins*,

N.C. *Documentary Service*, February 3, 1977, 6, as quoted in Grant, *White Women's Christ and Black Women's Jesus*, 77. Italics added.

24. Rosemary Radford Ruether, *Womanguides: Readings Toward a Feminist Theology* (Boston: Beacon Press, 1985), x.

25. Ruether, *Sexism and God-Talk*, 18–19.

26. Ibid., 24–27. This axis has four themes: (1) God's defense and vindication of the oppressed; (2) the critique of systems of power and power holders; (3) the vision of a new age *in history* free from oppression; and (4) critique of the religious ideology of domination.

27. Ibid., 22–33; On the correlation between the prophetic critique of oppression and the feminist critique of patriarchal oppression, see Ruether's "Feminist Interpretation: A Method of Correlation," in *Feminist Interpretation of the Bible*, ed. Letty M. Russell (Philadelphia: Westminster Press, 1985), 111–124.

28. Bernadette J. Brooten, "Early Christian Women and Their Cultural Context: Issues of Method in Historical Reconstruction," in *Feminist Perspectives on Biblical Scholarship*, ed. Adela Yarbro Collins, Society of Biblical Literature, Biblical Scholarship in North America, no. 10, (Chico, Calif.: Scholars Press, 1985), 79–84; and Phyllis Trible, *Texts of Terror: Literary-Feminist Readings of Biblical Narratives* (Philadelphia: Fortress Press, 1984).

29. Elisabeth Schüssler Fiorenza, *In Memory of Her: A Feminist Theological Reconstruction of Christian Origins* (New York: Crossroad, 1983), 99–159; and idem, *Bread Not Stone: The Challenge of Feminist Biblical Interpretation* (Boston: Beacon Press, 1984), 84–92.

30. Brooten, "Early Christian Women and Their Cultural Context," 73–74; and Schüssler Fiorenza, *Bread Not Stone*, 70–79.

31. Daly, *Beyond God the Father*, 72, 74.

32. Anne Carr, *Transforming Grace: Christian Tradition and Women's Experience* (San Francisco: Harper & Row, 1988), 172; see 158, 178, 183.

33. Brian Wren, *What Language Shall I Borrow? God-Talk in Worship: A Male Response to Feminist Theology* (New York: Crossroad, 1989), 124.

34. Carr, *Transforming Grace*, 145.

35. Valerie Saiving, "The Human Situation: A Feminine

View," in *Womanspirit Rising,* ed. Christ and Plaskow, 37. Feminine sins (i.e., those which are "outgrowths of the basic feminine character structure") are "better suggested by such items as triviality, distractibility, and diffuseness; lack of organizing center or focus; dependence on others for one's own self-definition" (ibid.).

36. Ruether, *Sexism and God-Talk,* 180.

37. Carr, *Transforming Grace,* 186.

38. Rosemary Radford Ruether, *Women-Church: Theology and Practice of Feminist Liturgical Communities* (San Francisco: Harper & Row, 1985), 4–5.

39. Cone and Wilmore, *Black Theology: A Documentary History,* 101.

40. William Jones, *Is God a White Racist? A Preamble to Black Theology,* C. Eric Lincoln Series on Black Religion (Garden City, N.Y.: Doubleday & Co., Anchor Books, 1973), 76.

41. Ibid., xiv.

42. See also Joseph Johnson's preached words of liberation, especially in "Jesus, the Disturber," which contains a litany of black leaders whose acts of liberation continued in the world the ministry of Jesus (Joseph A. Johnson, *The Soul of the Black Preacher* [Philadelphia: Pilgrim Press, 1971], 68–75).

43. Cone, *The Spirituals and the Blues,* 38.

44. James H. Cone, *For My People: Black Theology and the Black Church,* Bishop Henry McNeal Turner Studies in North American Black Religion, vol. 1 (Maryknoll, N.Y.: Orbis Books, 1984), 63.

45. This point has been much debated. Cecil Cone summarizes the opposing sides: "On one side scholars claimed to find important survivals from African religion in North America. Their opponents asserted that the special conditions of slavery on this continent (in contrast to the Caribbean and South America) virtually destroyed the African religious heritage here" (Cecil Cone, *The Identity Crisis in Black Theology* [Nashville: AMEC, 1975], 26). The majority opinion supports the belief that important survivals from African religion were brought to North America by the slaves. See Cone, *The Identity Crisis,* 26–38; Joseph Washington, "How Black Is Black Religion?" in *Quest for a Black Theology,* ed. James Gardiner and J. Deotis Roberts (Philadelphia: Pilgrim Press, 1971), 22–34; and Gayraud S. Wilmore,

*Black Religion and Black Radicalism: An Interpretation of the Religious History of Afro-American People,* 2nd. ed. (Maryknoll, N.Y.: Orbis Books, 1983), 1–28.

46. Wilmore, *Black Religion and Black Radicalism,* 239.

47. Washington, "How Black Is Black Religion?" 25–28.

48. Wilmore, *Black Religion and Black Radicalism,* 240.

49. James H. Cone, "Biblical Revelation and Social Existence," *Interpretation* 28 (1974): 422–440.

50. Cone, *For My People,* 63.

51. Major Jones, *The Color of God: The Concept of God in Afro-American Thought* (Macon, Ga.: Mercer University Press, 1988), 92.

52. Albert Cleage, "The Black Messiah and the Black Revolution," in *Quest for a Black Theology,* ed. Gardiner and Roberts, 20.

53. Even though black theology was birthed within the black church, many blacks contend that the influence of black theology has been greater in white seminaries than in black denominations in the last twenty years (J. Deotis Roberts, *Black Theology in Dialogue* [Philadelphia: Westminster Press, 1981], 115; see also Cone, *For My People,* 24–27). Wilmore, however, reminds critics of black theology that "from the beginning Black Theology intended to speak to the Black Church and community about the ethnic pride, political realism, and religious radicalism hidden in the deepest recesses of the Black experience but almost forgotten by Black people in their rush to embrace White standards and values" (Wilmore, "Introduction," in *Black Theology: A Documentary History,* 68).

54. Washington, "How Black Is Black Religion?" 28.

55. Ruether, *Sexism and God-Talk,* 135. She says this with the caveat, "Once the mythology about Jesus as Messiah or divine *Logos,* with its traditional masculine imagery, is stripped off . . . " (ibid.).

56. Cone, "Biblical Revelation and Social Existence," 439. See also James H. Cone, *Speaking the Truth: Ecumenism, Liberation, and Black Theology* (Grand Rapids: Wm. B. Eerdmans Publishing Co., 1986), 4, 6, 8–10.

57. James H. Cone, *A Black Theology of Liberation,* 2nd ed. (Maryknoll, N.Y.: Orbis Books, 1986), 125; see also idem, *God of the Oppressed* (New York: Seabury Press, 1975), 135.

58. Biblical references are from Cone, "Biblical Revelation and Social Existence," 423–430; the designation "prophetic-liberative" is from Ruether, *Sexism and God-Talk*, 22–27; idem, "Feminist Interpretation: A Method of Correlation," 111–124. See also Mary Hembrow Snyder, *The Christology of Rosemary Radford Ruether: A Critical Introduction* (Mystic, Conn.: Twenty-Third Publications, 1988), 28–49.

59. On Jesus as the Suffering Servant of Isa. 40–55, see Cone, *God of the Oppressed*, 170–177.

60. James H. Cone, *Black Theology and Black Power* (New York: Seabury Press, 1969), 36.

61. Cone, *God of the Oppressed*, 113–114.

62. Cone, *The Spirituals and the Blues*, 67.

63. Ibid., 52.

64. Cone, *God of the Oppressed*, 135.

65. Cone, *Black Theology and Black Power*, 68; see also idem, *A Black Theology of Liberation*, 121; idem, *For My People*, 67; and Gayraud S. Wilmore, "The Black Messiah: Revising the Color Symbolism of Western Christology," *Journal of the Interdenominational Theological Center* 2 (1974), 13, 14, 16, 18. For Cone and Wilmore, blackness is symbolic rather than literal. Cone writes: "The focus on blackness does not mean that *only* blacks suffer as victims in a racist society, but that blackness is an ontological symbol and a visible reality which best describes what oppression means in America" (*A Black Theology of Liberation*, 7).

66. Jones, *The Color of God*, 23.

67. Cone, *God of the Oppressed*, 138.

68. Ibid., 160–161.

69. Ruether, *Sexism and God-Talk*, 135.

70. Schüssler Fiorenza, *In Memory of Her*, 121.

71. Ibid., 122–128.

72. Ruether, *Sexism and God-Talk*, 136–137; see Schüssler Fiorenza, *In Memory of Her*, 140–142, on the integral relationship between poverty and patriarchy.

73. Elizabeth Moltmann-Wendel, *A Land Flowing with Milk and Honey: Perspectives on Feminist Theology* (New York: Crossroad, 1989), 127–129. Although Moltmann-Wendel is German, she interacts almost entirely with North American feminists.

74. Schüssler Fiorenza, *In Memory of Her*, 136–138.

Moltmann-Wendel (*A Land Flowing*, 121–124) provides a succinct statement of the impact of other women on Jesus.

75. Schüssler Fiorenza, *In Memory of Her*, 143–145. In another discussion (Mark 12:18–27), Jesus accused the Sadducees of not understanding the scriptures or the power of God because they assumed that the law of levirate marriage—according to which a brother must marry a widow to preserve the patriarchal lineage of his deceased brother—would persist in the age to come. Jesus unmasks the Sadducees' faulty assumption that, if there is marriage in the age to come, sexist laws will continue to apply.

76. Schüssler Fiorenza, *In Memory of Her*, 144–147. See also Luke 12:51–53.

77. Ibid., 147–150; and Ruether, *Sexism and God-Talk*, 136.

78. Ruether (*Sexism and God-Talk*, 121; *Womanguides*, 108) regards servanthood not as servile status but in the prophetic sense of the servant who has a relationship with God that frees him or her from all human masters.

79. Schüssler Fiorenza, *In Memory of Her*, 151; see 148–151.

80. Ibid., 133; see also Elizabeth A. Johnson, *Consider Jesus: Waves of Renewal in Christology* (New York: Crossroad, 1990), 105.

81. E.g., Proverbs 8; Sirach (Ecclesiasticus) 24. See also Luke 11:49, where Wisdom herself speaks.

82. Schüssler Fiorenza, *In Memory of Her*, 135.

83. Ibid., 130; 135. Schüssler Fiorenza rejects the death of Jesus as sacrifice or atonement for two reasons. Theologically, Sophia did not require sacrifice. Historically, the theological interpretation of Jesus' death as sacrifice was fairly late.

84. Ruether, *Sexism and God-Talk*, 122–126; and idem, *Womanguides*, 109.

85. E.g., Ruether, *Sexism and God-Talk*, 138.

86. Cone, *For My People*, 7.

87. Martin Luther King, Jr., *Strength to Love* (Philadelphia: Fortress Press, 1981), 9–16.

88. Virginia Ramey Mollenkott, *Women, Men, and the Bible*, rev. ed. (New York: Crossroad, 1988), 46–47.

89. Letty M. Russell, *Human Liberation in a Feminist Perspective—A Theology* (Philadelphia: Westminster Press, 1974), 138.

90. Letha Scanzoni and Nancy Hardesty, *All We're Meant to Be: A Biblical Approach to Women's Liberation*, (Waco: Word Books, 1974), 56–59.

91. Russell, *Human Liberation*, 138–139.

92. Patricia Wilson-Kastner, *Faith, Feminism, and the Christ* (Philadelphia: Fortress Press, 1983), 100–101.

93. King, *Strength to Love*, 46. Darkness here symbolizes the ignorance of racists: like Jesus' crucifiers, they know not what they do.

94. King, *Strength to Love*, 43; see also J. Deotis Roberts, *Liberation and Reconciliation: A Black Theology* (Philadelphia: Westminster Press, 1971), 152–153.

95. Wilson-Kastner, *Faith, Feminism, and the Christ*, 115.

96. J. Deotis Roberts, *A Black Political Theology* (Philadelphia: Westminster Press, 1974), 136–138; and idem, *Liberation and Reconciliation*, 140.

97. Roberts, *Liberation and Reconciliation*, 138.

98. Wilson-Kastner, *Faith, Feminism, and the Christ*, 112; see Russell, *Human Liberation*, 137.

99. King, *Strength to Love*, 51.

100. Ibid., 54–55. Roberts writes: "For blacks there is no split between personal and social existence. . . . Jesus as the Liberator is also the Savior" (*A Black Political Theology*, 136–137).

101. "Statements from Black and White Caucuses, National Council of Churches Conference on the Church and Urban Tensions, Washington, D.C., September 27–30, 1967," in *Black Theology: A Documentary History*, ed. Cone and Wilmore, 44.

102. Vincent Harding, "Black Power and the American Christ," in *Black Theology: A Documentary History*, ed. Cone and Wilmore, 36.

103. Daly, *Beyond God the Father*, 79; see also Rita Nakashima Brock, *Journeys by Heart: A Christology of Erotic Power* (New York: Crossroad, 1988), xii.

104. Albert Cleage, *The Black Messiah* (New York: Sheed & Ward, 1968), 160.

105. Rita Nakashima Brock, "The Feminist Redemption of Christ," in *Christian Feminism: Visions of a New Humanity*, ed. Judith L. Weidman (San Francisco: Harper & Row, 1984), 61.

106. Cleage, *The Black Messiah*, 3.

107. Daly, *Beyond God the Father*, 69–81.

108. Ibid., 69–75.

109. Brock, *Journeys by Heart*, 64–67.

110. Brock uses "Christa" which, she recalls, was a term first used in reference to the female crucifix in the Cathedral of Saint

John the Divine in New York City. Brock writes, "In using Christa instead of Christ, I am using a term that points away from a sole identification of Christ with Jesus. In combining it with community, I want to shift the focus of salvation away from heroic individuals, male or female" (*Journeys by Heart*, 113).

111. Ibid., 52.

112. Ibid., 76–81. The name "Legion" (a military term) and the sarcastic reference to "pigs" heighten the political dimension of this story.

113. Ibid., 87.

114. Ibid., 100.

115. Ibid., 103–104.

116. Cleage, "The Black Messiah and the Black Revolution," 14–16; and idem, *The Black Messiah*, 38–43.

117. Cleage, *The Black Messiah*, 60.

118. Ibid., 215; and Cleage, "The Black Messiah and the Black Revolution," 18.

119. Cleage, *The Black Messiah*, 64–69, 79–81, 94–95, 205.

120. Ibid., 71–84, 24–28.

121. Ibid., 99.

122. In a statement in October 1968, the NCBC theological commission expressed its indebtedness to Cleage. See Hiley H. Ward, *Prophet of the Black Nation* (Philadelphia: Pilgrim Press, 1969), 144.

123. Boesak, *Farewell to Innocence*, 42. Roberts (*Liberation and Reconciliation*, 56–57, 137–138) rejects Cleage's interpretation because it romanticizes the potential of the black nation for solidarity, failing to take its sinfulness into account, and because it disallows for ultimate reconciliation by isolating the black nation from the rest of humankind.

124. Cone, *A Black Theology of Liberation*, 123. Also, Wilmore distances himself from Cleage's interpretation, yet offhandedly reiterates it: "To call Christ the Black Messiah is not to infer that he looked like an African, although that may well have been the case considering the likelihood of the mixture of the Jewish genetic pool with that of people from the upper Nile, Nubia and Ethiopia" (Wilmore, "The Black Messiah: Revising the Color Symbolism of Western Christology," 13; see 13–18).

Chapter 6

# Continuing
# the Conversation

Now that we have overheard the conversations of theologians in each context, it is time to begin to set these contexts in conversation with each other. We will do so in two parts. First, we will provide an interpretative summary of the conversation between these contexts and the biblical text. Second, we will ourselves engage the conversation between the contexts. This will involve raising four issues of importance to these theologians and suggesting ways in which these issues can become the basis for the expansion and refinement of their conversations in Christology.

## Part I: A Conversation with the Text

The differences between cosmic Christ and Black Messiah, or Elder Brother and Pain-Love, might give the impression that these Christologies have nothing in common. It is true that these portraits differ substantially from each other. However, nearly all of them represent conversations between contemporary contexts and the life, death, and resurrection of Jesus. It is these biblical categories of life, death, and resurrection that will allow us to draw together the disparate strands of these Christologies in a summary and comparative analysis.

## The Life of Jesus

With few exceptions, it is liberation theologians who incorporate Jesus' life most fully into their Christologies. Jesus' life is for them a verbal denunciation of institutions and ideologies coupled with the annunciation of God's reign through social praxis and miracles. This combination of words and deeds expresses Jesus' conviction that the reign of God was at hand.

### Words

Jesus' preaching was a prophetic protest. Because he refused to ignore poverty and to overlook injustice, Jesus denounced oppressive *institutions* that preserved their own holiness at the expense of human wholeness. Jesus decried the Torah, Temple, and banquet table whenever they became institutions that excluded people on the basis of health, race, social status, or illegitimate vocations, such as prostitution and tax collection.

Women were excluded from these institutions simply because of gender. Men, not women, were the authoritative interpreters of Torah. While men had to meet certain requirements of health and vocation to serve in the Temple, women of all social positions were excluded. Although women prepared the table, men were the leaders of the home. Jesus did not tolerate these injustices. He denounced all patriarchal institutions, including patriarchal marriage, divorce, and hierarchically ordered biological households.

Alongside the denunciation of institutions, over which the oppressed had no control, Jesus also denounced *ideologies*, over which the oppressed could exercise control. From his first sermon in Nazareth onward (Luke 4:16–30), Jesus rejected an individualized application of the Deuteronomic formula that equated economic prosperity with divine blessing and poverty or sickness with divine disapprobation. He argued instead—to the bemused disciples' chagrin—that camels pass through the eye of a needle more easily than the rich enter heaven (Mark 10:17–31). Jesus also refused to allow the oppressed to accept and to interiorize their oppressors' assessment of them. He urged them not to lose hope in God's reign of justice and to realize that poverty and social ostracism—due to health, status, or vocation—are not inevitable. If the oppressed would embrace this ideology of God's reign, they could begin to break the cycle of oppression.

## Deeds

Jesus complemented this denunciation of institutions and ideologies with a positive embodiment of God's reign. The characteristic feature of this reign was the *social reintegration* of those who were excluded from full participation in the people of God. Social reintegration is especially apparent in Jesus' eating habits; he seemed always to be accused of eating with "tax collectors and sinners" and even commended an unnamed woman who caressed his feet while he ate at someone else's home (Luke 7:36–50). The festive banquet table, filled with those who were plucked unexpectedly from the streets—poor, crippled, blind, and lame—became for Jesus the quintessential symbol of God's reign (Luke 14:12–24).

Jesus combined these table habits with miracles. Most liberation theologians regard Jesus' miracles as partial liberations that anticipate the final integral liberation of God's reign, when God will annihilate poverty and sickness. As the tangible power of God's reign, these miracles conjoined physical healing and social reintegration. The paradigmatic miracle in this respect is the healing of the hemorrhaging woman who was impoverished by unsuccessful visits to doctors and whose bleeding required social isolation according to Torah. By not only healing her but also addressing her directly as a "daughter" (of Abraham), Jesus reintegrated her into the social and religious world of early Judaism (Mark 5:24b-34).

This emphasis on social reintegration is corroborated by insights from other than liberation theologians. Jesus' holistic model of healing is epitomized by the African healer, who lives at the crux of village life and whose task it is to maintain the balance of social equilibrium in the community. Like these healers, Jesus placed healing in the context

of a living community; that is why he addressed the hemorrhaging woman with a familial epithet, "daughter," sent
the Gerasene demoniac back to his village and friends
(Mark 5:19), and ordered a healed leper to go to the Jewish
priest (Mark 1:44).

Rita Nakashima Brock, a feminist theologian, highlights
the social dimension of miracles by contending that Jesus
did not dispense power unilaterally. Rather, he depended
on relationships with the sick for his ability to heal. For
instance, Jesus was unable to heal the sick in Nazareth
without their participation (Mark 6:1–6). Brock also suggests that Jesus' own experience of weakness allowed him
to empathize with the sick. This suggestion finds unexpected corroboration in the observation of Matthew Schoffeleers that many African healers gain their powers from
their own experience of suffering.[1] Could it be that shared
weakness, even more than heroic strength, was the source
of Jesus' healing power?

This brief analysis hardly exhausts the significance of
Jesus' life for other contextual theologians. The Japanese
novelist Shusaku Endo portrays Jesus as imbued with compassion rather than fiery denunciation. For many Africans,
Jesus' life is important as a demonstration of his humanity:
he goes through the requisite rites of passage in order to
become fully human and African. For several feminist and
black theologians (both North American and South African), Jesus' ministry of reconciliation is as significant as his
mission of liberation. Nevertheless, the lines of Jesus' life
have been laid out most exhaustively by liberation theologians such as Boff, Segundo, and Sobrino in Latin America;
Cone, Schüssler Fiorenza, and Ruether in North America;
Kappen in Asia; and Mofokeng in South Africa.

## The Crucifixion of Jesus

The death of Jesus features more prominently than the
life or resurrection in contextual portraits of Jesus. Interpretations can be ordered along two lines. The first views
Jesus' death as the inevitable result of his *historical* conflict
with the powerful of his society. The second interprets
Jesus' death as God's *identification* with humankind.

## Jesus' Death as Historical Conflict

Many of the theologians mentioned in this book have pressed the relevance of Jesus as a *human* being rather than a divine being. In this respect, we may recall M. M. Thomas's Christ-centered humanism or the attempt to entwine Jesus within African kinship patterns. Segundo speaks for liberation theologians when he asserts: "If people came face to face with a specific, limited human being . . . and came to see him as God . . . it was because that human being was of interest, was humanly significant."[2]

The death of Jesus must be understood first and foremost as the result of a conflict between the historical Jesus and the powerful elite of his day. Jesus and the Jewish leaders met in conflict primarily over their views of God. In other words, the *historical* conflict that led to Jesus' death was precipitated by a *theological* conflict. According to Song and Endo, the leaders believed in a God of retribution and judgment, while Jesus knew God to be loving and compassionate. According to feminists, Jesus rejected a patriarchal God who buttressed the hierarchy of power and instead followed Sophia-God, who gathered the poor and heavy laden under her wings. According to Latin American liberation theologians, Jesus rejected the God of the status quo and championed the God of the oppressed who had rescued the Israelites from Egyptian slavery and who now offered the reign of justice to the poor. In Sobrino's words, the trial of Jesus was "a choice between two deities: either a God wielding oppressive power or a God offering and effecting liberation. Framed in this context of a basic theological conflict, Jesus' trajectory to the cross is no accident. He himself provokes it by presenting the basic option between two deities."[3]

However, first-century Palestine did not permit the bifurcation of theology and politics. Therefore, although theology lay at the base of the conflict, politics was its medium. Jesus was brought to trial initially for blasphemy, a theological crime, but he was convicted as king of the Jews, a political charge. From the standpoint of the leaders, Jesus' death was necessary because he simultaneously undermined their religiopolitical leadership and conscientized the poor to resist oppression. Jesus' opposition to the Jewish leaders was *political* because it challenged their *religious* authority, as keepers of Torah and Temple, that upheld their status in the fragile equilibrium between the Jewish nation and Rome. Jesus also threatened the leaders' authority by mobilizing the poor with the conviction that God was prepared to overturn the status quo: "The first shall become last."

In regions such as Latin America, the interpretation of Jesus' death as historical conflict is painfully relevant. Countless people, named and unnamed, have reenacted the death of Jesus in the context of historical conflict, including Archbishop Oscar Romero and Jesuit priest-theologian Ignacio Ellacuría of El Salvador.

## Jesus' Death as Identification with Suffering

Another line of interpretation, which emphasizes the identification of Jesus with human suffering, has its biblical foundation in the portrait of the suffering servant in Isaiah 53:

> He was despised and rejected by others;
>     a man of suffering and acquainted with infirmity;
> and as one from whom others hide their faces
>     he was despised, and we held him of no account.
>
>                                                   (Isa. 53:3)

Against this background, Jesus is referred to variously as the Suffering Servant, the Oppressed One (Cone), Eternal Companion (Endo), or Pain-Love (Song).

Suffering people identify with Jesus at the cross, his deepest point of suffering. In sermons and spirituals, black preachers and slaves identified their suffering with the suffering of Jesus. Mofokeng and Tutu document Good Friday services in South Africa, where the recounting of Jesus' suffering and death is accompanied by perspiring, crying, and fainting because "it is their own painful life story that they are reliving and narrating. . . . They are hanging on the cross as innocent victims of white evil forces. . . . Jesus' cry of abandonment is their own daily cry."[4] A South African theologian and poet, Gabriel Setiloane, expresses this identification eloquently:

> And yet for us it is when
>    He is on the cross,
> This Jesus of Nazareth, with holed hands
>    and open side, like a beast
>    at a sacrifice:
> When He is stripped naked like us,
> Browned and sweating water and blood
>    in the heat of the sun,
> Yet silent,
> That we cannot resist Him.
>
> How like us He is, this Jesus of Nazareth,
> Beaten, tortured, imprisoned,
>    spat upon, truncheoned,
> Denied by His own,
>    and chased like a thief in the night.
> Despised, and rejected like a dog
>    that has fleas,
> for NO REASON.[5]

The biblical portrait of Jesus as suffering servant finds its Asian counterpart in Jesus as the pain-love of God. God meets Asians not as a God who demands the sacrifice of a son but as a God whose "gravity-bound" love for humankind leads to full identification with them at the cross. And it is here that Asians meet God, when they respond to the one who suffers *with* them rather than merely on their behalf.

At the same time, some theologians contest that many people identify with Jesus as a passive victim and, consequently, passively endure suffering themselves. Such passive identification serves to perpetuate oppression by allowing it to reign unchallenged. Feminists are especially sensitive to a close identification with Jesus' suffering. For too long, women have been told that Christlikeness demands the passive endurance of suffering.

Other theologians are reluctant to minimize Jesus' identification with human suffering. Nevertheless, they distinguish the innocent suffering of victims from the redemptive suffering of Jesus. Innocent suffering does not look beyond oppression; it is meaningless and perpetuates violence through passivity. In contrast, Jesus *chose* to suffer redemptively in solidarity with the oppressed in order to attain liberation. Redemptive suffering was espoused by Martin Luther King, Jr., who believed that nonviolent resistance to suffering could overcome hatred with love, segregation with reconciliation, and darkness with light.

The two interpretations of Jesus' death as the outcome of historical conflict and as God's identification with human suffering dovetail in two respects. They do so first at the point of redemptive suffering. Jesus did not suffer without liberating; nor did he liberate without suffering. What this means for the church *today* is that it cannot expect to liberate while distancing itself from suffering, while acting on behalf of but not with the poor, or while enduring suffering passively without cause.

Second, proponents of both interpretations of Jesus' death agree that the suffering of people *today* is the context for discerning the existential meaning of Jesus' crucifixion. Sobrino conjectures that the unexpected surprise of God's presence even at the crucifixion means that God is present *today* unexpectedly as well. Therefore, "it is when that surprise is maintained, when service is rendered to the oppressed, that we 'stand by God in his hour of grieving.'"[6] Song concurs: "In the people in pain and suffering, in the people tortured and put to death, we witness Jesus tortured and nailed to the cross. And in this Jesus and in such people we encounter the loving and suffering God."[7]

### The Resurrection of Jesus

Interpretations of Jesus' resurrection are more difficult to assess than the life or death because they vary so widely. Some theologians, such as Kappen and Balasuriya of Asia or Schüssler Fiorenza and Ruether of North America, tend to minimize its importance. Others, such as Brock and Cleage of North America, interpret the resurrection as a contemporary communal experience rather than a historical physical event. Nevertheless, interpretations of the resurrection that contextual theologians proffer gather around two poles: (1) human and cosmic reconciliation; and (2) justice.

## Resurrection and Reconciliation

Jesus as the risen Lord is, for many contextual theologians, the mediator of reconciliation. Although it includes humankind, this reconciliation expands to encompass the entire cosmos.

In their opposition to the ideology of domination, many North American theologians emphasize Jesus' victory over racial and gender dualisms. His resurrection overturned the bigotry and alienation that crucified him, so that his historical ministry of reconciliation might become a permanent process in the world. Jesus is now the universal Lord who crosses all racial and gender barriers and whose true humanity—neither male nor female, black nor white—is available to all who participate as partners in the ministry of reconciliation. Those who join this process become the new humanity, part of the cosmic movement toward reconciliation in which God is making all things new (Rev. 21:5).

Human and cosmic reconciliation are integral to the African interpretation of the risen Jesus as ancestor. Having passed through the requisite rites of passage that confirmed his humanity—genealogy, birth, circumcision, baptism, and death—and having lived an exemplary life, Jesus became preeminent among the ancestors by virtue of his resurrection. As proto-ancestor, Jesus destroys tribalism and reconciles all tribes and clans under his ancestral leadership. Jesus' preeminence extends also to the cosmic sphere, where he destroys all malevolent powers that terrorize humankind. Apart from his work within each sphere, he reconciles the human and divine spheres by mediating divine blessing to humans and by interceding on their behalf before the ancestors.

Asian theologians who portray Jesus as cosmic Christ naturally interpret reconciliation as cosmic in scope. The risen Christ is the firstfruit of a reconciliation that encompasses all things. They also emphasize that Christ's unifying presence in humankind preceded its division into separate religious traditions. "In him God, nature, history, and all human beings of all time are mysteriously intertwined in a manner that we cannot fully fathom."[8]

### Resurrection and Justice

Despite the discontinuity between the spheres of the historical and risen Jesus, it is the same person, with the same opposition to oppressive ideologies and institutions, who lives beyond the grave. In three respects, the resurrection continues rather than concludes the relationship between Jesus and justice.

First, the resurrection *validates* the life and death of Jesus. Although he died in apparent failure, abandoned by God and most of the community he had gathered, the resurrection demonstrates that God "gave confirmation to Jesus' concrete way of living, to his preaching, his deeds, and his death on the cross."[9]

Second, the resurrection gives the words and deeds of Jesus *universal* validity. No longer are they the preaching and miracles of an itinerant Palestinian prophet but the universal will of God. Liberation, reconciliation, and compassion are now no longer characteristics of Jesus' life alone; they have become the standard for human activity.

Third, the resurrection sets in motion an inexorable movement toward final liberation and reconciliation because it anticipates *within history* the future reign of God. That reign was historical during Jesus' life, became universal history at the resurrection, and will culminate in the future, historical appearance of God's reign. Therefore the church must not withdraw from but must participate fully in concrete, historical liberation. Although opting for particular historical movements for justice will undoubtedly raise many questions, the church must risk error to participate in the power politics of justice for the oppressed as a witness to the power of the resurrected Christ.

For nearly all contextual theologians, the life, death, and resurrection of Jesus constitute an integral unity. The resurrection of Jesus retrospectively confirms Jesus' ministry, presently universalizes that ministry in history, and prospectively anticipates the fulfillment of that ministry in the future, historical establishment of God's reign and the new humanity. The church's responsibility is to align itself actively with the historical, crucified, and risen Jesus.

## Part II: Conversation Between Contexts

### *Issue No. 1: Sources and Method*

The conversation between these contexts reveals shared sources and method. Contextual theologians begin with experience, engage the Bible and Christian tradition as sources, and incorporate a community as the locus of the theological process. To these sources and method held in common, theologians from each context bring their own contributions. These unique insights, born out of one context, can enhance theological reflection in other contexts.

### *Experience*

Contextual theologians begin with a precommitment to a specific experience of a racial, socioeconomic, cultural, or gender group. For feminist theologians, it is women's experience. For North American and South African black theologians, it is black experience. For African theologians, it is their cultural experience. For Latin American liberation theologians, it is the experience of being poor and oppressed. For Asian theologians, it is the experience of poverty and religiosity. We would suggest that the understanding of experience can be enhanced by further conversation in two areas: social analysis and popular artistic expressions.

Latin American liberation theologians contribute the most well developed example of social analysis. They have analyzed thoroughly tiers of dependency—the internal domination of the class struggle and the external domination by foreign powers and multinational corporations.

Theologians in other contexts recognize as well the importance of social analysis, but they have yet to develop its potential. Although Asian theologians selectively adopt Marxist social analysis, they are reluctant to utilize it fully because of its Western bias. Still, they have yet to substitute an Asian method of social analysis.[10] Cone criticizes the virtual absence of social analysis in North American black theology: "We were naive, because our analysis of the problem was too superficial and did not take into consideration the links between racism, capitalism, and imperialism."[11] Similarly, Obijole, Mosala, and others charge South African black theologians with being preoccupied with race but ignorant of class struggle.[12] And, by definition, African theologians are more interested in cultural rather than social analysis.

Our contention is that theologians in other contexts would do well to follow the lead of their Latin American counterparts. For instance, feminist theologians in North America might incorporate current social analysis, such as the Labor Department's study of Fortune 500 companies that indicated the presence of a glass ceiling that bars women and minorities from upper management. By incorporating such social analysis, feminist theology will become more socially relevant to all women and will expand to address patriarchy in arenas of society other than the church, which tends to be its present focus. A recent example of this is Rita Brock's attempt to utilize studies of child abuse as the basis for Christology.[13]

With their emphasis on culture, African theologians tend to be skeptical about the value of social analysis. We wonder whether this is judicious, given the immensity of problems such as starvation, deforestation, and a growing refugee population. A combination of cultural and social analysis would provide a holistic—and thus African—approach to the challenges of neo-colonialism.

Another contribution to the understanding of experience, the incorporation of popular artistic expression, has been made by Asian, North American black, and African theologians. Asian folktales, dances, and social biographies; black spirituals and blues; and the songs, dances, chants, and rhythms of African Independent Churches have become creative sources of theology.

Feminist theologians have just begun to incorporate popular artistic expressions of women. Katie Cannon constructs a womanist ethic from black women's literary works. Susan Thistlethwaite approaches the biblical text through the social biography of battered women in order to promote healing and liberation where there has been physical and verbal violence.[14] If these initial attempts expand to include artistic, musical, and biographical expressions of women from divergent racial and economic groups, feminist theologians can avoid the charge that their theology speaks only to white, middle-class, educated women.

Latin American liberation theology seems to lack a significant cultural component. This absence may be due to their ambivalence about popular religiosity because it has tended to inculcate submission and dependency among the oppressed. However, rather than baptizing popular culture entirely, they might incorporate as theological sources social biographies of the urban poor and *campesinos* as well as indigenous folktales and literature. One example is the writings of Manuel Quintín Lame, a chief of an indigenous ethnic group, the Páez Indians of Colombia. Lame was both a self-taught sage and a leader of rebellions to regain Indian land. His writing entitled "The Thoughts of the Indian Educated in the Colombian Forests" has been analyzed for its contribution to Latin American liberation theology.[15] If Latin American liberation theologians would complement their social analysis with popular expressions, they could develop a more substantial foundation for an *integral* liberation, which is, of course, the hope of Latin American liberation theology.

### Tradition

All contextual theologians utilize Western Christian tradition as a theological source, but they do so with ambivalence. At its worst, tradition has functioned to suppress and to control the oppressed. Within this tradition, slaves have been taught that their Christian duty is to obey passively in order to await their heavenly reward. Within this tradition, women have been barred from leadership positions in the church. Within this tradition, colonized peoples were told that they were pagan and that conversion required forsaking all vestiges of their former culture. At its best, Western Christian tradition has challenged slavery and the caste system and provided the foundation for the early feminist movement. How can theologians extricate themselves from its oppressive legacy in order to utilize tradition as a liberative source?

Feminist theologians provide a salutary solution to this quandary. Their first step in the theological method is critique. Passage by passage and image by image, they recognize and bring to light the oppressive character of tradition. Then, they are free both to recover liberative dimesions of the tradition and to revision traditional categories and symbols in more appropriate ways. This method of critique could be powerful for once-colonized peoples as they seek freedom from the hegemony of Western tradition.

### Community

Contextual theologians accord their community a prominent role in the theological process because a community prevents theology from becoming the individual reflection of academic theologians. Base communities in Latin America provide a place for theological reflection and concomitant action by and with the poor. Women-church offers a respite from patriarchal religion and a creative community for developing feminist liturgies. African Independent Churches are communities that embody indigenous African culture and values. The black church, with its sermons and spirituals, is a community where black theology is nurtured. However, these examples do not always live up to the ideal. In Boff's image of liberation theology as a tree, he compares the theologizing of base communities as the roots and that of academic theologians as the branches. Yet footnotes and references are replete with citations from other academic theologians rather than base communities. Black theologians admit that the black church is often at odds with black theology. African Independent Churches are still objects of description rather than genuine contributors to the theological process. Women-church is too recent a phenomenon for us to assess its impact on feminist theology.

Nevertheless, while most contextual theologians make provision for community, Asian theologians do not refer to an organized approach for convoking a community. This seems a natural step, given the interest of many Asian theologians in popular artistic expressions. Pieris's call for a community where theologians are poor, and the poor are theologians, indicates that community is still a reality to be fulfilled in Asian theology.[16]

## Issue No. 2: Use of the Bible

The purpose of this section is to engender conversation about the Bible across contextual boundaries. In particular, three aspects of biblical interpretation can contribute to cross-fertilization in the ongoing conversation about Christology: (1) implications of the method of interpretation that unify these Christologies; (2) the starting points of these Christologies; and (3) one area of biblical studies that would benefit from Western scholarship.

### Method

In the introduction to this book we suggested that contextual biblical interpretation is a *conversation* between context and text. Interpreter and text engage each other, losing themselves in the to-and-fro that develops a life of its own. Theologians from different contexts have refined this method to different extents. Nonetheless, this model can be distilled in three theses that unify all but a few contextual theologies. Each of these theses not only summarizes methods of biblical interpretation but also provides fodder for the ongoing conversation about the role of the Bible in constructing Christologies.

1. *All interpretations are suspect.* Contextual theologians assert that every interpretation must be evaluated in terms of the ideologies it supports.[17] History is replete with oppressive Christologies, such as the white Christ of Africa, the patriarchal Christ of North America, and the impotent Christ of Latin America.

Despite their negative influence, these oppressive Christologies comprise part of the context of contemporary theologians. However, the publications of contextual theology exhibit a tendency to analyze superficially this crucial aspect of context. Apart from feminist theologians, there are surprisingly few meticulous critiques of the oppressive interpretations that constitute the theological context in which contextual Christologies are emerging. Saúl Trinidad's "Christology, *Conquista*, Colonization" represents an initial Latin American attempt; black theologians devote scattered pages to the "White Christ, Black Jesus" problem,[18] but little else is available. If contextual theologians are in earnest about understanding their context, their conversations in Christology should include, we believe, critical, historical appraisals of oppressive Christologies that comprise an essential, albeit negative, aspect of their context.

2. *Because no interpretation is neutral, interpreters must develop a proper stance of advocacy.* Liberation theologians strive to develop an adequate praxis that ensures that their interpretation will not be oppressive. For liberation theologians, praxis entails solidarity with the poor as a prerequisite for developing interpretations that promote justice. Since praxis is always in a state of flux, we hope that the conversation will continue between theologians such as Pieris (Asia), Sobrino (Latin America), Schüssler Fiorenza (North America), and Mofokeng (South Africa) in order to discern precisely what shape praxis might take.

This thesis raises a question for other than liberation theologians: To what extent should interpreters of the Bible become advocates of their cultural heritage? Already this is a topic of considerable conversation in several contexts: the merits of Asian religions, the worth of African traditional religion, and the status of so-called heretical traditions in which women featured prominently. The role these cultural legacies play affects, even alters, Christologies. For example, Panikkar's commitment to mystery leads him to disregard the historical Jesus as the locus of revelation, while Nyamiti's commitment to African traditional religion prompts the portrayal of Jesus as an ancestor. The diversity of cultural heritages, coupled with the thorny question of their relative merits, should spark a lively conversation between theologians from various contexts.

3. *Interpretation should take place in grass-roots communities.* Third World theologians advocate a shift in theologi-

cal production from the elite to communities of the oppressed. Despite this universal commitment among contextual theologians, however, few studies of grass-roots Christologies are available. If theologians are to facilitate the transition from academic to grass-roots Christology, they should bring to the conversation more transcripts of grass-roots interpretation, such as Cardenal's *The Gospel in Solantiname*, and additional analyses of popular Christologies, such as Mbiti's "Some African Concepts of Christology," or de Araújo's "Images of Jesus in the Culture of the Brazilian People." Such analyses of popular Christologies will require, according to Nyamiti, researchers who live among indigenous communities "in close and sympathetic collaboration with them, so as to discover their understanding of Christ and His relevance to their current problems and aspirations."[19]

### Starting Points

The model of interpretation as conversation recognizes that interpreters are drawn to texts that address issues raised by their contexts. Often, however, a similar interest draws theologians to different texts. The comparison of contextual interests and biblical texts can, we believe, become an important topic of conversation. Two interests in particular provide potential points of departure: the human significance of Jesus and universal reconciliation.

Liberation theologians and African inculturation theologians share a common interest in the human significance of Jesus. However, they utilize different biblical starting points to establish Jesus' human significance for their contexts. Liberation theologians throughout the globe are suspicious of starting points for Christology that undervalue history as the locus of God's activity. Their starting point is the historical Jesus rather than the risen Christ. To understand Jesus they turn to the Synoptic Gospels and to Luke in particular. There they discern various aspects of Jesus' ministry, such as humanization, denunciation of patriarchy, and God's preference for the poor.

African theologians come to the Bible from a different perspective in an attempt to preserve community and its cultural heritage. They cite biblical texts that reinforce Jesus' membership in the human community, such as his submission to rites of passage (e.g., birth, circumcision, baptism, death). They are drawn especially to biblical passages that emphasize the exemplary life Jesus lived, for in African traditional religion humans achieve ancestral status, not merely by being human, but by becoming exemplary humans. This significant qualification of African life resonates with the Letter to the Hebrews' portrayal of Jesus as one who was tempted in all respects, but without sin, and who learned obedience through what he suffered (Heb. 4:14–16; 5:7–10).

Africans' interest in the exemplarity of Jesus' life arises from the belief that exemplary human beings become ancestors, who mediate between the ancestral and the human community. African theologians are drawn especially to the Letter to the Hebrews because their view of ancestors resonates remarkably with Hebrews' dual emphasis upon Jesus as earthly brother and heavenly priest. Like all ancestors, Jesus is able to mediate blessing and to destroy demonic evil because he first shared the humanity of his brothers and sisters. "Therefore he had to become like his brothers and sisters in every respect, so that he might be a merciful and faithful high priest in the service of God" (Heb. 2:17).

Another biblical book, the Gospel of John, also provides this dual emphasis on Jesus' humanity and mediation. Jesus is "the way, and the truth, and the life" (John 14:6), the gate of the sheepfold (John 10:9), and the source of abundant life (John 10:10). The example of his behavior (John 10:10) and his promise of watchful care (John 14:18) complete the accomplishments by which he becomes an ancestor.

This common interest in the human significance of Jesus is an unlikely point of contact between African theologians and liberation theologians. The fact that it leads to different biblical texts (Synoptic Gospels; John; Hebrews), because of different contemporary contexts, signals a promising venue for discussing how different biblical texts can illuminate matters of common interest.

The array of Asian biblical starting points is wider than those of African and liberation theologies. Pieris and

Thomas begin with entirely *different* starting points that yield divergent Christologies. Nevertheless both portraits of Jesus address Asian issues. Pieris finds Jesus' baptism into poverty and religiosity in the Synoptic Gospels. Thomas begins with Colossians 1 to validate the presence of Christ in movements for justice among all Asian religions. Although Pieris virtually ignores the risen Christ and Thomas refers sporadically to the words and deeds of Jesus, both develop Christologies that address the pressing issues of Asian poverty and religiosity.

The portrayal of Jesus as pain-love depends upon no single text or book but, at every turn, requires the reinterpretation of texts to emphasize Jesus' identification with suffering. Song reinterprets Jesus' quotation of Psalm 22:1, "My God, my God, why have you forsaken me?" to mean that the false God of retribution abandoned Jesus but not the Abba-God of parental care. Into Abba-God's hands Jesus committed his spirit: "*Father*, into your hands I commend my spirit" (Luke 23:46).

The biblical starting point for the cosmic Christ is more definite. Devanandan first appealed to Ephesians 1:9–10, "to gather up all things in him," in support of Christ's presence in the stirrings of other Asian religions. Panikkar refers to similar passages that imply Christ's presence beyond the historical Jesus and the Christian tradition: "What . . . you worship as unknown, this I proclaim to you" (Acts 17:23; see 14:16–17); and, "The true light, which enlightens everyone, was coming into the world" (John 1:9). The pivotal biblical source is Colossians 1:15–20, which gathers up the themes of unity and universal fulfillment in Christ into a singular poetic affirmation of the cosmic Christ.

A promising arena of conversation is the biblical portrayal of the cosmic Christ. Many contextual theologians refer to the reconciling dimension of Christ. Even liberation theologians refer sporadically to the cosmic reconciliation which the new humanity or reign of God in part anticipates.[20] Those references, however, tend to be slight. Therefore a conversation with proponents of the cosmic Christ might serve to deepen the meaning of reconciliation in contexts other than Asia. In turn, Asian theologians such as Panikkar might benefit from conversing with theologians who stress the humanity of Jesus, for, as we saw, Asian theologians have not yet determined the precise relationship between the historical Jesus and the cosmic Christ.

This survey reflects the diversity of biblical starting points that contextual theologians adopt: the Synoptic Gospels; John; Hebrews; Ephesians 1; and Colossians 1. We would suggest that theologians, rather than building on familiar texts, develop Christologies that incorporate several biblical interpretations of Jesus. If this wide diversity of starting points becomes a topic of conversation between contexts, it is likely that the fullness of the biblical witnesses to Jesus will be discovered more fully within each context.

## A Suggested Refinement

All of these Christologies emerge from contexts that are defined by suffering. Therefore it seems appropriate at this point to suggest that the negative portrayal of early Judaism in many of these Christologies contains the seeds of anti-Semitism which brings its own form of suffering. Because feminist theologians Ruether and Schüssler Fiorenza have attuned our ears to this problem, we shall endeavor only to expand their observations.

Schüssler Fiorenza cites Jewish feminist Judith Plaskow's warning that the early feminist image of Jesus depends on "an extremely negative depiction of the Jewish background, because the only way to depict him as a radical—that is as overthrowing tradition—is to depict the tradition as negatively as possible." In other words, feminists have utilized early Judaism as a negative foil for the positive, liberative dimensions of Jesus.[21]

This warning applies equally to many other contextual theologians who utilize early Judaism as a negative foil for Jesus. They claim that his God is "not God the law-giver but God the caring parent,"[22] nor is his message "the safe and solid ground of the law" but "a universal love that is superior to all laws."[23] In contrast to Jesus' interpretation of Torah, the Pharisees' interpretation is reduced to "a blind one that lacked any center of gravity."[24] Given this caricature of early Judaism, it is no wonder that Jesus rejects the "narrow ideology of the Zealots, the sectarian puritanism of the Essenes, the self-righteous legalism of the Pharisees, and the leisure-class mentality of the Sadducees."[25]

Frequently, the denigration of early Judaism results from the theologians' identifying their opponents with it.[26] At times this identification is obvious, such as when Cleage identifies the Pharisees with middle-class Uncle Toms, or when Balasuriya equates the religionism of the Jews with the religionism of modern Christianity.[27] In other instances the parallel is implicit. Song portrays Jesus in conflict with the God of the church which, of course, did not exist until after Jesus' death. Jesus rejected "the God of church authorities, the God secluded in the fortress of unintelligible doctrines and defended and protected by religious taboos and rituals." Here Song clearly identifies a negative appraisal of the God of modern Christianity with the God of early Judaism.

This negative assessment of early Judaism is an unfortunate legacy from the history of Christianity. It should not, however, be part of Christologies that develop in response to oppression. To mitigate the potential for anti-Semitism, we would suggest that contextual theologians extend their conversation to include Western scholars of early Judaism. A massive amount of research on early Judaism has developed within the last decade, often through cooperation between Jewish and Christian scholars. These scholars recognize the rich diversity of early Judaism and refuse therefore to reduce it to a religion of legalism. Were an author such as Pieris in conversation with this research, he would probably not refer to the "leisure-class spirituality of the Sadducees," for he would be aware that the priestly classes contributed to the Jewish rebellion in 66 c.e. by discontinuing sacrifices on behalf of the emperor or that the quick succession of high priests in the first century indicates that many of them refused to collaborate with Rome and, as a result, were replaced by high priests who would. This renaissance of research on early Judaism has spawned several newer books on Jesus that place him within rather than against Judaism.[28] Such a perspective informs Schüssler Fiorenza's reconstruction of Jesus' ministry, which she presents as a renewal movement within Judaism.

This suggestion may seem to demand a return to theological dependency on the West. It does not. Dependency occurs when oppressed nations are compelled to provide raw materials for oppressing nations. Extending the conversation in the way that we suggest designates the First World as the *exporter* of raw material—historical and sociological analysis on Jesus and Judaism—to the Third World. There, this raw material can be used in conjunction with experience, social biographies, indigenous art forms, and religious traditions.

### Issue No. 3: Liberation and Inculturation

Contextual theologians begin with their context. Yet they tend to give priority to select issues within that context. By virtue of the priorities they select, theologians can be divided into two groups: those who emphasize the socioeconomic and political issues (liberation contextual theologians) and those who emphasize the religiocultural issues (inculturation contextual theologians).[29] For example, African theologians are inculturationists who investigate African traditional religion and, as a result, portray Jesus as Elder Brother, ancestor, chief, or healer. Some Asian theologians adopt the inculturation approach. Endo presents Jesus as the Eternal Companion to meet the Japanese need for a God of love, not a God of wrath. Because Panikkar regards Asian religions as the primary issue, he depicts Jesus as the cosmic Christ who is present in these religions through the experience of mystery.

Unlike inculturationists, liberation theologians view the socioeconomic marginalization of oppressed peoples as the priority issue that their theology addresses. Thus, for liberation theologians, Jesus is liberator.

Liberation and inculturation theologians have, at times, been highly critical of each other. Frequently this debate has taken place between theologians of the same context. It is liveliest among African theologians of inculturation and South African black theologians of liberation. We may also recall the controversy at the 1979 EATWOT meeting be-

tween Asian theologians who gave priority to the religiocultural context and those who gave priority to the
socioeconomic. Liberation and inculturation theologians of
*different* contexts also criticize each other for the same reason. Asian theologians of inculturation fault Latin American liberation theologians for virtually disregarding the
religiocultural dimension embodied in the religiosity of the
poor.[30] Likewise, Mbiti, an African theologian, issues a negative assessment of Black theology in North America for
what he considers "an excessive preoccupation with liberation. . . . One gets the feeling that Black Theology has
created a semi-mythological urgency for liberation that it
must at all costs keep alive."[31]

Liberation theologians in turn critique inculturation
theologians. Éla, an African liberation theologian, indicts
those who emphasize culture without noticing socioeconomic and political oppression. "But how is it possible to
study the people's culture without becoming uneasy about
the marginalization of those masses whose folkways have
become the object of anthropological research?"[32] In his
opinion, people suffer far more from oppression and domination than from cultural alienation.

The unresolved nature of this debate between inculturation and liberation theologians demonstrates the need for further conversation. Continuing this conversation may, as Mbiti
cautions, raise "the dangers of encroaching upon one's theological territories."[33] Nevertheless the fruitfulness of such a
conversation is recognized by contextual theologians themselves, as the title of the most recent EATWOT meeting suggests: "Common and Distinct Elements and Cross-
Fertilisation Among Third World Theologies."

A conversation along these lines does not need to be in-
trusive. On the contrary, differences would alert theologians to other aspects in their context. In this respect, James
Cone has noted that liberation theology challenges inculturation theology to take seriously liberation as a common
theme in the gospel as well as a global theme in theology.
Inculturation theology also challenges liberation theology
to take seriously "the symbols and beliefs of the people
whom all liberation theologians claim to represent."[34]

The conversation will become all the more interesting as

variations on the liberation theme are taken into account, for liberation is not monolithic. Latin American liberation theology is the prototype of liberation theologies, but it is not definitive. Liberation theology in Latin America claims to be integral, including liberation of the individual and liberation of unjust structures. However, other liberation theologians perceive Latin American liberation theology to be targeting only socioeconomic and political structures, to the neglect of personal dehumanization.[35]

Asian theologians interpret liberation as humanization in order to incorporate the individual. Their context lends itself to this interpretation with its emphasis on personal salvation in many Asian religions. In addition, it is unrealistic to suppose that a small Asian Christian church can alter political structures in the way that Latin American liberation theology suggests. While structural liberation is difficult in Asia, liberation as humanization is more likely if the church would side with the poor and participate in all Asian movements for justice. In North America, feminist and black theologians emphasize that liberation entails a confrontation with the ideology of domination whose goal is to legitimize the domination of women by men and blacks by whites. In this instance, liberation involves the opening of minds long closed by generations of prejudice. African liberation theology in both South Africa and independent Africa comes the closest to providing a model of integral liberation, for it encompasses all aspects, including spiritual and physical wholeness, political structures, landownership, and equilibrium within the community.

What this review accomplishes is to demonstrate once again the diversity that provides fertile soil for continuing conversation. Even among those with a similar commitment to liberation, let alone among those who divide themselves over the issue of liberation versus inculturation, there is ample opportunity for enlightening conversation.

### Issue No. 4: Scandal of Particularity

During a seminar in Nairobi a graduate student from Madagascar confided that the most critical obstacle to his becoming a Christian had been Jesus' nonmembership in his African tribe. This issue, though framed by the student in African terms, pervades contextual theologies. The feminist theologian Letty Russell adopts G. Kittel's phrase "the scandal of particularity" to express this conundrum: How can one particular person, Jesus, become relevant to people of another tribe, race, or gender? The answers to this question, as diverse as the contexts in which they are raised, indicate the presence of an opportunity for further conversation.

For African theologians, the problem of Jesus' non-African status is a perennial issue. They answer that Jesus' adoption of a particular culture is the key to his relevance for Africa.[36] Also, Jesus' participation in Palestinian culture means that he now communicates through, not apart from, culture.[37] He cannot now come to Africa as a disembodied message or Western symbol, for "the Christ of faith can be authentically seen by an African only through his culture and thinking categories."[38] In addition, they acknowledge that Jesus can become one of them because he himself has gone through the rites of passage that made him a mature member of his own community.

In contrast to Africans, Asian theologians usually respond to the scandal of particularity by underscoring the universal significance of Jesus. For some, suffering is the enduring element of Jesus' life because it is the universal experience of suffering that engages the hearts of Asians. For others, Jesus' universal presence exists within religious traditions other than Christianity. The nature of that presence is subject to divergent interpretations. For Panikkar, Christ is a universal presence that is accessible at the deepest experience of mystery. He is the unknown reality to which Christians give the name Christ. Thomas, in contrast, conjectures that it is the example of Jesus, not the unknown Christ, whom Asians, such as Mahatma Gandhi, have acknowledged. Jesus' example, then, provides a persistent impetus for justice beyond the borders of the church. However, Thomas and others discern Christ's cosmic lordship in secular and religious movements for justice, even where he is not consciously acknowledged.

Through human suffering, mystical experience, historical example, and cosmic lordship, Christ has a universal impact on the transformation of Asia.

Feminists find Jesus' particularity especially scandalous. "For women the scandal is seen . . . most importantly in his *maleness*. . . . How is it possible for this male to be the bearer of God's togetherness with women and men when he represents only one half of the human race in this respect?"[39] Despite their reservations about Jesus' maleness, feminist proponents of liberation and reconciliation turn readily to the particularity of his life to mitigate this scandal. They refer to his life to establish that Jesus must be seen as a human who incorporated male and female qualities in his person, praxis, relationships, and view of God. His humanness rather than his maleness shapes Jesus' universal significance. Analogously, the community he called into existence is universal in scope—a new humanity of female and male released from the ideology of domination.

Black theologians in South Africa and North America proffer three ways in which the particularity of Jesus has significance for the black community. First, Cleage argues that "the historic truth" of Christianity is "that Jesus was the non-white leader of a non-white people struggling for national liberation against the rule of a white nation, Rome."[40] Therefore Cleage appeals directly to the particularity of Jesus' blackness to support his contention that Jesus' presence is located in the Black Power movement.

Although no black theologian accepts Cleage's interpretation, Cone adapts it by interpreting blackness as a universal symbol of God's identification with the oppressed. The particular, historical Jesus, who suffered with the oppressed to the point of death, is now the universal Christ who continues his work among the oppressed. In this respect, the risen Christ is black, for blackness is the quintessential symbol of oppression in North America and South Africa.

There is a third strain among black theologians that regards Christ's symbolic blackness as an integral but partial step toward universal reconciliation. Although Christ as liberator is "particularized for the black Christian in the black experience of the black Messiah,"[41] he is also the universal Christ, "the desire of all nations," who breaks through color lines to reconcile all people.[42]

The historical particularity of Jesus' life and death becomes universal as a model for liberation in Latin America. The life of Jesus demonstrates that the reign of God occurs in concrete human liberation which takes place, first and foremost, in history. His life is, therefore, a model of liberation for Latin American Christians. The death of Jesus confirms that the reign of God has a political dimension, for no matter how much Jesus used religious language to proclaim God's reign, he was ultimately crucified as a political criminal. His death demonstrates that political activity is a necessary medium of liberation. Without the resurrection, however, the life and death of Jesus can be considered worthwhile but particular, expendable models of behavior. The resurrection confirms and continues *within history* the inexorable process toward liberation that Jesus' life and death initiated.

These responses to the scandal of particularity raise another question: Does Jesus' relevance to a particular culture or group of people undermine his potential for universal significance? For Asians, the context of religiosity points naturally to Jesus' presence beyond the particular Christian community. Also, theologians who stress reconciliation have already made provision for Jesus' universal vision of a new humanity. But the response to the scandal of particularity by Africans and liberation theologians necessitates further elucidation.

African theologians can respond in two ways to the particularity of Jesus. They can answer in general that, if Jesus comes to Africa through African culture, he comes also to other peoples through their own cultures. They also answer with categories from within African culture. Jesus enters African life through the rites of passage, and his exemplary life and resurrection transform him into the greatest of ancestors. As Proto-Ancestor, he brings all Africans into a new family that transcends national and tribal boundaries. Thus, Jesus' particular entry into African rites of passage leads to his universal position as the greatest of ancestors who restores proper equilibrium between all human communities.

Many liberation theologians throughout the globe raise the question of Jesus' particularity to a new level because they contend that the universal significance of Jesus is evident today in God's particular preference for the oppressed. In other words, the universal message of Jesus' life, death, and resurrection is that God is not, after all, universal. If God has a preference for the poor, then God opposes the powerful elite. If the risen Jesus lounges on the streetcorners of the ghetto, then he is not to be found in the backyards of the suburbs.

This contention seems to limit the universal significance of Jesus. It does not, however. What it does demand is that universality be understood in historical terms. From this perspective, God's universal love takes on different forms in concrete situations, just as it did during Jesus' ministry. Jesus was for the poor by shouldering their cause, but he was for the rich by denouncing their dehumanizing commitment to money. His contentious denigration of the powerful and his blessing of the poor were both motivated by a love that yearned for all people to share in the full humanity of God's reign.

The majority of contextual theologians refer specifically to the relationship between Jesus' particularity and universality. African and liberation theologians move from the particularity of Jesus to his universality. The scenario is different for Asian theologians, who emphasize the universal presence of Christ within the suffering and religiosity of Asia. The particularity of Jesus plays for them a modest role. These tendencies cannot, however, obscure the different hues of this issue for each context. Therefore, this common concern can be a productive topic of conversation in the ongoing global attempt to ascertain the enduring relevance of Jesus.

## A Final Word

Jesus foresaw a day when "people will come from east and west, from north and south, and will eat in the kingdom of God." By joining the global conversation in Christology, Christians have the unique opportunity of anticipating that banquet. But Jesus' words do not stop there; he continues, "Indeed, some are last who will be first, and some are first who will be last."[43] Conversations can be unsettling. Conversations can also be life changing.

## NOTES

1. Brock, *Journey by Heart*, 80; and Schoffeleers, "Folk Christology," 162.

2. Segundo, *Historical Jesus*, 17.

3. Sobrino, *Crossroads*, 203–204; Song, *Jesus, the Crucified People*, 58–79; and Schüssler Fiorenza, *In Memory of Her*, 133, 148–151.

4. Mofokeng, *Crossbearers*, 28.

5. Setiloane, "I Am an African," 79.

6. Sobrino, *Crossroads*, 223.

7. Song, *Jesus, the Crucified People*, 215.

8. Tissa Balasuriya, *Planetary Theology* (Maryknoll, N.Y.: Orbis Books, 1984), 186.

9. Sobrino, *Crossroads*, 377.

10. Their concern is that Marxism is too reductionistic because it accomplishes only a sociological analysis. Pieris calls for a corresponding psychological analysis. "A 'liberation-theopraxis' in Asia that uses only the Marxist tools of social analysis will remain un-Asian and ineffective. It must integrate the psychological tools of introspection that our sages have discovered" (Pieris, *An Asian Theology*, 80–81). The same is true of a "social reading" of the Bible; it must not succumb to "the sociological reductionism of a strictly Marxist approach." A "religious reading" must accompany the social reading (George Soares Prabhu, "Towards an Indian Interpretation of the Bible," *Biblebhashyam* 6 [March 1980]: 168).

M. M. Thomas is a rare example of an Asian theologian who uses social analysis throughout his works. See Thomas, *The Christian Response to the Asian Revolution*; idem, *Salvation and Humanisation*; and idem, *Towards a Theology of Contemporary Ecumenism*.

11. Cone, *For My People*, 88.

12. See Obijole, "South African Liberation Theologies of Boesak and Tutu," 201–215; and Mosala, *Biblical Hermeneutics and Black Theology*, 13–42.

13. Brock, *Journeys by Heart*, 1–57.

14. Susan Brooks Thistlethwaite, "Every Two Minutes: Battered Women and Feminist Interpretation," in *Weaving the Visions: New Patterns in Feminist Spirituality*, ed. Judith Plaskow and Carol Christ (San Francisco: Harper & Row, 1989), 302–313.

15. See Gonzalo Castillo-Cárdenas, *Liberation Theology from Below: The Life and Thought of Manuel Quintín Lame* (Maryknoll, N.Y.: Orbis Books, 1987). The book consists of two parts: an introduction to Lame and his writing, and a translation of Lame's *Pensamientos*.

Castillo-Cárdenas raises the same question about the ability of liberation theologians to embrace the cultural and ethnic diversity within Latin America. "Can the ideological perspective adopted by liberation theology take full account of the uniqueness and the specific historical potential of the 'Indian consciousness' that permeates Lame's thought, as a reality distinct, for example, from 'class consciousness'?" (ibid., 95).

16. One example of Asian Christian communities is the collection of stories about house churches in China. Raymond Fung, comp. and ed., *Households of God on China's Soil*, WCC Mission Series, no. 2 (Geneva: WCC Publications, 1982).

17. On this suspicion, see Juan Luis Segundo, *Liberation of Theology* (Maryknoll, N.Y.: Orbis Books, 1976); and Schüssler Fiorenza, *Bread Not Stone*.

18. E.g., Boesak, *Farewell to Innocence*, 41–45; and idem, *Black and Reformed*, 10–15.

19. Nyamiti, "African Christologies Today," 35.

20. E.g., Boff, *Liberator*, 209–217.

21. Schüssler Fiorenza, *In Memory of Her*, 106.

22. Song, *Jesus, the Crucified People*, 73.

23. Boff, *Liberator*, 75.

24. Echegaray, *Practice of Jesus*, 56. According to F. Eboussi Boulaga of Africa, the Pharisaic interpretation consists of external legalism: "places the whole content of revelation in a corpus of usages, precepts, formulas, dispositions, and habits, which it identifies immediately with the will of God" (*Christianity With-*

*out Fetishes: An African Critique and Recapture of Christianity* [Maryknoll, N.Y.: Orbis Books, 1984], 102).

25. Pieris, *An Asian Theology*, 63.

26. Rosemary Radford Ruether, *To Change the World: Christology and Cultural Criticism* (New York: Crossroad, 1981), 37.

27. "Jesus was opposed to the religionism of the Jews. They were proud of being called the chosen people and proud of their religion as a legal system whose external performance was thought to be salvific. But all religionism is incompatible with Jesus' view. . . . Insofar as Christianity is religionist, it militates against Jesus' respect for and God's love of all human beings" (Balasuriya, *Planetary Theology*, 184).

28. E.g., James H. Charlesworth, *Jesus Within Judaism: New Light from Exciting Archaeological Discoveries* (New York: Doubleday & Co., 1988); John Riches, *Jesus and the Transformation of Judaism* (London: Darton, Longman & Todd, 1980); E. P. Sanders, *Jesus and Judaism* (Philadelphia: Fortress Press, 1985); and Géza Vermès, *Jesus the Jew: A Historian's Reading of the Gospel* (Philadelphia: Fortress Press, 1983).

29. R. Schreiter (*Constructing Local Theologies*, 12–16) names these two approaches to contextual theology as "ethnographic"—one that deals with issues of cultural identity and as "liberation"—one that deals with issues of "oppression and social ills."

30. Pieris describes Latin American liberation theology as being a "Christ-*against*-religions" theology rather than a "Christ-*of*-religions" theology. See Pieris, *An Asian Theology*, 88–93. See also *International Review of Mission* 69 (1980): 519.

31. John S. Mbiti, "An African Views American Black Theology," in *Black Theology: A Documentary History*, ed. Cone and Wilmore, 479.

32. Éla, *My Faith*, 173.

33. Mbiti, "An African Views American Black Theology," 482.

34. James H. Cone, "A Black American Perspective on the Future of African Theology," in *African Theology en Route*, ed. Appiah-Kubi and Torres, 183–184.

35. Asian theologians are especially strong in incorporating the personal aspect along with the structural. ". . . the liberation envisaged here is a total liberation and that it should not be reduced to a more political or social one" (Vellanickal, "Jesus the Poor and His Gospel to the Poor," 54). In contrast to an either/or

approach to liberation of the individual or the structures, Pieris states that "biblical revelation seems to advocate a unitary perception of all these aspects of liberation . . . —personal/social, spiritual/material, internal/structural" (Pieris, *An Asian Theology*, 123).

In addition, there was strong reaction by Asian theologians to the preference given to a Latin American perspective on liberation theology at the 1980 WCC Melbourne Conference. "Liberation theology, born in Latin America, . . . cannot now take the place of western theology in Asia. Not because we do not stand in need of liberation. Simply because the liberation we must have is from *our* captivities, and for such liberation we need other perspectives and other sensitivities.

Our captivities include the captivity of the traditional Christian understanding of other religions. We need liberation into dialogue, for the liberation we seek cannot be apart from the total liberation of all our peoples" ("An Asian Comment . . . ," *International Review of Mission* 69 [1980]: 519).

36. Bediako reverses the order, particular-universal, suggesting that Jesus' universality, rather than his particularity, is the key to his relevance for Africa, for Jesus' significance as Jewish Messiah did not arise so much in the course of his life as in the achievement of his resurrection (Bediako, "Biblical Christologies," 111–112). According to Kurewa, the ascension and Pentecost represent the universalization and particularization: "What makes Jesus of Nazareth seem foreign is failure by the Church to recognize the theological significance of his ascension which removed him from the attachment to one culture and the theological significance of Pentecost which means all people on earth need to hear the gospel in thought-forms and in language of their own (Acts 2:8)" (Kurewa, "Who Do You Say that I Am?" 188).

37. Aylward Shorter, *Toward a Theology of Inculturation* (Maryknoll, N.Y.: Orbis Books, 1988), 80; see his cautions about using incarnation as the basis of inculturation (ibid., 81–83). See also Carvahlo, "What Do the Africans Say that Jesus Christ Is?" 22; and David Gitari, "The Claims of Jesus in the African Context," *International Review of Mission* 71 (1982), 12–14.

38. Okolo, "Christ, 'Emmanuel': An African Inquiry," 17. See also Ambrose M. Moyo, "The Quest for African Christian Theology and the Problem of the Relationship Between Faith and

Culture—The Hermeneutical Perspective," *Africa Theological Journal* 12 (1983): 102–103.

39. Russell, *Human Liberation*, 137–138.

40. Cleage, *The Black Messiah*, 3.

41. Roberts, *Liberation and Reconciliation*, 140.

42. Roberts, *A Black Political Theology*, 119–120; and idem, *Liberation and Reconciliation*, 136–138, 152–153.

43. Luke 13:29–30.

# Bibliography

### Chapter 1: Conversations in Christology

Abesamis, Carlos. "Doing Theological Reflection in a Philippine Context." In *The Emergent Gospel*, ed. Torres and Fabella, 112–123.

Brown, Robert McAfee. "Diversity and Inclusiveness." *Church and Society* 67 (1977): 52–58.

———."A Preface and a Conclusion." In *Theology in the Americas*, ed. Torres and Eagleson, ix–xxviii.

Bultmann, Rudolf. "Is Exegesis Without Presuppositions Possible?" In *Existence and Faith: Shorter Writings of Rudolf Bultmann*, edited by Schubert M. Ogden, 289–296. London: Hodder & Stoughton, 1961.

———."The Problem of Hermeneutics." In *Essays Philosophical and Theological*, 234–261. London: SCM Press, 1955.

Cadbury, Henry J. *The Perils of Modernizing Jesus*. New York: Macmillan Co., 1937.

Cardenal, Ernesto, ed. *The Gospel in Solentiname*. Maryknoll, N.Y.: Orbis Books, 1976–1982.

"Doing Theology in a Divided World: Final Statement of the Sixth EATWOT Conference." In *Doing Theology in a Divided World*, ed. Fabella and Torres, 179–193.

Dyrness, William A. *Learning About Theology from the Third World*. Grand Rapids: Zondervan Publishing House, 1990.

Endo, Shusaku. *A Life of Jesus*. New York: Paulist Press, 1973.

Fabella, Virginia, and Sergio Torres, eds. *Doing Theology in a Di-*

*vided World*. Papers from the Sixth International Conference of the Ecumenical Association of Third World Theologians, January 5–13, 1983, Geneva, Switzerland. Maryknoll, N.Y.: Orbis Books, 1985.

Gadamer, H.-G. *Truth and Method*. Second edition. New York: Crossroad, 1990.

Grant, Robert M., and David Tracy. *A Short History of the Interpretation of the Bible*. Second edition. Philadelphia: Fortress Press, 1984.

Kraft, Charles H. *Christianity in Culture: A Study in Dynamic Biblical Theologizing in Cross-Cultural Perspective*. Maryknoll, N.Y.: Orbis Books, 1979.

Mbiti, John S. "Theological Impotence and the Universality of the Church." In *Third World Theologies*, edited by Gerald H. Anderson and Thomas F. Stransky, 6–18. Mission Trends No. 3. New York: Paulist Press, 1976.

Pelikan, Jaroslav. *Jesus Through the Centuries: His Place in the History of Culture*. New Haven, Conn.: Yale University Press, 1985.

Schreiter, Robert. *Constructing Local Theologies*. Maryknoll, N.Y.: Orbis Books, 1985.

Schweitzer, Albert. *The Quest of the Historical Jesus: A Critical Study of Its Progress from Reimarus to Wrede*. New York: Macmillan Co., 1959.

Tano, Rodrigo. *Theology in the Philippine Setting*. Quezon City: New Day Publishers, 1981.

Thiselton, Anthony C. *The Two Horizons: New Testament Hermeneutics and Philosophical Description with Special Reference to Heidegger, Bultmann, Gadamer, and Wittgenstein*. Grand Rapids: Wm. B. Eerdmans Publishing Co., 1980.

Torres Gonzalez, Sergio. "Dar-es-Salaam 1976." In *Convergences and Differences*, Concilium Series, edited by Leonardo Boff and Virgil Elizondo, 107–115. Edinburgh: T. & T. Clark, 1988.

Torres, Sergio, and John Eagleson, eds. *Theology in the Americas*. Maryknoll, N.Y.: Orbis Books, 1976.

Torres, Sergio, and Virginia Fabella, eds. *The Emergent Gospel: Theology from the Underside of History*. Papers from the Ecumenical Dialogue of Third World Theologians, Dar es Salaam, August 5–12, 1976. Maryknoll, N.Y.: Orbis Books, 1978.

Walls, Andrew F. "Towards Understanding Africa's Place in

Christian History." In *Religion in a Pluralistic Society,* edited by John S. Pobee, 180–189. Leiden: E. J. Brill, 1976.

Wessels, Anton. *Images of Jesus: How Jesus Is Perceived and Portrayed in Non-European Cultures.* Grand Rapids: Wm. B. Eerdmans Publishing Co., 1990.

## Chapter 2: Jesus in Latin America

Arias, Esther, and Mortimer Arias. *The Cry of My People: Out of Captivity in Latin America.* New York: Friendship Press, 1980.

Arias, Mortimer. *Announcing the Reign of God: Evangelization and the Subversive Memory of Jesus.* Philadelphia: Fortress Press, 1984.

Batstone, David. *From Conquest to Struggle: Jesus of Nazareth in Latin America.* Albany, N.Y.: State University of New York Press, 1991.

Beeson, Trevor, and Jenny Pearce. *A Vision of Hope: The Churches and Change in Latin America.* Philadelphia: Fortress Press, 1984.

Boff, Leonardo. *Desde el Lugar del Pobre.* Second edition. Bogotá: Ediciones Paulinas, 1986.

————. *Jesus Christ Liberator: A Critical Christology for Our Time.* Maryknoll, N.Y.: Orbis Books, 1978.

Boff, Leonardo, and Clodovis Boff. *Introducing Liberation Theology.* Maryknoll, N.Y.: Orbis Books, 1987.

Bussmann, Claus. *Who Do You Say? Jesus Christ in Latin American Theology.* Maryknoll, N.Y.: Orbis Books, 1985.

Cleary, Edward. *Crisis and Change: The Church in Latin America Today.* Maryknoll, N.Y.: Orbis Books, 1985.

Cook, Michael. "Jesus from the Other Side of History: Christology in Latin America," *Theological Studies* 44 (1983): 258–287.

Costas, Orlando. *Christ Outside the Gate: Mission Beyond Christendom.* Maryknoll, N.Y.: Orbis Books, 1982.

Croatto, J. Severino. "The Political Dimension of Christ the Liberator." In *Faces of Jesus,* ed. Míguez Bonino, 102–122.

Eagleson, John, and Philip Scharper, eds. *Puebla and Beyond: Documentation and Commentary.* Maryknoll, N.Y.: Orbis Books, 1979.

Echegaray, Hugo. *The Practice of Jesus.* Maryknoll, N.Y.: Orbis Books, 1984.

Ellacuría, Ignacio. "The Political Nature of Jesus' Mission." In *Faces of Jesus,* ed. Míguez Bonino, 79–92.

Freire, Paulo. *Education for Critical Consciousness.* New York: Seabury Press, 1973.

———. *Pedagogy of the Oppressed.* New York: Penguin Books, 1970.

———. *The Politics of Education: Culture, Power, and Liberation.* South Hadley, Mass.: Bergin & Garvey, 1985.

Galilea, Segundo. *The Beatitudes: To Evangelize As Jesus Did.* Maryknoll, N.Y.: Orbis Books, 1984.

———. *Following Jesus.* Maryknoll, N.Y.: Orbis Books, 1981.

———. "Jesus' Attitude Toward Politics: Some Working Hypotheses." In *Faces of Jesus,* ed. Míguez Bonino, 93–101.

Gudorf, C. E. "Liberation Theology's Use of Scripture: A Response to First World Critics," *Interpretation* 41 (1987): 5–18.

Gutiérrez, Gustavo. "Latin America's Pain Is Bearing Fruit," *Latinamerica Press* (May 26, 1983): 5–6, 8.

———. *The Power of the Poor in History: Selected Writings.* London: SCM Press, 1983.

———. "Statement by Gustavo Gutiérrez." In *Theology in the Americas,* ed. Torres and Eagleson, 309–313.

———. *A Theology of Liberation: History, Politics, and Salvation.* Rev. ed. Maryknoll, N.Y.: Orbis Books, 1973.

Mackie, Steven. "Praxis as the Context for Interpretation: A Study of Latin American Liberation Theology." *Journal of Theology for Southern Africa* 24 (1978): 31–43.

Míguez Bonino, José. *Doing Theology in a Revolutionary Situation.* Philadelphia: Fortress Press, 1975.

———. *Room to Be People.* Philadelphia: Fortress Press, 1979.

———, ed. *Faces of Jesus: Latin American Christologies.* Maryknoll, N.Y.: Orbis Books, 1984.

Richard, Pablo. *Death of Christendoms, Birth of the Church.* Maryknoll, N.Y.: Orbis Books, 1987.

Secretariat for Latin America. *The Medellín Conclusions.* The Church in the Present-Day Transformation of Latin America in the Light of the Council. Second General Conference of Latin American Bishops. Third edition. Washington, D.C.: National Conference of Catholic Bishops, 1979.

Segundo, Juan Luis. *The Historical Jesus of the Synoptics.* Jesus of Nazareth Yesterday and Today, Volume II. Maryknoll, N.Y.: Orbis Books, 1985.

Skidmore, Thomas, and Peter Smith. *Modern Latin America.* New York: Oxford University Press, 1984.

Sobrino, Jon. *Christology at the Crossroads.* Maryknoll, N.Y.: Orbis Books, 1978.

———. *Jesus in Latin America.* Maryknoll, N.Y.: Orbis Books, 1987.

———. *The True Church and the Poor.* London: SCM Press, 1984.

Tamez, Elsa. *The Bible of the Oppressed.* Maryknoll, N.Y.: Orbis Books, 1982.

Tamez, Elsa, ed. *Through Her Eyes: Women's Theology from Latin America.* Maryknoll, N.Y.: Orbis Books, 1989.

Trinidad, Saúl. "Christology, *Conquista*, Colonization." In *Faces of Jesus*, ed. Míguez Bonino, 49–65.

## Chapter 3: Jesus in Asia

Abesamis, Carlos. "Faith and Life Reflections from the Grassroots in the Philippines." In *Asia's Struggle For Full Humanity*, ed. Fabella, 123–139.

Amalorpavadass, D. S. "The Bible in Self-Renewal and Church Renewal for Service to Society." In *On Interpreting the Bible. Voices from the Third World*, 55–65. EATWOT, 1987.

———. "The Indian Universe of a New Theology." In *The Emergent Gospel*, ed. Torres and Fabella, 137–156.

———. "New Theological Approaches in Asia," *Verbum SVD* 21 (3/4, 1980): 279–301.

———, ed. Papers from the 1974 *Research Seminar on Non-Biblical Scriptures.* Bangalore: NBCLC, 1975.

Asian Report Group. "Toward a Relevant Theology in Asia." In *Irruption of the Third World*, ed. Fabella and Torres, 61–76.

Balasuriya, Tissa. *The Eucharist and Human Liberation.* London: SCM Press, 1979.

Banawiratma, J. B. "JESUS SANG GURU, Pertemuan Kejawen dengan Injil." Ph.D. Dissertation, Yogya, 1977.

Bastiaens, J., E. v. d. Peet, and E. Megant (under the direction of P. G. van Hooijdonk). "Jesus as Guru—A Christology in the Context of Java (Indonesia)," *Exchange* 13, no. 39 (1984): 33–57.

Bok, Kim Yung. "Minjung Social Biography and Theology," *Ching Feng* 28 (1985): 221–231.

Boyd, R. H. S. *An Introduction to Indian Christian Theology.* Revised edition. Madras: Christian Literature Society, 1975.

Bürkle, H. "The Debate of the 'Cosmic Christ' as Example of an Ecumenically Oriented Theology." In *Indian Voices in Today's Theological Debate*, edited by H. Bürkle and W. M. W. Roth, 198–214. Lucknow: Lucknow with ISPCK, Christian Literature Society, 1972.

Chandran, J. R. "Jesus: Freedom Fighter or Prince of Peace?" *Indian Journal of Theology* 24 (1975): 96–103.

de la Torre, Edicio. *Touching Ground, Taking Root: Theological and Political Reflections on the Philippines Struggle*. London: Catholic Institute for International Relations, 1986.

Devanandan, Paul D. "Called to Witness," *Ecumenical Review* 14 (1962): 155–163.

Digan, Parig. *Churches in Contestation: Asian Christian Social Protest*. Maryknoll, N.Y.: Orbis Books, 1984.

Duraisingh, J. C., and K. C. Abraham. "Reflections from an Asian Perspective." In *Irruption of the Third World*, ed. Fabella and Torres, 209–216.

England, John C., ed. *Living Theology in Asia*. Maryknoll, N.Y.: Orbis Books, 1982.

Fabella, Virginia, ed. *Asia's Struggle for Full Humanity: Towards a Relevant Theology*. Papers from the Asian Theological Conference, January 7–20, 1979, Wennappuwa, Sri Lanka. Maryknoll, N.Y.: Orbis Books, 1980.

Fabella, Virginia, and Sergio Torres, eds. *Irruption of the Third World: Challenge to Theology*. Papers from the Fifth International Conference of the Ecumenical Association of Third world Theologians, August 17–29, 1981, New Delhi, India. Maryknoll, N.Y.: Orbis Books, 1983.

Fabella, Virginia, and Sun Ai Lee Park, eds. *We Dare to Dream: Doing Theology as Asian Women*. Maryknoll, N.Y.: Orbis Books, 1989.

Galloway, Allan D. *The Cosmic Christ*. New York: Harper & Brothers, 1951.

Gispert-Sauch, G. "Inspiration and Extra Biblical Scriptures: Some Tentative Propositions," *Indian Theological Studies* 20 (1983): 16–36.

Kappen, Sebastian. *Jesus and Freedom*. Maryknoll, N.Y.: Orbis Books, 1977.

———. "The Man Jesus: Rupture and Communion," *Religion and Society* 23 (1976): 66–76.

Kitamori, Kazo. *Theology of the Pain of God*. Richmond: John Knox Press, 1965.

Koyama, Kosuke. *Mount Fuji and Mount Sinai: A Pilgrimage in Theology*. London: SCM, 1984.

———. *Three Mile an Hour God*. London: SCM, 1979.

———. *Waterbuffalo Theology*. London: SCM Press, 1974.

Kurian, K. Matthew. "Socio-Economic and Political Reality in Asia." In *Asia's Struggle for Full Humanity*, ed. Fabella, 59–74.

Lan, Kwok Pui. "God Weeps with Our Pain," *East Asia Journal of Theology* 2 (1984): 228–232.

Lee, Peter K. H. "Nothingness and Fulfillment: From Laozi's Concept of *Wu* to Jesus' Theology on the Kingdom of God." *Ching Feng* 29 (1986): 106–128.

———. "Rereading Ecclesiastes in the Light of Su Ting-P'o's Poetry." *Ching Feng* 30 (1987): 214–236.

Lee, Peter K. H., with Shih Heng-Ching. "Karma and Christ," *Ching Feng* 31 (1988): 24–47.

Lee, Peter K. H., with Wing Yuk. "Ta-T'ung and the Kingdom of God," *Ching Feng* 31 (1988): 225–244.

Legrand, L. "Christological Issues in the New Testament," *Indian Journal of Theology* 24 (1975): 71–78.

Mackie, Steven. "People Power and Lady Meng," *The Modern Churchman* 32 (1991): 1–10.

NBCLC. "The Indian Church in the Struggle for a New Society," *Indian Missiological Review* 4 (1982): 13–56.

Niles, D. Preman. "A Continuing Ecumenical Journey—Report of the Secretary for Theological Concerns, CCA January 1983," *CTC Bulletin* 4 (1983): 46–64.

Panikkar, Raimundo. *The Unknown Christ of Hinduism: Towards an Ecumenical Christophany*. Revised and enlarged edition. Maryknoll, N.Y.: Orbis Books, 1981.

Pieris, Aloysius. *An Asian Theology of Liberation*. Maryknoll, N.Y.: Orbis Books, 1988.

———. "Ecumenism and Asia's Search for Christ," *The Month* 239 (1978): 4–9.

———. *Love Meets Wisdom: A Christian Experience of Buddhism*. Faith Meets Faith Series. Maryknoll, N.Y.: Orbis Books, 1988.

———. "Towards an Asian Theology of Liberation: Some Religio-Cultural Guidelines." In *Asia's Struggle for Full Humanity*, ed. Fabella, 75–95.

Rayan, Samuel. *Breath of Fire, The Holy Spirit: Heart of the Christian Gospel.* Maryknoll, N.Y.: Orbis Books, 1978.

———. "Reconceiving Theology in the Asian Context." In *Doing Theology in a Divided World*, ed. Fabella and Torres, 124–142.

Samartha, S. J. *The Hindu Response to the Unbound Christ.* Bangalore: CISRS; and Madras: Christian Literature Society, 1974.

———. "Indian Realities and the Wholeness of Christ," *Indian Missiological Review* 4 (1982): 256–274.

Schumann, H. Wolfgang. *Buddhism: An Outline of Its Teachings and Schools.* London: Rider & Co., 1973.

Shoji, Tsutomu. "The Church's Struggle for Freedom of Belief—An Aspect of Christian Mission." In *Living Theology in Asia*, ed. England, 49–57.

Singh, Godwin R. "Editorial: Christology in the Indian Context," *National Christian Council Review* 107 (1987): 1–3.

Sittler, Joseph. "Called to Unity," *Ecumenical Review* 14 (1962): 177–187.

Song, C. S. *The Compassionate God.* Maryknoll, N.Y.: Orbis Books, 1982.

———. *Jesus, the Crucified People.* New York: Crossroad, 1990.

———. *The Tears of Lady Meng: A Parable of People's Political Theology.* Risk Book Series. Geneva: WCC Publications, 1981.

———. *Tell Us Our Names.* Maryknoll, N.Y.: Orbis Books, 1984.

———. *Theology from the Womb of Asia.* Maryknoll, N.Y.: Orbis Books, 1986.

———. *Third Eye Theology: Theology in Formation in Asian Settings.* Maryknoll, N.Y.: Orbis Books, 1979.

Thomas, M. M. "The Absoluteness of Jesus Christ and Christ-centred Syncretism." *Ecumenical Review* 37 (1985): 387–397.

———. *The Acknowleged Christ of the Indian Renaissance.* London: SCM Press, 1969.

———. *The Christian Response to the Asian Revolution.* London: SCM Press, 1964.

———. "The Meaning of Salvation Today—A Personal Statement," *International Review of Mission* 62 (1973): 158–169.

———. *Risking Christ for Christ's Sake: Towards an Ecumenical Theology of Pluralism.* Geneva: WCC Publications, 1987.

———. *Salvation and Humanisation.* Madras: Christian Literature Society, 1971.

———. "Theological Aspects of the Relationships Between Social Action Groups and Churches," *Religion and Society* 31 (1984): 17–23.

―――. *Towards a Theology of Contemporary Ecumenism.* Madras: Christian Literature Society, 1978.

―――. "Uppsala 1968 and the Contemporary Theological Situation," *Scottish Journal of Theology* 23 (1970): 41–50.

Ting, K. H. *Chinese Christians Speak Out—Addresses and Sermons.* China Spotlight Series. Beijing: New World, 1984.

―――. "Opening Address Before the Third Chinese National Christian Conference," *Voices From The Third World* 8 (1985): 88–104.

Vellanickal, Matthew. "The Hermeneutical Problem in Christology Today," *Biblebhashyam* 6 (1980): 5–17.

―――. "Jesus the Poor and His Gospel to the Poor," *Biblebhashyam* 9 (1983): 52–64.

Weber, Hans-Ruedi. *Asia and the Ecumenical Movement, 1895–1961.* London: SCM Press, 1966.

Wickremesinghe, C. Lackshman. "Alienated Church and Signs of the Times." In *Living Theology in Asia,* ed. England, 183–190.

―――. "The Cosmic Christ and Its Relation to Mission Today—Some Notes for Discussion," *CTC Bulletin* 5 (1984): 1–2, 39–46.

―――. "Living in Christ with People." In *A Call to Vulnerable Discipleship,* CCA Seventh Assembly (1981): 25–49.

Wilfred, Felix. "The Liberation Process in India and the Church's Participation," *Indian Theological Studies* 25 (1988): 301–333.

Young-Hak, Hyun. "A Theological Look at the Mask Dance in Korea." In *Minjung Theology: People as the Subjects of History,* edited by Commission on Theological Concerns of the Christian Conference of Asia, 47–54. Maryknoll, N.Y.: Orbis Books, 1981).

## Chapter 4: Jesus in Africa

AACC. *Engagement.* Second AACC Assembly "Abidjan 69." Nairobi: AACC, 1969.

―――. *The Struggle Continues.* Official Report of the Third Assembly of the All Africa Conference of Churches, Lusaka, Zambia, May 12–24, 1974. Nairobi: AACC, 1975.

Appiah-Kubi, Kofi. "Why African Theology?" *AACC Bulletin* 7 (1974): 3–8.

―――. "Indigenous African Christian Churches: Signs of Authenticity." In *African Theology en Route*, ed. Appiah-Kubi and Torres, 117–125.

Appiah-Kubi, Kofi, and Sergio Torres, eds. *African Theology en Route*. Papers from the Pan-African Conference of Third World Theologians, December 17–23, 1977, Accra, Ghana. Maryknoll, N.Y.: Orbis Books, 1979.

Bediako, Kwame. "Biblical Christologies in the Context of African Traditional Religions." In *Sharing Jesus in the Two Thirds World: Evangelical Christologies from the Contexts of Poverty, Powerlessness and Religious Pluralism*, edited by Vinay Samuel and Chris Sugden, 115–176. Grand Rapids: Wm. B. Eerdmans Publishing Co., 1984.

Biko, Steve. "Black Consciousness and the Quest for a True Humanity," *AACC Bulletin* 11, no. 1 (1978): 6–10.

Boesak, Allan. *Black and Reformed: Apartheid, Liberation and the Calvinist Tradition*. Maryknoll, N.Y.: Orbis Books, 1984.

―――. *Farewell to Innocence: A Socio-Ethical Study on Black Theology and Black Power*. Maryknoll, N.Y.: Orbis Books, 1977.

Bujo, Bénézet. *Afrikanische Theologie in ihrem gesellschaftlichen Kontext*. Düsseldorf: Patmos Verlag, 1986.

―――. "A Christocentric Ethic for Black Africa," *Theology Digest* 30 (1982): 143–146.

Buthelezi, Manas. "Daring to Live for Christ." In *Third World Theologies*, edited by Gerald H. Anderson and Thomas F. Stransky, 176–180. Mission Trends 3. New York: Paulist Press; and Grand Rapids: Wm. B. Eerdmans Publishing Co., 1976.

―――. "Reconciliation and Liberation in Southern Africa." In *African Challenge*, edited by Kenneth Y. Best, 43–49. Nairobi: AACC, 1975.

―――. "Towards Indigenous Theology in South Africa." In *The Emergent Gospel*, ed. Torres and Fabella, 56–75.

Carr, Burgess. "The Moratorium: The Search for Self-Reliance and Authenticity," *AACC Bulletin* 7 (1974): 36–44.

Carvalho, Emilio J. M. de. "What Do the Africans Say that Jesus Christ Is?" *Africa Theological Journal* 10 (1981): 17–25.

Christensen, Thomas G. "The Gbaya Naming of Jesus: An Inquiry Into the Contextualization of Soteriological Themes

Among the Gbaya of Cameroon." D.Min. Thesis, Lutheran School of Theology, Chicago, 1984.

Cone, James H. "A Black American Perspective on the Future of African Theology." In *African Theology en Route*, ed. Appiah-Kubi and Torres, 176–186.

Cone, James H., and Gayraud S. Wilmore, eds. *Black Theology: A Documentary History, 1966–1979*. Maryknoll, N.Y.: Orbis Books, 1979.

Daneel, Marthinus L. "Towards a Theologia Africana? The Contribution of Independent Churches to African Theology," *Missionalia* 12.2 (1984): 64–89.

Dickson, Kwesi A. *Theology In Africa*. Maryknoll, N.Y.: Orbis Books, 1984.

Dickson, Kwesi A., and Paul Ellingworth, eds. *Biblical Revelation and African Beliefs*. London: Lutterworth Press, 1969.

Donders, Joseph. *Non-Bourgeois Theology: An African Experience of Jesus*. Maryknoll, N.Y.: Orbis Books, 1985.

Éla, Jean-Marc. *African Cry*. Maryknoll, N.Y.: Orbis Books, 1986.

———. *My Faith as an African*. Maryknoll, N.Y.: Orbis Books, 1988.

"Final Communiqué." In *African Theology en Route*, ed. Appiah-Kubi and Torres, 189–195.

Goba, Bonganjalo. "The Black Consciousness Movement: Its Impact on Black Theology." In *The Unquestionable Right To Be Free*, ed. Mosala and Tlhagale, 57–69.

———. "A Black South African Perspective." In *Doing Theology in a Divided World*, ed. Fabella and Torres, 53–58.

———. "Corporate Personality: Ancient Israel and Africa." In *The Challenge of Black Theology*, ed. Moore, 65–73.

———. "Doing Theology in South Africa: A Black Christian Perspective," *Journal of Theology for Southern Africa* 31 (1980): 23–35.

de Gruchy, John. *The Church Struggle in South Africa*. Grand Rapids: Wm. B. Eerdmans Publishing Co., 1979.

Idowu, E. Bolaji. *African Traditional Religion: A Definition*. London: SCM Press, 1973.

Kabasélé, François. "L'au-delà des modèles." In *Chemins de la christologie africaine*, ed. Kabasélé et al., 203–228.

———. "Le Christ comme ancêtre et aîné." In *Chemins de la christologie africaine*, ed. Kabasélé et al., 127–141.

————. "Le Christ comme chef." In *Chemins de la christologie africaine*, ed. Kabasélé et al., 109–126.

Kabasélé, François, et al., eds. *Chemins de la christologie africaine*. Paris: Desclée, 1986.

Kibongi, R. Buana. "Priesthood." In *Biblical Revelation and African Beliefs*, ed. Dickson and Ellingworth, 47–56.

Kobia, Sam. "Elitism, Wealth and the Church," *AACC Bulletin* 11 (1978): 31–41.

Kolié, Célé. "Jésus guérisseur?" In *Chemins de la christologie africaine*, ed. Kabasélé et al., 167–199.

Kretzschmar, Louise. *The Voice of Black Theology in South Africa*. Johannesburg: Ravan, 1986.

Kurewa, J. W. Z. "Who Do You Say that I Am?" *International Review of Mission* 69 (1980): 182–188.

Lamb, David. *The Africans*. New York: Vintage Press, 1987.

Loader, J. A. "The Use of the Bible in Conventional South African Theology." In *Scripture and the Use of Scripture*, ed. Vorster, 1–25.

Lwasa, Damian. "Traditional and Christian Community in Africa." In *African Christian Spirituality*, ed. Shorter, 141–150.

Magesa, Laurenti. "Christ the Liberator and Africa Today." In *Jesus in African Christianity*, ed. Mugambi and Magesa, 79–92.

————. "Towards a Theology of Liberation for Tanzania." In *Christianity in Independent Africa*, edited by Edward Fasholé-Luke, et al., 503–515. Bloomington: Indiana University Press, 1978.

Maimela, Simon. "Black Power and Black Theology in Southern Africa," *Scriptura* 12 (1984): 40–53.

————. "Abp. Desmund Tutu—A Revolutionary Political Priest or a Man of Peace?" In *Hammering Swords Into Ploughshares*, ed. Tlhagale and Mosala, 41–59.

Mbiti, John S. *African Religions and Philosophy*. Garden City, N.Y.: Doubleday & Co., 1970.

————. "Some African Concepts of Christology." In *Christ and the Younger Churches*, edited by C. F. Vicedom, 51–62. London: SPCK, 1972.

————. "ὁ σωτὴρ ἡμῶν as an African Experience." In *Christ and Spirit in the New Testament*, edited by Barnabas Lindars and Stephen S. Smalley, 397–414. Cambridge: Cambridge University Press, 1973.

Mofokeng, Takatso A. "Black Christians, the Bible and Liberation." In *Towards Freedom, Justice and Peace*, Voices from the Third World, 15–24. EATWOT, 1987.

———. *The Crucified Among the Crossbearers: Towards a Black Christology*. Kampen: J. H. Kok, 1983.

Moloney, Raymond. "African Christology," *Theological Studies* 48 (1987): 505–515.

Moore, Basil, ed. *The Challenge of Black Theology in South Africa*. Atlanta: John Knox Press, 1973.

Mosala, Itumeleng J. *Biblical Hermeneutics and Black Theology in South Africa*. Grand Rapids: Wm. B. Eerdmans Publishing Co., 1989.

Mosala, Itumeleng J., and Buti Tlhagale, eds. *The Unquestionable Right To Be Free: Black Theology From South Africa*. Maryknoll, N.Y.: Orbis Books, 1986.

Mosothoane, E. K. "The Use of Scripture in Black Theology." In *Scripture and the Use of Scripture*, ed. Vorster, 28–37.

Motlhabi, Mokgethi. "The Historical Origins of Black Theology." In *The Unquestionable Right To Be Free*, ed. Mosala and Tlhagale, 37–56.

———. "Introduction." In *The Unquestionable Right to Be Free*, ed. Mosala and Tlhagale, viii–xiii.

Mugambi, J. N. K. *African Christian Theology. An Introduction*. Nairobi: Heinemann, 1989.

Mugambi, J. N. K., and Laurenti Magesa, eds. *Jesus in African Christianity: Experimentation and Diversity in African Christology*. Nairobi: Initiatives, 1989.

Mushete, Alphonse N. "The Figure of Jesus in African Theology." In *Christian Identity*, Concilium 196, edited by Christian Duquoc and Casiano Floristán, 73–79. Edinburgh: T. & T. Clark, 1988.

Muzorewa, Gwinyai. *The Origins and Development of African Theology*. Maryknoll, N.Y.: Orbis Books, 1985.

Ngubane, J. B. "Theological Roots of the African Independent Churches." In *The Unquestionable Right To Be Free*, ed. Mosala and Tlhagale, 72–100.

Nyamiti, Charles. "African Christologies Today." In *Jesus in African Christianity*, ed. Mugambi and Magesa, 17–39.

———. *Christ as Our Ancestor: Christology from an African Perspective*. Gweru, Zimbabwe: Mambo Press, 1984.

———. "A Critical Assessment on Some Issues in Today's African Theology," *African Christian Studies* 5 (March 1989): 5–18.

―――. "The Incarnation Viewed from the African Understanding of Person," *African Christian Studies* 6 (March 1990): 3–27, and *African Christian Studies* 6 (June 1990): 23–76.

Obijole, Olubayo. "South African Liberation Theologies of Boesak and Tutu—A Critical Evaluation," *Africa Theological Journal* 16, no. 3 (1987): 201–215.

Oduyoye, Mercy Amba. *Hearing and Knowing: Theological Reflections on Christianity in Africa.* Maryknoll, N.Y.: Orbis Books, 1986.

―――. "The Value of African Religious Beliefs and Practices for Christian Theology." In *African Theology en Route*, ed. Appiah-Kubi and Torres, 109–116.

Okolo, Ch. B. "Christ, 'Emmanuel': An African Inquiry," *Bulletin de Theologie Africaine* 2.3 (1980): 15–22.

Parratt, John. "African Theology and Biblical Hermeneutics," *Africa Theological Journal* 12 (1983): 88–94.

―――. *A Reader in African Christian Theology.* London: SPCK, 1987.

Penoukou, E. J. "Réalité africaine et salut in Jésus-Christ," *Spiritus* 23 (1982): 374–392.

Pityana, Nyameko. "What Is Black Consciousness?" In *The Challenge of Black Theology*, ed. Moore, 58–63.

Pobee, John. *Toward An African Theology.* Nashville: Abingdon Press, 1979.

Ramodibe, Dorothy. "Women and Men Building Together the Church in Africa." In *With Passion and Compassion: Third World Women Doing Theology*, Reflections from the Women's Commission of the Ecumenical Association of Third World Theologians, edited by Virginia Fabella and Mercy Amba Oduyoye, 14–21. Maryknoll, N.Y.: Orbis Books, 1989.

Sanon, Anselme T. "Jésus, maître d'initiation." In *Chemins de la christologie africaine*, ed. Kabasélé et al., 143–166.

Sarpong, Peter. *The Sacred Stools in Akan.* Accra-Tema: Ghana Publishing, 1971.

Sawyerr, Harry. *Creative Evangelism: Towards a New Christian Encounter with Africa.* London: Lutterworth Press, 1968.

Schoffeleers, Matthew. "Black and African Theology in Southern Africa: A Controversy Re-Examined," *Journal of Religion in Africa* 18 (1988): 99–123.

―――. "Folk Christology in Africa: The Dialectics of the Nganga Paradigm," *Journal of Religion in Africa* 19 (1989): 157–183.

Schreiter, Robert, ed. *Faces of Jesus in Africa.* Maryknoll, N.Y.: Orbis Books, 1991.

Sebidi, Lebamang. "The Dynamics of the Black Struggle and Its Implications for Black Theology." In *The Unquestionable Right To Be Free,* ed. Mosala and Tlhagale, 1–36.

————. "Towards an Understanding of the Current Unrest in South Africa." In *Hammering Swords Into Ploughshares,* ed. Tlhagale and Mosala, 253–263.

Setiloane, Gabriel M. *African Theology: An Introduction.* Johannesburg: Skotaville, 1986.

————. "I Am an African," *Currents in Theology and Mission* 13.2 (1986): 78–80.

Shorter, Aylward. "Ancestor Veneration Revisited," *African Ecclesiastical Review* 25 (1983): 197–203.

————. *Jesus and the Witchdoctor: An Approach to Healing and Wholeness.* Maryknoll, N.Y.: Orbis Books, 1985.

————, ed. *African Christian Spirituality.* London: Geoffrey Chapman, 1978.

Sprunger, A. R. "The Contribution of the African Independent Churches to a Relevant Theology for Africa." In *Relevant Theology for Africa,* edited by Hans-Jürgen Becker, 163–173. Durban, Natal: Lutheran Publishing, 1973.

Taylor, John V. *The Primal Vision: Christian Presence Amid African Religion.* Christian Presence Series. London: SCM Press, 1963.

Thomas, J. C. "What Is African Theology?" *Ghana Bulletin of Theology* 4 (1973): 14–30.

Tlhagale, Buti. "Nazism, Stalinist Russia and Apartheid—A Comparison." In *Hammering Swords Into Ploughshares,* ed. Tlhagale and Mosala, 265–278.

Tlhagale, Buti, and Itumeleng J. Mosala, eds. *Hammering Swords Into Ploughshares: Essays in Honor of Archbishop Mpilo Desmond Tutu.* Grand Rapids: Wm. B. Eerdmans Publishing Co., 1987.

Tutu, Desmond M. "Black Theology/African Theology—Soul Mates or Antagonists?" In *Black Theology,* ed. Cone and Wilmore, 483–491.

————. *Hope and Suffering: Sermons and Speeches.* Edited by John Webster. Grand Rapids: Wm. B. Eerdmans Publishing Co., 1983.

Udoh, Enyi B. "Guest Paradigm: An Alternative Christological Approach in Africa," *Reformed World* 39 (1987): 661–674.

Ukpong, Justin S. *African Theologies Now—A Profile.* Spearhead No. 80. Eldoret, Kenya: Gaba Publications, 1984.

Ungar, Sanford. *Africa: The People and Politics of an Emerging Continent.* New York: Simon & Schuster, 1986.

Vorster, W. S., ed. *Scripture and the Use of Scripture.* Pretoria: University of South Africa Press, 1978.

Waruta, Douglas. "Who Is Jesus Christ for Africans Today? Prophet, Priest, Potentate." In *Jesus in African Christianity,* ed. Mugambi and Magesa, 40–59.

## Chapter 5: Jesus in North America

Brock, Rita Nakashima. "The Feminist Redemption of Christ." In *Christian Feminism: Visions of a New Humanity,* edited by Judith L. Weidman, 55–74. San Francisco: Harper & Row, 1984.

———. *Journeys by Heart: A Christology of Erotic Power.* New York: Crossroad, 1988.

Brooten, Bernadette J. "Early Christian Women and Their Cultural Context: Issues of Method in Historical Reconstruction." In *Feminist Perspectives on Biblical Scholarship,* edited by Adela Yarbro Collins, 79–84. Society of Biblical Literature, Biblical Scholarship in North America, no. 10. Chico, Calif.: Scholars Press, 1985.

Bullock, Henry Allen. *A History of Negro Education in the South from 1619 to the Present.* Cambridge, Mass.: Harvard University Press, 1967.

Cannon, Katie. *Black Womanist Ethics.* American Academy of Religion Academy Series, no. 60. Atlanta: Scholars Press, 1988.

Carr, Anne. *Transforming Grace: Christian Tradition and Women's Experience.* San Francisco: Harper & Row, 1988.

Christ, Carol P., and Judith Plaskow, eds. *Womanspirit Rising: A Feminist Reader in Religion.* San Francisco: Harper & Row, 1979.

Cleage, Albert. *The Black Messiah.* New York: Sheed & Ward, 1968.

———. "The Black Messiah and the Black Revolution." In *Quest for a Black Theology,* ed. Gardiner and Roberts, 1–21.

Cone, Cecil. *The Identity Crisis in Black Theology.* Nashville: AMEC, 1975.

Cone, James H. "Biblical Revelation and Social Existence," *Interpretation* 28 (1974): 422–440.

——. *Black Theology and Black Power.* New York: Seabury Press, 1969.

——. *A Black Theology of Liberation.* Second edition. Maryknoll, N.Y.: Orbis Books, 1986.

——. *For My People: Black Theology and the Black Church.* Bishop Henry McNeal Turner Studies in North American Black Religion, volume 1. Maryknoll, N.Y.: Orbis Books, 1984.

——. *God of the Oppressed.* New York: Seabury Press, 1975.

——. *Speaking the Truth: Ecumenism, Liberation, and Black Theology.* Grand Rapids: Wm. B. Eerdmans Publishing Co., 1986.

——. *The Spirituals and the Blues: An Interpretation.* New York: Seabury Press, 1972.

Daly, Mary. *Beyond God the Father: Toward a Philosophy of Women's Liberation.* Boston: Beacon Press, 1973.

——. *Gyn/Ecology: The Metaethics of Radical Feminism.* Boston: Beacon Press, 1978.

Fanon, Frantz. *The Wretched of the Earth.* New York: Grove Press, 1963.

Gardiner, James, and J. Deotis Roberts, eds. *Quest for a Black Theology.* Philadelphia: Pilgrim Press, 1971.

Grant, Jacquelyn. *White Women's Christ and Black Women's Jesus: Feminist Christology and Womanist Response.* American Academy of Religion Academy Series, no. 64. Atlanta: Scholars Press, 1989.

Harding, Vincent. "Black Power and the American Christ." In *Black Theology*, ed. Cone and Wilmore, 35–42.

Hennelly, Alfred. *Theologies in Conflict: The Challenge of Juan Luis Segundo.* Maryknoll, N.Y.: Orbis Books, 1979.

Johnson, Elizabeth A. *Consider Jesus: Waves of Renewal in Christology.* New York: Crossroad, 1990.

Johnson, Joseph A. *The Soul of the Black Preacher.* Philadelphia: Pilgrim Press, 1971.

Jones, Major. *The Color of God: The Concept of God in Afro-American Thought.* Macon, Ga.: Mercer University Press, 1988.

Jones, William. *Is God a White Racist? A Preamble to Black The-*

*ology*. C. Eric Lincoln Series on Black Religion. Garden City, N.Y.: Doubleday & Co., Anchor Books, 1973.

King, Martin Luther, Jr. *Strength to Love*. Philadelphia: Fortress Press, 1981.

Loades, Ann. *Searching for Lost Coins: Explorations in Christianity and Feminism*. Allison Park, Pa.: Pickwick Publications, 1987.

Mollenkott, Virginia Ramey. *Women, Men, and the Bible*. Revised edition. New York: Crossroad, 1988.

Moltmann-Wendel, Elizabeth. *A Land Flowing with Milk and Honey: Perspectives on Feminist Theology*. New York: Crossroad, 1989.

Pero, Albert. "On Being Black, Lutheran, and American in a Racist Society." In *Theology and the Black Experience: The Lutheran Heritage Interpreted by African-American Theologians*, edited by Albert Pero and Ambrose Moyo, 150–169. Minneapolis: Augsburg Publishing House, 1988.

Position Paper of the African Methodist Episcopal Church. "Liberation Movements: A Critical Assessment and a Reaffirmation." In *Black Theology*, ed. Cone and Wilmore, 288–295.

Rich, Adrienne. *Of Woman Born: Motherhood as Experience and Institution*. New York: W. W. Norton & Co., 1976.

Roberts, J. Deotis. *A Black Political Theology*. Philadelphia: Westminster Press, 1974.

————. *Black Theology in Dialogue*. Philadelphia: Westminster Press, 1981.

————. *Liberation and Reconciliation: A Black Theology*. Philadelphia: Westminster Press, 1971.

Ruether, Rosemary Radford. "Feminist Interpretation: A Method of Correlation." In *Feminist Interpretation of the Bible*, edited by Letty M. Russell, 111–124. Philadelphia: Westminster Press, 1985.

————. *Liberation Theology: Human Hope Confronts Christian History and American Power*. New York: Paulist Press, 1972.

————. *Sexism and God-Talk: Toward a Feminist Theology*. Boston: Beacon Press, 1983.

————. *Women-Church: Theology and Practice of Feminist Liturgical Communities*. San Francisco: Harper & Row, 1985.

————. *Womanguides: Readings Toward a Feminist Theology*. Boston: Beacon Press, 1985.

Russell, Letty M. *Human Liberation in a Feminist Perspective—A Theology*. Philadelphia: Westminster Press, 1974.

Saiving, Valerie. "The Human Situation: A Feminine View." In *Womanspirit Rising*, ed. Christ and Plaskow, 25–41.

Scanzoni, Letha, and Nancy Hardesty. *All We're Meant to Be: A Biblical Approach to Women's Liberation*. Waco: Word Books, 1974.

Schüssler Fiorenza, Elisabeth. *Bread Not Stone: The Challenge of Feminist Biblical Interpretation*. Boston: Beacon Press, 1984.

———. *In Memory of Her: A Feminist Theological Reconstruction of Christian Origins*. New York: Crossroad, 1983.

Seper, Franjo Cardinal. "Vatican Declaration," *Origins, N.C. Documentary Service*. February 3, 1977: 6.

Slee, Nicola. "Parables and Women's Experience," *Modern Churchman* 26 (1984): 20–31.

Snyder, Mary Hembrow. *The Christology of Rosemary Radford Ruether: A Critical Introduction*. Mystic, Conn.: Twenty-Third Publications, 1988.

"Statements from Black and White Caucuses, National Council of Churches Conference on the Church and Urban Tensions, Washington, D.C., September 27–30, 1967." In *Black Theology*, ed. Cone and Wilmore, 43–47.

Thistlethwaite, Susan. *Sex, Race, and God: Christian Feminism in Black and White*. New York: Crossroad, 1989.

Trible, Phyllis. *Texts of Terror: Literary-Feminist Readings of Biblical Narratives*. Philadelphia: Fortress Press, 1984.

Walker, Alice. *In Search of My Mother's Garden*. New York: Harcourt Brace Jovanovich, 1983.

Ward, Hiley H. *Prophet of the Black Nation*. Philadelphia: Pilgrim Press, 1969.

Washington, Joseph. "How Black Is Black Religion?" In *Quest for a Black Theology*, ed. Gardiner and Roberts, 22–43.

Williams, Delores. "The Color of Feminism: Or Speaking the Black Woman's Tongue," *Journal of Religious Thought* 43 (1986): 42–58.

Wilmore, Gayraud S. "The Black Messiah: Revising the Color Symbolism of Western Christology," *Journal of the Interdenominational Theological Center* 2 (1974): 8–18.

———. *Black Religion and Black Radicalism: An Interpretation of the Religious History of Afro-American People*. Second edition. Maryknoll, N.Y.: Orbis Books, 1983.

Wilson-Kastner, Patricia. *Faith, Feminism, and the Christ*. Philadelphia: Fortress Press, 1983.

Wren, Brian. *What Language Shall I Borrow? God-Talk in Worship: A Male Response to Feminist Theology*. New York: Crossroad, 1989.

## Chapter 6: Continuing the Conversation

Balasuriya, Tissa. *Planetary Theology*. Maryknoll, N.Y.: Orbis Books, 1984.

Boulaga, F. Eboussi. *Christianity Without Fetishes: An African Critique and Recapture of Christianity*. Maryknoll, N.Y.: Orbis Books, 1984.

Castillo-Cárdenas, Gonzalo. *Liberation Theology from Below: The Life and Thought of Manuel Quintín Lame*. Maryknoll, N.Y.: Orbis Books, 1987.

Charlesworth, James H. *Jesus Within Judaism: New Light from Exciting Archaeological Discoveries*. New York: Doubleday & Co., 1988.

Cone, James H. "A Black American Perspective on the Future of African Theology." In *African Theology en Route*, ed. Appiah-Kubi and Torres, 492–501.

Fung, Raymond, comp. and ed. *Households of God on China's Soil*. WCC Mission Series, no. 2. Geneva: WCC Publications, 1982.

Gitari, David. "The Claims of Jesus in the African Context," *International Review of Mission* 71 (1982): 12–19.

Mbiti, John S. "An African Views American Black Theology." In *Black Theology*, ed. Cone and Wilmore, 477–482.

Moyo, Ambrose M. "The Quest for African Christian Theology and the Problem of the Relationship Between Faith and Culture—The Hermeneutical Perspective," *Africa Theological Journal* 12 (1983): 102–103.

Prabhu, George Soares. "Towards an Indian Interpretation of the Bible," *Biblebhashyam* 6 (March 1980): 151–170.

Riches, John. *Jesus and the Transformation of Judaism*. London: Darton, Longman & Todd, 1980.

Ruether, Rosemary Radford. *To Change the World: Christology and Cultural Criticism*. New York: Crossroad, 1981.

Sanders, E. P. *Jesus and Judaism*. Philadelphia: Fortress Press, 1985.

Segundo, Juan Luis. *The Liberation of Theology.* Maryknoll, N.Y.: Orbis Books, 1976.

Shorter, Aylward. *Toward a Theology of Inculturation.* Maryknoll, N.Y.: Orbis Books, 1988.

Thistlewaite, Susan Brooks. "Every Two Minutes: Battered Women and Feminist Interpretation." In *Weaving the Visions: New Patterns in Feminist Spirituality,* edited by Judith Plaskow and Carol Christ, 302–313. San Francisco: Harper & Row, 1989.

Vermès, Géza. *Jesus the Jew: A Historian's Reading of the Gospel.* Philadelphia: Fortress Press, 1983.

For other books and articles, see "Bibliography on Christology in Africa, Asia-Pacific and Latin America," *Theology in Context Supplements* 5 (1990), published by the Institute of Missiology.

# Index
# of Scripture References

# Index
## of Proper Names

# Index
# of Subjects

African Independent
    Churches, 94, 99, 111–12
African traditional religion,
    94–95, 104–105, 106,
    137–39
All Africa Conference of
    Churches (AACC), 19, 92,
    94
anti-Semitism, 184–86
ancestors, 94–95, 102, 104–
    106, 107, 173, 182, 191–
    92

Bible: and Asian social
    biography, 58–59; in black
    theology, 138–39, 141–42;
    in feminist theology, 132–
    35; in independent sub-
    Sahara Africa, 95–97;
    interpretation of, 14–16,
    22–23 n3, 179–84, 184–
    86; in Latin America, 30–
    32; in South Africa, 99–
    100. *See also* anti-Semitism;
    Judaism
Black Consciousness

movement, 98–99, 100,
    114–16
Black Power movement, 137,
    140, 147–48, 150–51, 190
black religion, 137–39
Buddhism, 55, 58–59, 67, 70

Christian Conference of Asia
    (CCA), 19, 71
Christology. *See* Jesus
Civil Rights movement, 136–
    37, 148
class struggle, 27–28, 60, 176
colonialism: in Africa, 89–92,
    96; in Asia, 55–57
context: Africa, 89–92; Asia,
    55–57; importance of, for
    theology, 15–18; Latin
    America, 26–29; North
    America, 128–31
conscientization, 32, 35, 74–
    75
conversion, 38–41, 64–65
cross. *See* Jesus, death of
crucifixion. *See* Jesus, death of
culture of silence, 32, 34

229